One Country or Two?

One Country or Two?

Edited by

R. M. Burns

with an introduction by

John J. Deutsch

McGill-Queen's University Press
Montreal and London
1971

This book has been published with the help of
a grant from the Social Science Research Council
of Canada using funds provided by the Canada
Council.

ISBN 0 7735 0104 5
Library of Congress Catalog Card No. 76-174566

PRINTED IN CANADA

Foreword

AS THIS VOLUME is prepared for publication those who have contributed to it have been faced with the question of the effect of the events of the autumn of 1970 on the state of Canadian nationhood, both within and without the Province of Quebec. We have had to ask ourselves what all this has meant for the analysis we undertook some time before.

Most of the writing was done before the Liberal victory in the provincial election which is dealt with elsewhere in this volume. And while the implications of that may have seemed reasonably clear, at least for the short term, those of the FLQ affair and the proclamation of the War Measures Act on 16 October 1970 are more obscure. In an election you can, at least, count the votes.

The central concern of these essays is the effect of Quebec political attitudes upon the various threads of the fabric of Canadian nationality. The events of October must be looked at with that in mind. We have been forced to ask ourselves how these events have influenced the present regard of French-speaking Canadians for their place in Canada and to what extent the attitudes of English-speaking Canadians in other parts of Canada have been influenced with regard to Quebec. Have the people of Canada accepted this as the inevitable climax of a series of events which will in some way perhaps enable us seriously to re-assess the influences that brought them about? Or do they regard them as but one more step in the road to national dissolution?

Of course we don't know. Jealous regard for civil liberties, the inherent empathy of many with the cause of self-determination, and the revulsions of humanity to acts of violence, have operated in many conflicting ways not only within groups but in individuals, leaving the way open for new cleavages and new alignments.

There seems very little doubt that the actions of the Governments of Canada and Quebec in the situation that developed have had the support of a great majority of the Canadian people, within and without that province. The question that is now more important and must concern us all for the future is to what extent that action has resulted in a polarization of forces for and against the preservation of a national political identity. To what extent are the forces set in motion by these events likely to continue and to what extent are they likely to develop their own reactions?

There seems fair reason to believe that the events of which we write have resulted in a wave of sympathy and understanding in English-speaking Canada for the dilemma of Quebec. It has been a time, perhaps, when the people of other provinces have moved from the viewpoint of their own interests and have seen events through the eyes of the people of Quebec. But we do not know, when the quiet has returned, if this will continue and be preserved. Will the rest of Canada become tired of trouble and resent the cost of the inevitable measures that the country must take to correct the errors of the past? Already there are some signs in the West that it could be so. Or will the understanding which was the immediate product of the crisis be prolonged through the period of reconstitution?

In Quebec, on the other hand, will the reactions of relief at the decisive, if restrictive, moves of October be replaced by a resentment of the federal role and by the acceptance of the economic nationalism embodied in the view of such as René Lévesque and the Parti Québécois?

These are but a few of the questions the answers to which are still unknown and which we must face as we seek to solve the equation of our political identity. We believe that what we have written is still valid as a presentation of the facts and attitudes as they have seemed to each of us, and that the solutions to our problems remain fundamentally subject to the same forces and the same boundaries although the intensity and the dimensions may have changed. These problems have not been essentially changed by recent happenings, only the urgency has been made more plain. We can only speculate and hope that responsibility and reason will ultimately prevail.

R. M. BURNS

Contents

Contributors

JOHN J. DEUTSCH Principal of Queen's University, former Director of the Economic Council of Canada

W. R. LEDERMAN Professor of Constitutional Law and former Dean of the Faculty of Law, Queen's University

R. L. WATTS Professor of Political Studies and Dean of the Faculty of Arts and Science, Queen's University

RICHARD SIMEON Assistant Professor, Department of Political Studies, Queen's University

F. J. E. JORDAN Associate Professor of Law, Queen's University

J. R. MALLORY Professor of Political Science, McGill University, and former Chairman of the Department

JOHN MEISEL Professor of Political Studies, Queen's University, and Co-Editor of the *Canadian Journal of Political Science*

T. H. B. SYMONS President and Vice Chancellor of Trent University, Peterborough, Ontario

G. A. RAWLYK Professor of History, Queen's University, and Acting Chairman of the Department, 1970–71

J. A. ARCHER Principal, Regina Campus, University of Saskatchewan

R. M. BURNS Director, Institute of Intergovernmental Relations, Queen's University

Introduction

John J. Deutsch

> *In terms of* realpolitik, *French and English are equal in Canada because each of these linguistic groups has the power to break the country.*
> Pierre Elliott Trudeau

SHORTLY AFTER the "Confederation of Tomorrow Conference" which was convened by Premier Robarts in Toronto in November 1967, the *Toronto Daily Star* published an editorial (on 4 December) under the headline, "We must prepare for Quebec's departure." The editorial stated that "simple prudence now requires us to face the possibility that Quebec may secede from Canada. . . . Therefore we should prepare against the failure of our troubled partnership with French Canada even while trying to salvage it."

Premier Robarts's conference was a significant turning point in the mounting dialogue between English and French Canada, but the spectre referred to in the *Toronto Daily Star* editorial continued to rise over the Canadian scene in increasingly menacing shapes and forms during the succeeding months and years. The editorial struck a sensitive chord in many Canadians, including the former Premier of Ontario, Leslie M. Frost. Whenever we met, Mr. Frost returned repeatedly to the implications of the *Star*'s warning, and raised the question of how we might best proceed to give timely heed to this stark possibility.

Early in 1969, Mr. Frost wrote to me to say, "It did not seem to me that there was any appreciation (at the Robarts Conference) of what the situation would be if Quebec separated. As I see it now, I doubt that there could be the use of force, or that there would be a parallel to the United States in 1861. If that is so, then the question really is Quebec's. . . . If emotions are the deciding factor, then reasoning becomes pretty difficult. On the other hand, standing out very clearly is the fact that the French–English partnership, stretching back to the days of 1763, has been of the utmost value to both. If it had not been for this, probably our English-Canadian culture would have long ago been absorbed into the United States. Conversely, the partnership has meant that the French-Canadian culture has been preserved. If it had not been for Canada and what led up to Canada, Quebec unquestionably would be like Louisiana. . . . My view is that anything we do should be calculated to strengthen and preserve the partnership, and to avoid its break-up, which could be disastrous to the Canadian way of life. We discussed the desirability of a dispassionate academic approach. Little effort has been made to really place the facts on the table face up." In another letter, Mr. Frost remarked, "Studies by coolheaded, thoughtful people at a time such as this might be very valuable in days to come."

I arranged a meeting between Mr. Frost and a number of colleagues and friends who, like myself, were keenly interested in these matters. Mr. Frost strongly encouraged the group to prepare a series of thoughtful essays on topics which are highly pertinent to the whole question of Quebec Separatism and its consequences for Canada. The purpose of the essays would be to face directly and boldly a number of the hard and basic issues that are involved in any process that could lead to the break-up of the country; issues that are not, and perhaps could not, be matters for official discussion or even general public debate. It was felt that the time had come to confront some of the inescapable realities in order to assist in the critical task of coming to workable and mutually tolerable solutions before the hour is too late. The goal would be to elucidate some of the fundamental forces which operate in the vast and intricate relationships which comprise the Canadian nation, to examine the inherent dynamics of a federal system in the complex circumstances of the Canadian case, to consider the conditions and processes for accommodation and peaceful change, to weigh the possibilities for success, and to assess the consequences of failure. It is logical to presuppose a large program of research as a part of so sweeping an enterprise, but it was felt that timeliness and immediate relevance should take precedence over documentation and structured analysis.

It was decided to prepare the essays on the basis of the body of information already available, and out of the perceptions of specialists who have devoted much of their scholarly careers to these matters.

This series of essays has been designed to examine the critical elements in the developing crisis between French and English Canada. What are the inherent problems of a federal system in adapting to the powerful forces of rapid and far-reaching change in a modern post-industrial society? What are the new and significant factors in the long history of French–English tensions within the Canadian federation? What are the basic aspirations of the various groups and regions which comprise the federation, and what are their attitudes towards the French fact and towards each other? What is the essential nature of the forces of division and the circumstances which could lead to a break-up? What would be the process of disintegration, and what would be the aftermath? What are the fundamental forces of cohesion? What are the possibilities and the means of accommodation for the preservation of national unity in these rapidly changing times? The authors of these essays hope that a discussion of these sensitive questions openly and explicitly will contribute a sense of constructive reality to the great Canadian debate which will take place in the months and years to come.

A federal system of government is always and everywhere subject to powerful forces making for instability. This form of government is invariably the outcome of a compromise between substantial divergencies based on language, religion, race, economics, or geography; and important cohesive tendencies based on significant common interests. At any given time this compromise rests on a particular balance between the divisive and cohesive forces. The distinctive groups or regions seek to pursue their own ends and maintain their own identities to an extent which is consistent with the degree of centralization required for the effective realization of worthwhile common purposes. This balance, however, is continuously liable to be upset by social, political, and economic changes. Consequently, federal systems are constantly confronted with the difficult task of working out new compromises and new accommodations between special interests and common goals.

These inherent characteristics of a federal system are present in all federal countries. Canada is no exception. In order to gain a sense of perspective on the Canadian difficulties in our time, it is particularly instructive to examine the experience and the history of federal systems around the world in various circumstances and periods. Professor Watts, in his essay, "The Survival or Disintegration of Federations," describes the circumstances which have brought about the establishment of federations over the past several centuries, the stresses and strains they have encountered, the processes of accommodation and survival, and the causes of disintegration and failure.

In Professor Watts's survey, it is particularly noteworthy that all federations have had to contend, at one time or another, with serious dangers of disintegration. It is a sobering fact that in most cases the efforts to cope with these dangers have ended in failure. The failures have been of two kinds; one type of failure has occurred where the federal structure was replaced by what was in effect a unitary form of government, and the other type has occurred where the forces of disintegration brought about the break-up of the federal state. Examples of the first type of failure are to be found in the history of a number of South American countries, and pre-war Germany. Examples of the second type are present in the failures of federal systems during recent years in the Caribbean, Central Africa, and in Asia.

The federal systems which have survived for a substantial period of history include those of the United States, Switzerland, Australia, and Canada. Each of these has had to contend, at one time or another, with dangerous separatist movements. In two of the four cases—the United States and Switzerland—the forces of division were ultimately contained by violence and civil war. In the other two cases—Canada and Australia—the regional manifestations of separatism which have occurred from time to time were held in check in the last resort, until relatively recently, by the final constitutional authority of the Imperial power. These plain facts are constant reminders of the dangers and risks inherent in federal systems, even in highly developed and mature democratic countries. These dangers and risks are not uniquely associated with the overwhelming problems of an Indian sub-continent, the Congo, or Nigeria.

The history of federal systems shows that the danger of disintegration mounts as language, religious, and other cultural differences are being threatened and exacerbated by increasing economic and political disabilities. Political disabilities may arise from unequal changes in populations, from changes in the bases of political power, from changes in the working of political processes, and from changes in communications. Economic disabilities may develop from new technologies, from the effects of central economic policy, from social changes, and from changes in markets at home and abroad. A federal system, in order to remain viable, must have the capacity to adjust to these many and complex changes in such a way as to maintain important regional cultural, language, religious, or economic interests while, at the same time, making possible the continued pursuit of worthwhile common purposes for the nation as a whole. This means that there must be enough flexibility in the constitutional arrangements to allow timely redistributions of powers between the centre and the regions, either through formal amendments or through changing interpretations and practice. Also, this means that there must continue to exist, throughout the unsettling processes of change and adaptation, the continued acceptance and recognition of regional identities and interests, and a continued common commitment to significant national aims. When these basic requirements can no longer be fulfilled, the federal system is in imminent danger of disintegration or violent confrontation.

The essays in this volume examine the problems and processes of adjustment in the Canadian federal system, in our time of massive social and economic changes. These changes have impinged with particularly far-reaching effects on the French-speaking population of Quebec. Therefore, the essays deal mainly, though not exclusively, with consequences of this special impact on French-speaking Canadians and their relations with the rest of Canada. Given the characteristics of the federal system, these problems have inherent in them the possibilities of the break-up of the Canadian nation. It is an explicit purpose of the essays to discuss the nature and extent of these possibilities, the attitudes of the various regions and groups in the country, the procedures and processes that would operate, the difficulties that would arise, and the outcome that might be expected under various circumstances. Along with this frank and explicit treatment of the dangers and problems, there is an evaluation of the possibilities for workable adjustments, and an appreciation of the enduring forces for cohesion. In other words, what is sought is to expose some of the hard issues that all Canadians must weigh in their choice of one country or two in this particular time of accelerated and revolutionary change.

Professor Lederman discusses the role and particular genius of our inherited political institutions in the preservation of a united country, and in the provision of the practical means by which the aspirations of two cultures and of widely separated regions can come to realization in the circumstances of our time. Professor Jordan examines an important part of the vast infrastructure that was constructed in the building of the nation, the St. Lawrence–Great Lakes Waterway, and considers the complex problems that would arise should Quebec want to separate. The attitudes in the Eastern and Western regions of the country are discussed by Professor Rawlyk for the Maritimes, by Principal Archer for the Prairie Provinces, and by Professor Burns for British Columbia. The special circumstances of the English-speaking minority in Quebec are examined by Professor Mallory. The significant response of the pivotal province of the federation, Ontario, to the rising fears and aspirations of the French-speaking minority, both within its own borders and in the larger Canada, is presented by President Symons. Professor Meisel describes the basic aims of the French-speaking people in the light of their historical development in North America, and considers the nature of the accommodation with English-speaking Canada, which will be necessary for the survival of "one" country. Professor Simeon speculates about the manner of Quebec's going, and about the risks and consequences in various circumstances, should the processes for adjustment and accommodation fail. In a postscript, Professor Simeon adds some thoughts on the significance of recent traumatic events.

One way to gain an understanding of the contemporary problems of the Canadian federation is to contrast the circumstances of today with those which made it possible to build the new political structure of Confederation in 1867. During the middle of the nineteenth century, there were various special circumstances and particular developments which made it possible and expedient to devise a federal solution to the political and economic problems of the separate British North American colonies. At that time, there were a number of important common purposes for which a new central government was needed. Under the Imperial system of the day, the common interests to be served comprised those of the British Government, as well as those of the governments and peoples of the several colonies. The common interests included (i) the provision of greater security against the possibility of an expansionist and aggressive American Government, following the Civil War; (ii) the promotion of inter-regional trade in the face of unfavourable developments abroad, resulting from the loss of colonial preferences in the United Kingdom, and the abrogation of the Reciprocity Treaty by the United States; (iii) the promotion of economic growth by the construction of costly inter-regional transportation facilities, and the settlement of the empty lands of the West; and (iv) the establishment of a new political structure to overcome the political deadlock between the French and English in the United Province of Canada. The pursuit of these common interests, and the pressures exerted by the Imperial authorities brought about the adoption of a federal constitution embodied in the BNA Act.

Under this federal constitution, the new central government was given the powers required to carry out the common purposes through its jurisdiction over external relations, defence, money and banking, all forms of taxation, national transportation facilities, national public works, and western settlement. The provincial governments were given authority over regional and local affairs through exclusive jurisdiction over education, social and cultural matters, municipal government, provincial natural resources, property and civil rights, and local public works.

This federal system, with its prescribed distribution of powers, represented the compromise reached in 1867 between common purposes and regional interests. The federal system of 1867 contained another compromise—the vitally important compromise between the English-speaking and French-speaking Canadians. The constitutional arrangements provided for the protection of the language, culture, and religion of the French-speaking population, specifically in Quebec. In fact, this protection had meaning, not simply because of the constitutional guarantees, but because of the circumstances of the time. This is an immensely important feature of the arrangements of 1867.

The inhabitants of the British North American colonies in the mid-nineteenth century constituted an overwhelmingly rural society engaged very largely in agricultural and other primary occupations. Except for a few small cities and a few substantial towns, the population was widely dispersed and lived in isolated pioneering conditions. These circumstances were particularly characteristic of Quebec, despite the fact that the original French-speaking settlers had come there more than two centuries previously. In this type of society, the problem of ensuring the survival of the language, culture, and religion of the French-speaking people was relatively easy. These attributes and values had a large measure of natural protection by isolation from both the English-speaking majority and the larger world outside. This isolation was strongly reinforced by a magisterial Church, which ministered to the spiritual, educational, cultural, and social needs of virtually the entire French-speaking population, and carefully protected it against alien influences from at home and abroad. Furthermore, the Church was, in many respects, an autonomous institution which derived its authority with the people, not from an English-controlled power in London or Ottawa, but from a spiritual source in Rome. In these circumstances, the political compromise of 1867, between the French-speaking minority and the English-speaking majority, had meaning and reality.

The present-day problems of the Canadian federal system can usefully be approached and understood by looking at what has happened to the 1867 compromise during the intervening years. Basically, three things have happened. There is the all-pervasive and revolutionary impact of modern industrialism; there is the enormous rise in the role of government in modern society; and there is the profound decline in the role of the Church.

After the middle of the nineteenth century, Canadian development was brought about, to an increasing extent, by the application of the advanced industrial techniques, the capital, the enterprise, the skills, and the manpower of the United Kingdom, Western Europe, and the United States. Indeed, one of the primary aims in the establishment of the new central government was to facilitate the use of these powerful means to promote economic growth in the difficult circumstances of a vast East-West nation, with huge undeveloped natural wealth but with great physical barriers, a small and widely dispersed population, and a rigorous climate. By the end of the First World War, the purposes of national development had been accomplished to a significant extent through the settlement of the immense western lands, and the establishment of a modern industrial and financial economy in southern Ontario and on the banks of the St. Lawrence around Montreal. However, the full impact of modern industrialism did not arrive until the Second World War, when Canada became a major economic arsenal for the Allied powers, and until the immediate post-war decades when Canada was drawn fully into the rapidly expanding commerce of the industrially developed world. These dynamic and powerful influences had immense effects on the nature of the economy, the distribution of the population, and the structure of the Canadian society.

The very rapid application of advanced technologies brought about a precipitous decline in agriculture and in rural pursuits. These followed a massive migration from the countryside into the cities, on a scale seldom equalled anywhere. Almost overnight, Canada was transformed into a predominantly urban society, with its more diverse and sophisticated occupations and its different needs, values, attitudes, and preoccupations. At the same time, the revolution in electronics and developments in communications and transportation were annihilating space and time with far-reaching effects on the relations between peoples, both inside and outside Canada. Canadian society, both economically and culturally, became immensely more open to the large world outside, especially to the large and vibrant world of the United States.

It is not at all surprising that these almost cataclysmic events have had profound effects on the relations between the diverse regions of the country, and on the Canadian federal system. The changes resulting from World War II and its aftermath set in motion powerful centralizing forces both in the economy and in society. Rapid urbanization was accompanied by the growing predominance of the great

metropolitan cities, especially in the Great Lakes–St. Lawrence valley. This predominance was part of an increasing concentration of
manufacturing industry, finance, commerce, and communications in
Central Canada. The populations of the Maritimes and the Prairie
region declined relatively. The chronic economic disparities in the
eastern regions of the country persisted in the midst of an affluent
economy. In the Prairie Provinces, a decline in political influence
within the federation, and a continued industrial and financial
dependency on the rapidly expanding central metropolis in the
East, brought frustration, alienation, and fear of neglect. In British
Columbia, rising self-confidence based on a rapidly expanding self-
dependent raw material exporting economy has heightened tensions
with a distant, tax-gathering, and little comprehending East.

However, the effects of these recent changes on Quebec have been
far more profound and disturbing than anywhere else. The rate of
industrialization, urbanization, and social transformation would have
been, in any case, disturbing enough, but these changes brought also
the disappearance at the same time of many of the particular circumstances which made it possible to secure the language and culture of
a minority in the Canadian federation, under the compromise of
1867. Earlier, the large migration of population into the new lands
of the West and into Ontario, without significant French-speaking
participation, was followed by the loss of French language rights in
these regions. Now the threat of being overwhelmed had come to the
homeland itself.

In a very short period of time the economic, social, and cultural
isolation of the French-speaking population of Quebec was gone.
Already, not far short of one-half of the entire population of the
province lives in a single massive urban concentration located at a
prominent crossroad of world commerce and communications. The
French-speaking inhabitants of Quebec are now fully exposed to the
influences and requirements of a modern technology, which is dominated by an English-speaking culture; they are exposed to the multinational corporations by which much of this technology is propa-
gated; and they are exposed also to the revolutionary developments
in communications which are internationalizing culture, especially
the mass culture of the United States.

The vast changes wrought by modern industrialism were accom-

panied by an equally vast change in the role of government in our
society. A far-reaching change in the role of government is bound to
raise very difficult problems in a federal system which is based on
compromises between common central purposes and particular regional interests. The compromise of 1867 resulted in the allocation
of responsibilities to the provinces for the support of regional interests
which were relatively inexpensive at the time. However, during the
intervening years, the growth in the role of government which
accompanied industrial and social change impinged disproportion-
ately on the responsibilities which had been assigned to the provinces
—that is, education, social welfare, health, public utilities, resource
development, municipal and urban services of all kinds, and so forth.
In modern industrial societies, these responsibilities are the most
costly. The Canadian federal system, like other federal systems, has
been subjected to severe strains in the attempts to adjust to this
persistent development.

In Canada, as elsewhere, pressing human needs and political expediency have taken precedence over the theories and logic of
federalism in coping with this large problem. Because of the financial
and administrative limitations of the provincial governments, the
central government responded to popular wishes for action by using
its unlimited taxing and spending powers to assume much of the
expanding role of government in large fields of provincial jurisdiction. This development was greatly and rapidly intensified by the
special problems of the Great Depression, followed closely by those
of wartime national mobilization during World War II and the
implementation of the Welfare State during the 1940s and 1950s.
A situation emerged in which there was an almost overwhelming
concentration of financial power and authority in the hands of the
central government, and a correspondingly high degree of dependency on the part of the provincial governments. This situation was
strongly at variance with the basic premises of the federal system,
and resulted in increasing strains between the centre and the regions,
particularly Quebec, Ontario, and British Columbia.

Quebec was in a position in which it felt itself to be increasingly
unable to exercise its responsibilities in the fields of education, social
affairs, and local development which were vital for the preservation
of its language, its culture, and its political integrity during a period

of vast social change and rapidly increasing exposure to powerful cultural influences from outside. Consequently, after the death of Duplessis, which in many ways marked a dramatic and final break with the old regime, there began a period of intense negotiations with the central government designed to return the balance between centrally controlled common purposes and Quebec regional interests more closely to the logic of the compromise of 1867. In this, Quebec received a significant measure of support from the prosperous and rapidly growing provinces of Ontario, British Columbia, and Alberta. The problem of finding a generally acceptable new balance has been extremely difficult because of the wide divergence of interest between the weaker, slower-growing provinces which favoured strong central-ization, and the others, particularly Quebec, which emphasized greater regional self-determination. The task remains uncompleted and very troublesome.

The great upheavals in society and in the federal system, wrought by modern industrialism and the accelerating growth in the respon-sibilities of government, impinged most strongly on Quebec at a time when the vital and historic role of the Church was undergoing a rapid decline. The emotional, spiritual, and moral inspiration and support for the survival of a distinctive language and culture were disappearing at a time when the need for such transcendent influences was particularly great. This large vacuum was not left to exist for long. A new and rising intellectual élite was quick to sponsor another emotional and inspirational force of powerful appeal, namely secular nationalism. This great emotional force, which was to be raised to a dominant role, was based not on moral and spiritual authority but on the secular authority of the State. The powerful emotional appeal of nationalism was to invest the elevated State with pervasive powers to protect and cultivate the language, culture, and economy of a minority people against the massive influences and inroads of a larger English-speaking population in the rest of Canada, and also from a very much larger one in the rest of North America. The sacrifices needed would be asked not in the name of spiritual values but in the name of a glorious and omnipotent State.

Sacrifices there would be, because the achievement of the aims of a thoroughgoing secular nationalism would involve the use of gov-ernmental powers of restriction, protection, and the promotion of special purposes and interests which can be exercised only by a fully sovereign State separated from the rest of Canada. Separation would inevitably entail a serious disturbance of the massive economic relationships with the remainder of the country. Regardless of the longer-run economic arrangements with the remainder of Canada, the processes leading up to and immediately following upon an intensely nationalist-engendered separation would cause serious economic disturbances arising from flights of capital and enterprise, from uncertainties regarding future policies, and from conflicts between groups over matters ranging all the way from basic differences over political ideologies and the redistribution of falling incomes. Such disturbances would bring hardships to many—more to some than to others. The new ruling élites of all kinds, including an expanding bureaucracy and some of the new professional middle class, might even improve their position, but the weaker and more exposed groups and individuals, including the mass of ordinary workers, clerks, farmers, and many small businessmen, would suffer, in one way and another, most of the losses and failures. Of course, those who make the sacrifices would be asked to accept them in the cause of a glorious nationalist future.

Thus we come to the central question of these essays: one country or two? Simply put, the answer lies in the ability of the Canadian federal system to adjust to the enormous industrial and social changes which have transformed all of Canadian society. This calls for the working out of a new compromise between common purposes and regional interests which embodies the realities of today.

Such a compromise involves a set of considerations far more complex and difficult than those of the nineteenth century. It must provide the unqualified possibility for the French-speaking minority, particularly in Quebec, to maintain and foster its language and culture in a modern post-industrial society in which communications, information, and knowledge are the increasingly important means to progress and achievement. At the same time the new compromise must make it possible for the English-speaking regions to attain their common purposes in the achievement of national development and a Canadian national identity on the North American continent.

The circumstances of the French-speaking minority requires un-equivocal constitutional guarantees respecting the position of its

language in various parts of the country, together with the establishment of conditions in which French-speaking Canadians can participate adequately in all the significant activities of Canadian life.
This calls for both an understanding attitude on the part of the
majority, and a willingness to meet the costs that are involved as an
indispensable investment in the concept of Canada.

The adjustments in the Canadian federal system must include
arrangements and measures which reduce the highly centralizing
tendencies that have operated in the Canadian society in recent
decades. These centralizing tendencies have been both political and
economic. Disregard of strong regional interests in these respects in
the East and West will exacerbate the problem of reaching agreement with Quebec, whose interests, it is feared, dominate the attention of the central government and of the inhabitants of Central
Canada. Continued very large disparities in levels of income and
rates of economic growth between the regions lead to feelings of
frustration and alienation which are inconsistent with the spirit
needed to cope with the complex problems of change in the federal
system.

In the face of these tasks and difficulties, what are the basic
strengths and assets which will support the efforts to preserve one
country? There is no doubt that, despite the discontents and the lack
of a clear identity, there is among the great majority of English-
speaking Canadians a strong emotional attachment to the idea of a
Canada from sea to sea. Professor Norman Ward expressed this
widespread, but largely unspecified, emotional attachment very effectively: "So far as I am concerned, this is one whole country: and
that's the way it is going to be." This strong, and in many ways
uncompromising, sentiment, which is typical of many English-
speaking Canadians, is at one and the same time a source of strength
and a warning that any attempt to break the country in two is going
to be a very troublesome business.

There is an illuminating dichotomy here. Among English-speaking
Canadians, the attachment to a united Canada is primarily emo-
tional; the discontents and fears are largely economic. Among
French-speaking Canadians, the attachment to a united Canada is
primarily economic; the discontents and fears are largely emotional.
The essential purpose of the federal solution is to sustain one country

on the basis of these contrasts; one country, culturally dualistic and economically diverse. To be sure, in order to make this possible there must also exist important over-riding common interests and hopes.

Canada, more than any other modern nation, is still the land of tomorrow. The challenges and the possibilities that lie ahead can engage fully the energies and the skills of all Canadians of whatever region and of whatever culture or language. There are enormous things to be accomplished together. There is the unparallelled opportunity to apply advanced techniques to a vast unused store of natural wealth, and to use it for worthwhile ends and for the benefit of all Canadians. The scope here for greater Canadian initiative and self-reliance remains very large. There is the belated Canadian manifest destiny in the huge and difficult territories in the North. Above all, there is the possibility of building a distinctive modern society in the New World, with important values and purposes of its own. All this can be accomplished more surely by one country than two, even though there is not yet any clearly articulated sense of common nationality.

> *I know a man whose school could never teach him patriotism, but who acquired that virtue when he felt in his bones the vastness of his land, and the greatness of those who founded it.*

(Pierre Elliott Trudeau)

The British Parliamentary System and Canadian Federalism

W. R. Lederman

CANADA'S PRESENT CONSTITUTION, and her system of public law generally, are the products of a long history of development following for the most part the model afforded from time to time by the British constitution, as that constitution grew and developed over the centuries for the internal government of Britain herself. This process culminated for British North America in the winning of responsible government in 1848. This was the transfer to British North America of the full-fledged British cabinet and parliamentary system as it was in the middle of the nineteenth century. Here is the root of a vitally important difference between Canada and the United States today, for the American inheritance from Britain is dated in the late eighteenth century, stopping with the British constitution as it stood in 1776. Only about seventy years intervened between 1776 and 1848, but this particular seventy years saw critical changes in the British constitution; specifically they saw the development of the cabinet system in Britain, particularly after 1832, and the prompt transfer of that system to British North America. We will return later to the modern significance of this vital difference between the Canadian and American systems of government.

But the British North American colonies in the nineteenth century were also very much a part of the New World, and the example and influence of the United States in things constitutional and legal was strong. In 1867 the British North American colonies adopted the idea of federal union from the United States, though of course in the new Canadian federation parliamentary institutions on the British model were continued at the provincial level and were set up also at the national level of the central federal government.

So we may say that the two high points of Canadian constitutional development were responsible government in the 1840s and federation of the British North American colonies in the 1860s. Amid our present constitutional discontents in Canada we should pause to remember that Quebec and French Canada have been well served by parliamentary democracy (with its concomitant cabinet system) and by federalism. These two institutions were and are important bulwarks protecting the distinctive French-Canadian way of life in Canada and North America. Of course, there were other objectives being sought as well in the historical movements of the nineteenth century directed to winning responsible government and bringing about federation. The acquisition and development of the Northwest is an example. But none of the other objectives was more constant or more important than the objective of assuring reasonable security for the essentials of the French-Canadian way of life, as those essentials were conceived to be at the time. The leaders of English Canada entered into close and continuing partnerships with the leaders of French Canada to accomplish this end in the case of both these developments. The extent to which they succeeded in safeguarding the French-Canadian way of life was very significant and should not now be disparaged.

Moreover, responsible parliamentary government and federalism are vital cohesive factors for all the various parts of Canada today, and indeed they may have even greater importance than in the past. Even if Quebec were to separate, these cohesive influences would remain operative for the other provinces and regions of Canada. But the main thrust of my comments is to argue that both the lessons of our history and the pressures of the modern world demonstrate that the best security French Canadians can now have for their way of life lies in the continuing federal unity of Canada, including Quebec. No doubt it is true that the range of political and constitutional options, as we approach extreme solutions, may be decisively limited by the balance of overall economic costs and benefits for Quebec and other parts of Canada. The economic considerations are obviously important and at some point may become critical to what happens. Nevertheless, I argue from the conviction that political and social traditions and their expression in constitutions and laws are supreme over economics.

This has been shown in our history by the fact that Canadians have always paid, and willingly, an economic price for maintaining a national identity separate from the United States of America. If we maintain present Canadian unity, I believe that Canadians can continue so to govern themselves that the economic price of remaining separate from the United States will stay within acceptable limits on into the future. Our system of government is just as democratic as that of the Americans; moreover, the Canadian parliamentary and cabinet system is more efficient than the American congressional and presidential system. In addition, the Canadian type of federalism has turned out to be more balanced, that is, more sensitive and responsive to cultural duality and regionalism, than is the case with the modern federalism of the United States.

But if Quebec insists on separation, then these issues are shrouded in rather ominous uncertainty, with the continued distinctiveness of Quebec in the greatest peril of all. In other words, there would then be a serious question whether Quebec alone, or the other parts of Canada (separately or together), could so reorganize their life and industry through the medium of democratic governmental institutions as to keep the costs of avoiding absorption by the United States within acceptable limits, economic and otherwise. Probably Canada without Quebec could do so if the other provinces and regions stayed together in a federal parliamentary union. I am sanguine enough to believe that the will to maintain such a union would be there. But the better and much more likely alternative for all is the continuation of the present Canadian federation, with Quebec as a vital member. We must seek the political and constitutional adjustments that would facilitate this.

It is true, of course, that we cannot simply rest on past successes in accommodating the French Fact in British North America, but, nevertheless, it is still worth looking in some detail at certain highlights of the nineteenth century in this respect, because those were troubled times too and there *are* lessons for today and tomorrow in what was accomplished then. We shall look at the winning of responsible government, the achievement of federation of the British North American colonies, and at the contrasts between the Canadian and American constitutions in these and certain other matters.

We consider first the development of the cabinet system in Britain, that is, the nature of the relation between the Crown and Parliament —the executive and legislative bodies in the state. This was one thing in the late eighteenth century wherein the internal British governmental system provided the model for the new American constitution. But the relations of Crown and Parliament in Great Britain had become something quite different some seventy years later, when these relations provided the model for responsible government as granted to the British North American colonies in the period from 1841 to 1848.[1]

The nature of the eighteenth-century British constitution can be seen in the position of King George III. He was the real executive head of the nation, though it was true that parliamentary legislative power prevailed over the royal prerogative power and Parliament held the purse strings. The royal prerogatives still included control of colonial administration and policy, foreign relations, and the command of the armed forces. The executive power and initiative generally were thus very much in the hands of the king. He selected his own ministers or advisers, some from the House of Commons, some from the House of Lords, and some who were not in either House. It is true enough that he usually had a "First Minister." There were no political parties in the modern sense, and there was no prime minister in the modern sense—indeed George III, in effect, acted as his own prime minister. The chosen group of royal advisers came and went as individuals or in various combinations pretty well as the king determined they should. When meeting, they considered only matters on which the king had requested their advice. The executive primacy of the king was not affected by whether or not he attended cabinet meetings—in any event he settled the questions to be considered, and the resulting advice was reported to him, whereupon he could accept it or reject it.

It is true that the king had some need of a sympathetic House of Commons and of some ministers who sat in the House, so that on occasion he could obtain the statutes and money votes he wanted. But in the eighteenth century the king first selected his ministers and then, if necessary, constructed a sympathetic House of Commons at the next election. The parliamentary constituencies at this time were extremely unequal in population and a great many of them could be managed, either because they were "rotten" boroughs up for sale or "nomination" boroughs where the choice of member was controlled by a local patron. By the use of patronage and preferment for various public offices, the king and his ministers could assure themselves a House of Commons that would go their way.

If there was a defeat in the House in these earlier times, the ministry did not resign but waited for the right moment to call an election and reconstruct the membership of the House. No British ministry resigned as a result of a defeat in the House between 1783 and 1830. At the time of George III then, the executive powers of the Crown and the legislative powers of Parliament were autonomous and separate. They had to seek one another's co-operation from time to time, but there was no regular or consistent system for the co-ordination of executive and legislative functions. This is one reason why George III was able to make his arbitrary American policy prevail, with the eventual result that the American colonists were provoked to successful revolution. It is true that the Prime Minister, Lord North, and all his colleagues except the Lord Chancellor resigned in 1782 when confronted with a very hostile House of Commons. But this was most unusual, and in any event the American Revolutionary War had then been lost.

In constitutional terms, the chief complaint of the American colonists was that the British government in London would not export the internal British constitution of the day to the American colonies.[2] London would not give the colonial assemblies the same control over their respective local affairs that the British House of Commons possessed over the internal affairs of Britain, including legislative and financial means of imposing some control on the royal governors appointed and instructed from London. George III and his ministers resisted this solution to the bitter end, claiming that the British constitution could not be exported in full to a colony, since no royal governor could be accountable to two masters, the king and parliament in London on the one hand, and the respective colonial assemblies on the other.

When the American colonists won the revolutionary war and

broke with Britain, they promptly adopted the main features of the eighteenth-century British constitution. In the American constitution of 1789, the position stipulated for the American president in relation to the American congress is essentially the same as that of George III in relation to the British parliament. There is, of course, the difference that the president is elected separately from congress for a four-year term, so that heredity was replaced by democratic electoral processes in this respect. But once elected, the American president possesses separate and independent executive power following the eighteenth-century English model.

There is a serious defect in this model, the lack of systematic co-ordination between the legislative and executive functions or branches of government. This defect became fixed—indeed frozen—in the written constitution of the United States in 1789. However, the unwritten British constitution continued to develop and change through practice and custom, so that, by the time some sixty more years had passed, this defect had been remedied in Britain. As we shall see, the new and better system was passed on to the British North American colonies in the 1840s. As we shall also see, the new system served French Canada well. The main features of this later part of the story are as follows.

The development of the full-fledged cabinet system in Britain owes a great deal to William Pitt. He became Prime Minister in 1783, and with only one brief break of three years (1801–1804) he remained in office until 1806. Shortly after 1783, George III suffered permanently declining health, and his repeated illnesses left Pitt virtually in a position of primacy. Pitt had the personal qualities to take advantage of this, and he developed and consolidated the power of the office of Prime Minister. He established the principle of cabinet solidarity: that the cabinet must take a single position on matters of policy and stand together in support of that position. He also effectively asserted his own control as Prime Minister over the composition and agenda of the cabinet. These were long steps forward toward the modern cabinet system, and both the Prince Regent and William IV accepted the new custom and practice—they had no interest in re-asserting George III's earlier authority. However, Pitt continued to manipulate electoral representation in the House of Commons in the old way, to ensure himself the favourable House that was recognized as necessary. He ignored several defeats in the House of Commons.

It was not until after 1830 that the further principle was established, by practice and custom, that the prime minister must resign, or ask for dissolution and an election, if an important cabinet-sponsored measure was defeated on a vote in the House of Commons. The resignation of the Duke of Wellington as Prime Minister in 1830 was the first instance of this. The Great Reform Act of 1832 reorganized the parliamentary constituencies and widened the franchise so that Parliament became more democratic and much less subject to manipulation of membership by a prime minister. Very quickly after 1832, the precedents for resignation or dissolution on defeat in the House multiplied and the rule became firm. Thus, in Britain by the 1830s, the defect of the eighteenth-century British constitution had been cured. Effective co-ordination and harmony between the executive and legislative powers in the state had been achieved on a systematic basis which held the executive accountable to the elected chamber of the legislature as indicated.

Let us look now at relevant developments in British North America after the American Revolution.[3] At first Britain continued to govern the remaining British North American colonies along the old lines, though there were some minor administrative reforms. To make a long story short, we find that the same constitutional conflicts that had preceded the Revolution in the American colonies surfaced again in the British North American colonies during the 1820s and 1830s. The governor, appointed and instructed from London, held the whole of the executive power in a colony, along with his appointed executive council. This oligarchy came into conflict in the old way with the elected assembly of the colony. As in 1776, the British government could see no way out of this dilemma—the colonial governor still could not serve two masters. The result was rebellion in both Upper and Lower Canada in 1837. It is noteworthy that the rebel leaders, Mackenzie in Upper Canada and Papineau in Lower Canada, both advocated the American constitutional system as the solution. The rebellions quickly failed, but they did prompt the British Government to send Lord Durham to British North America as Governor General, charging him to report on the situation and propose remedies.

As explained earlier, this was the very decade in which the final steps rounding out the full modern cabinet system were taken in Britain itself. Moreover, while full collective cabinet responsibility thus became established in practice, there was little public explanation or articulation of what had happened. Indeed, many in Britain still considered cabinet accountability to the House of Commons to be what it was in the time of Pitt or even the earlier years of George III. But Lord Durham, being a Radical and a reformer in British politics, was well aware of the new position. Another person who knew of it was Robert Baldwin, one of the leaders of the "Reform" party in Upper Canada. His reform group, which had wide support, preferred the British to the American constitution and wished loyally to maintain the British connection. Robert Baldwin made representations to Durham, on the latter's invitation, urging that the grant of cabinet or responsible government to each of the colonies for all purposes of internal self-government was the great and necessary measure to be taken. No doubt this influenced Lord Durham greatly; in any event this was the principal recommendation of the Durham Report to the British Government in 1839. Speaking of the nature of cabinet or responsible government in the Report, Lord Durham said:

In England, this principle has so long been considered an indisputable and essential part of our constitution, that it has really hardly ever been found necessary to inquire into the means by which its observance is enforced. When a ministry ceases to command a majority in Parliament on great questions of policy, its doom is immediately sealed; and it would appear to us as strange to attempt, for any time, to carry on a government by means of ministers perpetually in a minority, as it would be to pass laws with a majority of votes against them. The ancient constitutional remedies, by impeachment and a stoppage of supplies, have never, since the reign of William III, been brought into operation for the purpose of removing a ministry. They have never been called for, because in fact, it has been the habit of ministers rather to anticipate the occurrence of an absolutely hostile vote, and to retire, when supported only by a bare and uncertain majority.[4]

Professor A. H. Birch points out that, even for Britain herself, this is the first authoritative statement in a great public document of the nature of the collective responsibility of the cabinet. Commenting on the passage just quoted from Durham's Report, Professor Birch says: "This statement is worth quoting in full because it was the first clear assertion of what later became known as the convention of collective responsibility. In giving the impression that this was a long-established principle of the British constitution, Durham (who was a Radical) was rather misleading. In fact it had been established only during the previous three or four decades, and securely and irrevocably established only since the Reform Act of 1832."[5] So, the Canadian reformers and Durham himself were indeed very much up-to-date respecting the state of the British constitution on its home ground. The newness of this development at the time in Britain explains some of the misunderstandings of the period, in both Britain and Canada, about what "responsible government" did mean.

Finally, there was a vital refinement to Durham's proposal. In proposing that the colonial governor should govern under the advice of a cabinet dependent on the elected assembly of his colony, Durham reserved certain subjects, those of persisting importance being foreign relations, foreign trade, and the constitution of the colonial system of government itself. On these matters the governor would continue to take his instructions from London, but on all other matters he would act under the advice of his colonial prime minister and cabinet, according to the newly established principles of cabinet government. This federal formula for executive responsibility helped to solve the dilemma of the first British Empire; that dilemma being the old idea that a colonial governor could not respond to two masters if there was to be an Empire at all. He *could* respond to two masters *on different subjects*. Thus Lord Durham pointed the way to full colonial domestic self-government coupled with the maintenance of the British connection. There was now no need for a second American Revolution. It should be noted that Lord Durham's constitutional solution was largely made possible by the emergence in Britain herself, just a very few years before his mission to British North America, of the full-fledged cabinet system.

Nevertheless, in 1839 and 1840 the outlook for the French Canadians was dark and gloomy indeed. Unfortunately Lord Durham's Report had another principal feature. In the aftermath of armed rebellion, he advocated the anglicization of the French Canadians. To this end, he proposed the union of Upper and Lower Canada to form the United Province of Canada. In the electorate for the parliament of the United Province, the English Canadians of Upper and Lower Canada would be a majority and the French Canadians a perpetual minority. Even before receiving Durham's Report, the British Government had decided on union, and in the Imperial Act of Union of 1840 they went even further than Durham had proposed. They provided that Upper and Lower Canada (Canada West and Canada East) were to have an equal number of members in the union parliament, though the population of Lower Canada was considerably greater than that of Upper Canada at the time. Thus the English element of the combined electorate was given even greater influence than it would have enjoyed on strict principles of representation by population. Moreover, it was provided that English was to be the sole language of the new parliament.[6]

At this point, something of great importance happened. After Papineau fled, Louis La Fontaine, who had not taken part in the rebellion, became the most influential political leader of the French Canadians. Meanwhile, the British Government made it clear that they were not accepting Lord Durham's proposal for responsible government in Canada—they still considered the constitutional dilemma of the old Empire insoluble, and did not perceive that Durham had found a solution. The Reform party of Robert Baldwin in Upper Canada realized that they would have to organize and fight political battles in the new united parliament to win responsible government. This meant they needed allies in Lower Canada, and so they sought a reform alliance with La Fontaine and his followers. The Baldwin party in Upper Canada was concerned to get rid of the Family Compact, and the La Fontaine party in Lower Canada was just as anxious to eliminate the corresponding oligarchy there, the *château clique*.

The events of the next few years can be given briefly as follows. Baldwin and Hincks assured La Fontaine that responsible government, if it were won for Canada, would provide the French Canadians with enough real political power that they could effectively protect and preserve the French-Canadian culture and way of life. Indeed, they argued that this was the best if not the only way open to do so. La Fontaine was persuaded and managed to carry his followers with him. He and Baldwin held to the alliance with great mutual sympathy and integrity, and responsible government was achieved in a very few years, with the results for French Canada that Baldwin and Hincks had predicted and supported. The vital historical fact, then, is that the dominant political leaders of English Canada at this time took the initiative and joined hands with the dominant political leaders of French Canada to ensure the continuance and protection of the French way of life in Lower Canada. English Canadians and French Canadians together used the winning of responsible government to frustrate the British Government's plan to anglicize the French Canadians. Professor Chester Martin's account of the formation and development of this alliance is worth quoting in full.

Hincks's first letter to La Fontaine, dated April 12, 1839, was written without previous acquaintance. Between that date and the first session of the Canadian Assembly in June, 1841, no fewer than thirty-four of these confidential letters are to be found in the La Fontaine Papers. So discreet and secret was this intercourse that it could not be entrusted to the post office of those days. The good offices of trusted friends and a visit of La Fontaine to Toronto during the summer of 1840 enlarged the confidential circle to include Morin, Cherrier, Viger, Woodruff, and a few others. With the meeting of La Fontaine and Baldwin the alliance took on a deeper and more intimate relationship. Domestic bereavement for both charged this friendship as time went on with mutual sympathy and affection. Baldwin's incorruptible character, his uncompromising rectitude, his inflexible "principle," remained the sheet-anchor of the Canadian reform party until responsible government was won. But the strategy was the strategy of Francis Hincks, and the political alliance which he advocated became a landmark in Canadian politics.

The induction of a group of young French Canadians, trained in the Papineau school of uncompromising obstruction, into the Eleusinian mysteries of responsible government was no easy task. La Fontaine's long association with Papineau, his ineradicable bitterness intensified by Durham's proscription of "his people," the brutal terms of the union and the manner of its passing in

Lower Canada, must have given many a rankling reflection to a
young patriot of La Fontaine's sensibilities. How he responded to
the crisis, how he mastered his old prepossessions and turned with
his new friends to face the unpredictable prospects of the union,
with smouldering faith but with a grim sense of destiny for his
country, is traceable in the La Fontaine Papers. How he succeeded
in purveying that faith to others, in training them to discipline
and forbearance and acquiescence if not confidence in the mysteries of a new technique, remains a more baffling problem, one
to which Canadian history has not yet found the answer.

The burden of Hincks's argument was threefold: that the
union which outraged La Fontaine's instincts and many of his
dearest interests in detail could yet, through the co-operation of
trusted allies restore French Canada to an honourable and honoured place in Canadian politics; that responsible government,
with all its indirection and conventions would be more effective
for this purpose than uncompromising obstruction; and finally
that the British connexion, exploited though it had been by the
château clique, could be a better guarantee for the rights of "his
people" at the darkest hour of their fortunes than the most logical
application of the "elective principle" under a hypothetical republic. All three of these arguments were fairly won: sometimes by
ingratiating candour, sometimes by the adroit indoctrination of
events, and not infrequently by invoking the serene faith, the
incorruptible character, of Robert Baldwin.[7]

There is no need to retrace in detail here the last few steps during
the 1840s toward responsible government. A new British government
adopted Durham's plan in 1846 and instructed the British North
American governors accordingly. The reform parties won elections
both in Nova Scotia and Canada in 1847 and 1848, whereupon the
respective governors installed responsible ministries in office, first in
Nova Scotia and a few weeks later in Canada, in the early months
of 1848. It should be noted that this was a victory for democracy, as
well as for efficiency in the co-ordination of legislature and executive.
While there were property qualifications on the franchise in Canada
at the time, farmers and small shopkeepers were able to meet the
requirements and possessed the vote. Thus both representative

assembly and cabinet came under the control of a broadly based electorate. In these circumstances the Jacksonian democracy of the United States ceased to be attractive as an alternative for British North America. The executive oligarchies of the colonies were replaced by cabinets responsible through the elected assemblies to the electorate itself.

The first Prime Minister of the United Province of Canada was Louis La Fontaine, as Canada East had elected the larger number of Reform party members. It was, however, a partnership, being the La Fontaine–British ministry. Specific results beneficial to French Canada were quick in coming under the new ministry. "During their administration, three legislative measures of particular significance to French Canada were given royal assent. One permitted the last of the exiled rebels of 1837–38 to return home, the second gave official recognition to the French language. The third, and most controversial, was the Rebellion Losses Act, by which Lower Canadians were permitted to put forward claims for compensation for damages sustained during the Rebellions."[8]

French Canada had come a very long way indeed in ten years. Thus we see that Baldwin and La Fontaine had made cultural duality and racial collaboration part of the pattern of Canadian life, along with democratic responsible government. This pattern of life has endured, though it has been ineffectively challenged from time to time. One challenge was immediate. The Montreal English merchants, angry at the Rebellion Losses Act and despairing because of the abrupt ending of Imperial trade preferences by the British government, proposed union with the United States in their Annexation Manifesto of 1849. They got nowhere. Professor J. M. S. Careless describes and interprets the reaction to the Annexation Manifesto as follows:

The peak came in October, when in Montreal the Annexation Association issued a jolting manifesto. Pointing darkly to "ruin and decay" throughout Canada, the barren hope of the canals, the vital need for new markets and capital, the document called for "friendly and peaceful" separation from Britain and union with the United States. Its three hundred and twenty-five signatories included a future father of Confederation, Alexander Tilloch

Galt, a later conservative prime minister, J. J. C. Abbott, and two subsequent leading liberals, Antoine-Aimé Dorion and Luther Holton; but the list read chiefly like a roster of Montreal's business élite. Response was rapid. There was a clamour of anti-annexation meetings and addresses, drowning minor echoes elsewhere of the Montreal declaration. Indignant argument and agitation went on through the winter. Yet well before the year's end it was evident that the Annexation Manifesto had been scarcely more than a final bout of Montreal fever, not the herald of a new popular upheaval.

It had shown, in fact, that the mass of Canadians were essentially satisfied with their political state, whatever the burdens of depression. In French Canada, the very success of responsible government, of La Fontaine's leadership, of the Rebellion Losses Act, had left small margin for Papineau and the *rouges'* annexationism. A largely cautious, conservative-minded people were in the mass but little stirred by visions of democratic and republican perfection; and they saw joining the United States as the virtual extinction, not the realization, of the national identity which they had so resolutely defended. *Survivance* within the Canadian union looked far more feasible and desirable than the radicals' dream of *nationalité* within the American union. Furthermore, the fact that *rouges* revived the old anti-clericalism of the *patriotes*, and warmly hailed the liberal, anti-papal revolution of 1848 in Rome, turned the potent influence of the church with increasing effect against them.

In Upper Canada among all parties, the strength of British allegiance, the ingrained resistance to the United States, and the feeling also for a separate identity in America, had brought the emphatic rejection of annexationism. Besides, now that responsible rule had so clearly been established, any former association of annexation with self-government had lost much of its meaning. Joining the republic meant, instead, associating with slavery and sectional conflict, and (as the Toronto *Globe* energetically informed the West) abandoning the free, efficient system of British cabinet and parliamentary rule for a rigid, unwieldly, even old-fashioned, American written constitution.[9]

So much then for the winning of responsible government and its service to the preservation of the French-Canadian way of life. The other great landmark of our constitutional history is the achievement of federation of the British North American colonies in 1867 and the years following, and this too served the same purpose in a very significant way, though of course federation had other motives and purposes as well.

The story of the achievement of confederation is better known than is that of the winning of responsible government. My present purpose, then, is simply to recount enough of the confederation story to show that, once again, there was at work a close, sympathetic, and effective partnership between the political leaders of English Canada and French Canada concerned to ensure continuing security for the French-Canadian way of life.

It would be wrong to suggest that, after the advent of responsible government, all was smooth sailing in the United Province of Canada. In fact, though much was accomplished, the successive governments, partnerships between English Upper Canadians and French Lower Canadians though they were, became increasingly unstable. For many purposes Upper and Lower Canada were still treated as separate. At times the political claim was made that there should be a majority from each section (a "double majority") to pass new legislation, but this never became a consistent practice. By the late 1850s, Upper Canada had quite considerably surpassed Lower Canada in population, so that now the shoe of under-representation by population was pinching the Upper Canadian foot, reversing the position of 1841. This was aggravated by some instances where the informal double-majority idea was ignored when it did seem relevant. Perhaps the most striking of these was the Taché School Act of 1855, where a big majority of Lower Canadian votes was used by John A. Macdonald to ensure the passage of legislation applying to Upper Canada alone and requiring in Upper Canada tax-supported separate schools for Roman Catholics. There was a considerable storm of protest in Upper Canada about the way this was done, but the legislation was never repealed and indeed its essential provisions were eventually guaranteed by section 93 of the British North America Act of 1867 and stand today as part of the school law of

Ontario. In 1855, however, this did sharpen the campaign in Upper
Canada for representation by population, led by George Brown of
the *Globe* newspaper.[10]

George Brown had succeeded Baldwin as the chief Reform Party
leader in Upper Canada while John A. Macdonald became the
principal leader of the Upper Canadian Conservatives. In Lower
Canada, George Etienne Cartier had succeeded La Fontaine as the
most influential leader of the French Canadians. Brown and Macdonald were bitter political rivals in Upper Canada, but nevertheless
as the 1850s passed into the 1860s they both became exasperated over
the frequency with which governments in the United Province were
falling. At this period, both leaders on occasion publicly advocated a
federal solution of some kind. In the early 1860s, also, Brown and
Macdonald tentatively sounded one another out through interme-
diaries about reform along federal lines, but nothing came immediately of these indirect soundings. Finally, matters came to a head
in May and June of 1864. Taché and Macdonald had formed a
ministry on 30 March, but it was defeated on a vote in the House on
14 June. There was no prospect that another election would bring
different political party groupings and more stability.

In these circumstances, George Brown took a "dramatic initiative."[11] He passed the word through friends to John A. Macdonald
that he, Brown, would be interested in the possibility of a coalition
government dedicated to major constitutional reform along federal
lines. Macdonald responded positively and quickly, he and Galt
opened negotiations with Brown and soon they were joined by
Cartier. In the background Lord Monck, the Governor General,
gave enthusiastic encouragement. So the Taché–Macdonald–Brown–
Cartier coalition ministry was formed, with Brown and two other
Upper Canadian Reformers in cabinet positions. This meant a break
between Brown and former political allies in Lower Canada. The
intention and mandate of the new coalition was to pursue a federal
solution for the political and constitutional ills of the United Province
of Canada. Brown's preference was for a federal union of Upper and
Lower Canada, with the union to be widened later to the East and
to the West in British North America, if possible. John A. Macdonald
preferred to seek the wider union first, and to fall back, if necessary,
on the federation of Upper and Lower Canada only. This was just

a difference in emphasis about what was politically more practical, so the coalition government started out on Macdonald's course, which was consistent enough with Brown's basic approach. From this point on, the consummate political skill of John A. Macdonald, and his vision of a new British country from sea to sea, were the guiding factors in achieving the wider union, so that the alternative of a federal union of Upper and Lower Canada alone never had to be considered.

It is true that John A. Macdonald would have preferred legislative union of British North America, and on occasion he said so rather wistfully. The United States was in the midst of a bloody civil war and this was hardly an encouragement to Canadian federalists at the time. But both Macdonald and Brown knew all along that a federal solution designed to give very significant autonomy to Lower Canada was essential. Both accepted this. The French Canadians were to be asked to give up their very powerful position in the parliament of the United Province of Canada for a lesser influence in the new parliament of a federated British North America composed on principles of representation by population. They had to be given in return an autonomous provincial parliament for Lower Canada in which the same population principle would ensure a French-Canadian majority position with power over subjects vital to the French-Canadian way of life, like education and laws covering property and civil rights. To this extent Brown was willing to give federalism priority over the principle of representation by population, and likewise Macdonald surrendered his preference for legislative union. At this point, we must appreciate the vital part played by Cartier. Professor J. M. S. Careless pays him the following tribute.

> Without his willingness to pledge support of the French-Canadian majority—and thereby mortgage his entire political future with his people—the new government and its project would have been wholly impossible. Essentially it took two to end deadlock, the two who could swing the votes of the two opposed sectional majorities: Brown to make the offer, Cartier to receive it. In agreeing to that offer, the Bleu leader was accepting both the loss of the entrenched French position in the existing union and the establishment of rep by pop within a new federation. It was an act of highest political

courage, and, one might add, of undeluded vision. Brown gained new respect and fellow-feeling for Cartier on their joining forces, for, as one sectional leader, he knew what it had cost the other to come to terms. The two of them brought the majority votes, Grits and Bleus, that made the Confederation ministry politically viable. It could not have existed or pursued its ends without them both.[12]

Once again then, as in the 1840s, the English-Canadian political leaders of Upper Canada formed a partnership with the French-Canadian political leader of Lower Canada to ensure security for the French-Canadian way of life in the new constitutional arrangements contemplated. Perhaps the geographical extent and natural regionalism of British North America from sea to sea would have required a federal solution in any event, but the duality of cultures in the United Province of Canada made federalism essential regardless of geography.

The present constitutional debate in Canada has been marked by much adversely critical reference to historical sins of omission and commission by British Canadians against their French-Canadian fellow citizens. No doubt the record is not spotless; certain valid causes of complaint have occurred and some still exist. But we have heard too much in recent years of these things and not enough of the other side of the story. There has been too much disparagement along historical lines of British Canadians—some of it coming from French Canada but some of it being undue self-disparagement by British Canadians themselves. As I have tried to show, and the two cases covered are only examples, there have been very important positive factors in the historical record to the credit of British Canadians in relation to French Canadians. I have written in the conviction that it is time to recall the establishment of responsible government and confederation with pride in the common achievements they represent for British and French Canadians alike. It is time also to appreciate the great positive potential of parliamentary democracy, the cabinet system, and federalism for ensuring the continuance of Canadian unity today and tomorrow.

More needs to be said, in conclusion, on this last point. Though the main outlines of the confederation plan were given in the British North America Act, much vital fleshing out of the full meaning of the division of legislative powers between the federal parliament and the provincial legislatures remained to be done. By judicial interpretation and governmental practice, before the nineteenth century had ended, we had developed in Canada a well-balanced federalism in which the full autonomy of the provinces in their allotted legislative sphere was made explicit. Sir Oliver Mowat, as Premier of Ontario, was the principal champion of a strong position for the provinces in the later years of the nineteenth century, and the powers of the Government of Quebec benefited from the successes of the Mowat Government in some of the constitutional cases it took to court. Some think judicial interpretation went too far in favour of the provinces. Be that as it may, the rules of the game started to change anyway with growing demands from the public for greatly increased activity and responsibility by *all* governments. This caused a shift in the nature of Canadian federalism, a process still going on, from dual federalism to co-operative federalism, in the sense in which Professor R. L. Watts has used these terms.[13] He explains that both types of federalism are based on the principle that the country concerned has one basic constitutional system under which the central government on the one hand and the respective regional governments on the other "are assigned co-ordinate authority such that neither level of government is legally or politically subordinate to the other." But the classical dual federalism assumed also that the central and regional governments could and would operate in separate spheres without any functional dependence one upon the other. This may have been accurate to a considerable degree in the Canada of one hundred years ago, but it has simply not been the truth of the relationship in recent decades. The provincial governments on the one hand and the federal government on the other, though still co-ordinate in constitutional status, have become dependent on one another in many ways. Federal and provincial finances, laws, and responsibilities interact and interpenetrate in numerous areas of urgent social concern, making a genuinely co-operative federalism necessary, if federalism we are to have at all. But this is a very demanding and delicately poised form of government and requires the spirit of true partnership from our political leaders, both federal and provincial, if it is to work successfully. While primary leadership must come from the federal government on the public control of many of the problem areas of modern society, nevertheless the provinces (large or small) must be treated as equals and not as subordinates. They have their own contribution to make.

We are developing in Canada sophisticated processes of intergovernmental consultation, so that there may be collaboration and agreement in providing the public control measures (both federal and provincial) for sweeping problem areas like poverty, pollution, regional economic disparities, urban reform and renewal, privacy, the new electronic technologies of communication and information processing, and so on. In fact, co-operative federalism, Canadian style, is already emerging as the pattern of the future for a united Canada.[14] The present systematic review of constitutional issues is bringing federal and provincial ministers and principal civil servants together in many more intergovernmental consultations than ever before. This may or may not result in some formal changes in the federal constitution of the country. I strongly suspect that, in the end, we shall find the historical importance of these many meetings of ministers and officials to be elsewhere. We may find their importance to lie in the development of more regular and effective intergovernmental co-operation for the co-ordinated use of existing federal and provincial powers, or at least for the use of federal and provincial powers that are not much changed from what they are now.

This should not be viewed as an anti-democratic development, though some commentators and editors would have us believe that this is so. Because of the cabinet system, the ministers who engage in intergovernmental consultations are responsible to their respective democratic parliamentary bodies for the policies they sponsor, the concessions they make, and the agreements they sign.[15] The policies and agreements can be considered and debated under many different procedural arrangements in the legislative bodies concerned, to ensure the accountability of cabinets to their respective parliaments and so to the people themselves. I hope I am right when I think that I see emerging in Canada a more effective co-operative federalism that Quebec needs as much as, if not more than, the rest of us. A dynamic, balanced co-operative federalism of this type offers the best security now available for the French-Canadian way of life.

By contrast, the United States has really ceased to be a federal country in the Canadian "distribution-of-powers" sense. The legislative supremacy of the national congress over the state legislatures is now established to the extent that statutes of the congress almost invariably prevail over state laws on just about any subject. American writers speak of this as the demise of dual federalism.[16] This may well be a perfectly proper and desirable development for the United States, as their response to the modern demand for governments to be ever more active with social control measures of all kinds. Indeed, in the absence of a cabinet system in Washington and the state capitals, to accept the legislative supremacy of the national congress may be the only way the American constitutional system can respond to the modern need for social legislation of a sweeping nature in so many fields. The president and the state governors are often not in harmony with or in control of their respective legislative bodies, so they are unable to conclude intergovernmental agreements as partners and make them stick, either as a matter of money or legislation. Canadian cabinets can make their agreements stick with both money and legislation.

This leads to the thought that it is highly important in Canada today to improve the procedures of our parliamentary bodies (federal and provincial) to ensure that the elected members (including the cabinet ministers) are better informed and more sensitive concerning the problems of our society and the needs of the people. We do see major improvements in parliamentary procedure being developed. Real progress has been made recently in the Parliament of Canada and changes are also under way in the Legislative Assembly of Ontario. It is most important that these reforms should continue so that, among other things, democratic controls should operate well on the processes of co-operative federalism.

If we make a success of the Canadian type of balanced co-operative federalism, this will be a useful example and prototype for the extension of the rule of law in other areas of the world—areas where local autonomy is highly prized but where there is yet critical need for wider regional authority and unity as well. American congressional supremacy within the United States does not offer such a model to the world.

If Quebec were to separate, then it might well happen that both Quebec and other parts of Canada would soon be absorbed piecemeal into the United States. There are worse fates possible in the modern world. The American constitution does provide one of the world's great systems of democratic government, in spite of serious defects that have been mentioned. Nevertheless, we in Canada do have a distinctive society in North America that differs in vital ways from that of the United States. Our evolutionary tradition of constitutional change and our better systems of government and law have much to do with these distinctions. The lesson of our history and present situation is that all Canadians, including those of British and French origin, should hold together in a federal Canada, separate from the United States. To borrow the words of Professor Careless, Canadians have a "feeling" for "a separate identity in America."[17]

NOTES

1. See A. H. Birch, *Representative and Responsible Government* (Toronto: University of Toronto Press, 1965), chap. 10; and John P. Mackintosh, *The British Cabinet* (London: Stevens, 1962), chap. 2.

2. L. W. Labaree, *Royal Government in America* (New Haven: Yale University Press, 1930), pp. 394–395.

3. In general, see Chester Martin, *Foundations of Canadian Nationhood* (Toronto: University of Toronto Press, 1955), Parts I and II.

4. Quoted in Birch, *Representative and Responsible Government*, p. 132.

5. Ibid.

6. See generally on this period, J. M. S. Careless, *The Union of the Canadas, 1841–1857* (Toronto: McClelland & Stewart, 1967).

7. Martin, *Foundations of Canadian Nationhood*, pp. 160–161.

8. Margaret Elizabeth Abbott Nish, *Racism or Responsible Government: The French Canadian Dilemma of the 1840s* (Toronto: Copp Clark, 1967), p. 131.

9. Careless, *Union*, pp. 129–130.

10. Careless, *Brown of The Globe*, 2 vols. (Toronto: Macmillan of Canada, 1959–62), 1:203–204; and *Union*, pp. 216–217.

11. Careless, *Brown*, 2:chap. 4 [the phrase "dramatic initiative" is the author's]; and Donald Creighton, *John A. Macdonald: the Young Politician* (Toronto: Macmillan, 1952), chap. 12–13.

12. Careless, *Brown*, 2:145–146.

13. Ronald Lampman Watts, *New Federations: Experiments in the Commonwealth* (Oxford: Clarendon Press, 1966), pp. 12–13.

14. See W. R. Lederman, "Some Forms and Limitations of Co-operative Federalism," *Canadian Bar Review* 45 (1967): 409–436; and Queen's University at Kingston, Institute of Intergovernmental Relations, *Report: Inter-*

governmental Liaison on Fiscal and Economic Matters (Ottawa: Queen's Printer, 1969).

15. For example, Premier Lesage first agreed to the Fulton–Favreau Formula for Amendment, at Charlottetown in 1964, and then repudiated it after encountering strong opposition in his own party on his return to Quebec.

16. See, for example, Bernard Schwartz, *American Constitutional Law* (Cambridge: Cambridge University Press, 1955), pp. 167–175.

17. In this essay nothing has been said of the respective judicial systems of the United States and Canada, but here also there is the same story, lesson, and result as in the case of the cabinet system. The later nineteenth century was a period of great reform in England resulting in radical simplification of judicial procedure and organization of the courts. Both before and after Confederation, the British North American parliaments followed the British example with reform statutes of their own on the British model. The United States, however, took English courts and procedure as it found them in the late eighteenth century before the great era of reform referred to. In many states of the Union, the court systems and procedure are still pretty much in the unreformed condition of overlapping powers, confusion, and complexity inherited from eighteenth-century England. See Lederman, "The Independence of the Judiciary," *Canadian Bar Review* 34 (1956): 769 and 1139.

The Survival
or Disintegration
of Federations

R. L. Watts

IS A FEDERATION a stable form of political union? What factors contribute to the survival or failure of a federation? These are questions of fundamental importance to Canadians today. While every federation is to a large extent the product of a unique conjunction of conditions and institutions, there may be some valuable lessons for us to be drawn from the persistence or disintegration of other federal political systems. It is significant that four of the longest surviving constitutional systems anywhere in the world today are federal in form: the United States adopted its federal constitution in 1787, Switzerland in 1848, Canada in 1867, and Australia in 1900. It is equally significant that a number of apparently stable federal constitutional systems have experienced the secession of component regions or total disintegration: recent examples are the secession of Jamaica which led to the disintegration of the West Indies Federation in 1962, the secession of Malawi and Zambia in 1962 and 1963 which broke up the Federation of Rhodesia and Nyasaland, the expulsion of Singapore from the Federation of Malaysia in 1965, and the secession of Biafra from Nigeria in 1966 triggering off a protracted civil war. If Canada is to avoid a similar experience we might well look at the factors which have contributed to the success or failure of other federations.

FEDERAL FAILURES

What are the indications of stress or failure in a federal political system? Ultimately civil war or disintegration clearly indicates that a federation has failed. But such a situation is usually preceded by other indications that the federation is under stress. The first is the existence of continued political cleavage between regional groups within the federation, exemplified by a tendency for political controversies to focus continually on inter-regional resentments and by the drawing of party loyalties on primarily regional lines. Of course, even relatively stable federations have experienced inter-regional disputes or controversies from time to time, but where there is a failure to resolve these, the cumulative sharpness in inter-regional political cleavages is a sign of increasing stress within the federation. Such a trend in turn may become more acute when governments, faced by continued political cleavage and unable to find solutions to apparently irreconcilable regional demands, simply avoid making decisions upon these questions. The consistent failure of a political system to meet the demands presented to it may create a feeling of frustration. This may lead certain segments of the population to the view that governmental decisions are no longer legitimate or binding, a view which then expresses itself in the organization of secession movements or in an increasing resort to violence by those opposed to governmental decisions. A further indication of serious stress within a federal system is the growth of demands for the conversion of the constitutional structure to an alternative form of union: for a looser form of union such as a confederacy or economic community, or for a tighter union such as a centralized unitary system or even a military administration. Finally, the most extreme indication of stress within a federal system is the eruption of political cleavage into outright civil war.

The examples of such stresses or even outright failure in federal or confederal systems are numerous. Even the long-standing federations of the United States, Switzerland, and Australia have experienced their moments of extreme stress. Although in most periods the American federal system has moderated political conflict, in the mid-nineteenth century relations between the Northern and Southern states deteriorated to the point where a long and bitter civil war, the ultimate mark of political failure, was fought over the issue of slavery, 1861–1865. In the decade preceding 1861, the conditions which previously had encouraged moderation had gradually given way to those which sharpened political cleavages and encouraged intransigence. More and more there was a political polarization until on almost every issue the Northern and Southern states split into two irreconcilable camps. In the end, faced by the determination of the Southern states to secede, the federal Government had to turn to military means to preserve the Union. In the century since, the American political institutions have on the whole moderated political conflict and encouraged compromises and consensual decisions. But now, a century since the Civil War, there are signs that the United States may again be entering a period of increasing political polarization which the political institutions are failing to moderate.

Switzerland is often taken for granted as a unique model of long-standing multicultural co-existence and harmony. What is frequently forgotten is that the history of the Swiss confederacies from 1291 to 1847 was studded with inter-cantonal military struggles from time to time, and that the present Swiss federal constitution was adopted following a civil war in 1847 in which the federal troops crushed a rebellion by the Sonderbund, a separatist league of seven cantons. The confederacy established under the Pact of Restoration, 1815, had been under considerable strain from 1830 on. In the years following 1830 those cantons which had accepted liberal reforms brought pressure to bear for the revision of the 1815 Pact along more liberal lines, but the conservative Catholic cantons dug in their heels. The result was a growing cleavage between the liberal and conservative cantons. Events came to a head when the liberals clashed head-on with the Catholic conservatives over such issues as the taxing of Church property, the abolishing of monasteries and the exclusion of Jesuits. When seven Catholic cantons, including the three original cantons of the Confederacy of 1291, formed a separate league, the Sonderbund, in order to defend themselves against the pressure of the liberal cantons and to put down internal liberal movements, the central Diet demanded that the Sonderbund dissolve itself. Following a blunt refusal, a federal army of 100,000 was sent in to crush the rebellion in November 1847. The campaign was briefer than the American Civil War—it lasted only nineteen days—but here too it was ultimately only by force that the union was preserved.

While Australia has never suffered the tragedy of a civil war, it has experienced a secessionist movement. Western Australia, a state which is remote from the other major centres of Australian population, was from the beginning slow to take up the enthusiasm for federation. After the creation of the federation, Western Australians, cut off from the rest of Australia and therefore parochial and isolationist in their outlook, developed over a period of several decades a growing dissatisfaction with federal policies and particularly with the trend towards financial, economic, and political centralization. This trend was the subject of growing protest from Western Australia until finally the people of that state actually voted for secession at a referendum held in 1933. Following upon this vote the state Government presented a formal petition to the United Kingdom Government to pass an act detaching Western Australia from the federation. The British Parliament, however, refused to receive the petition since it did not have the support of the Australian Commonwealth Government. Subsequently, with the gradual restoration of prosperity, the increase of federal financial aid to the state, and the improvement of communications between east and west, the secession movement in Western Australia lost much of its passion until the remnants of secessionist sentiment have now almost completely faded away.

The newer parliamentary federations established during the last twenty-five years in the former British colonial areas also illustrate the ways in which separatist movements may arise and federations disintegrate. Within most of them linguistic, racial, or religious divisions have been at the root of severe internal tensions. On the Indian sub-continent, the British search in the 1930s and 1940s for some form of federation within which the Hindus and Muslims might remain politically associated proved fruitless, and the political partition of the sub-continent which followed this failure was marked by a bloodbath in which something like one million people were killed and more than twelve million became refugees. The resulting legacy of hostility between India and Pakistan has continued to the present day.

Within India itself, since 1947, the explosive impact of linguistic divisions has made itself felt in the irresistible demands of regional linguistic groups for the reorganization of state boundaries in order that most states might represent homogeneous unilingual units. Linguistic division has also expressed itself in the tension between the generally Hindi-speaking majority in the North and the Dravidian-speaking peoples of the South, where during the last decade or so the separatist movement for an independent Dravidasthan has made a powerful political impact.

In Pakistan, too, linguistic regionalism and even separatism have been a disruptive political force. Linguistic distinctiveness, accentuated by a feeling on the part of the Bengalis that they have suffered exploitation at the hands of the West Pakistanis, has been at the root of the continued demands by East Pakistanis for greater provincial autonomy and of occasional suggestions in favour of secession. These tensions produced the political instability which, first in 1958 and again in 1969, induced the establishment of military rule with the avowed intention of preventing the break-up of the fragile union of West and East Pakistan. More recently, these pressures erupted in the tragic strife in East Pakistan in the spring of 1971.

Other new federations have also provided examples of the ways in which federations may split or disintegrate. The West Indies Federation of 1958, for example, illustrated the strains which may arise within a federation in which there are wide disparities in the size and wealth of the component territories. Jamaica, the largest of the territorial units, possessed more than half the federal population and area and provided 42 per cent of the federal revenue. The result was continued and heated controversy over the appropriate regional representation in the central institutions. The small islands distrusted Jamaica, and Jamaica in turn resented the degree to which its influence in the federation was reduced in order to accommodate the fears of the smaller islands. Ultimately this dispute reached such proportions that in a referendum held in 1961 a majority of Jamaicans voted for secession. Faced with this democratic expression of Jamaican opinion, the British Government, without consulting the federal Government, hastily agreed to permit Jamaica to secede, disregarding the very different stand which it had taken following the Western Australian secession referendum of 1934. The British Government assumed that after the secession of Jamaica the remainder of the West Indies Federation would carry on, but once one territory had been permitted to secede, it proved impossible to refuse others, and on 31 May 1962—the very date which had been set some time before for its independence—the West Indies Federation was dissolved.

The Federation of Rhodesia and Nyasaland, created in 1953, was

ostensibly an inter-racial partnership of territories in which there had
previously been contrasting traditions in the relation of settlers to
Africans. The federation foundered, however, because of the insistence of the settlers of Southern Rhodesia that they should have the
role of "senior" partners. The result was increasing African disillusionment with the federation. This expressed itself in the growth in
the two northern territories of African nationalist movements dedicated to separation. As constitutional advances in the internal government of those two territories brought into political power African
nationalist leaders committed to secession, the British Government
found itself forced to accede first to an independent Malawi in 1962
and then to an independent Zambia and the dissolution of the federation in 1963.

The Federation of Malaya, created in 1948, contained a delicate
racial balance in which the Malays constituted 50 per cent, the
Chinese 37 per cent, and the Indians 11 per cent. (These percentages
are derived from the 1957 census.) From the mid-1950s on, this balance was maintained by the dominance of the conservative Alliance
Party, uniting the existing three major communal parties within a
multiracial alliance in which the Malays acted as senior partners. The
economic and military desirability of adding Singapore to the federation created a problem because Singapore's predominantly Chinese
population and radical politics threatened to upset the delicate balance. Consequently, the federation was widened in 1963 into a
Federation of Malaysia, adding not only Singapore but two Borneo
states as well in order to offset the fears of Chinese preponderance.
Furthermore, Singapore as a component state was given a "special
status" with considerably more autonomy in its own affairs than the
Malayan states. But this special status was accompanied by constitutional and political limits on the role which the Singapore Chinese
were permitted to play in federal politics. These limits provoked inter-
racial tensions and a struggle for power between the mainland Malays
and the Singapore Chinese which culminated, in August 1965, in the
expulsion of Singapore from the federation.

A very recent example of a federation under severe stress has
been Nigeria. Although, in all, some 248 languages are spoken in
Nigeria, Nigerian politics, following the adoption of a federal form
of government in 1954, was characterized by the rivalry of the three

main cultural groups, each politicized through its own regionally based political party and each fearful of domination by the other two groups. Until 1965 the tenuous balance was maintained by the fact that the Northern People's Congress, representing the largest but economically most backward of the three groups, found it politically expedient in central politics to rely upon a coalition with the National Convention of Nigerian Citizens, whose strength was based on the Ibos, the most aggressively modernized group, mainly concentrated in Eastern Nigeria. But by 1965 the Northern People's Congress found it could dominate central politics without being dependent on its Southern partners. At the same time, Southern politicians, who had previously accepted a Northern majority in central politics as a temporary expedient in the expectation that demographic trends would soon reduce the proportion of seats held by the North, had become alarmed when new census results presented the prospect of prolonged Northern dominance. Distrust and intransigence on each side made the achievement of a federal consensus increasingly difficult. The resulting unrest induced a group of Ibo officers in the army to end constitutional government by a military *coup* early in 1966 in which the key non-Ibo political and military leaders were assassinated. But when, a few months later, these officers attempted to establish a centralized unitary government, the army itself became the victim of inter-regional distrust and resentment. The non-Ibo troops mutinied, a widespread massacre of Ibos followed, and the Ibos retreated to Eastern Nigeria, declaring it an independent Biafra and so triggering off a bitter civil war which lasted until 1970.

CONDITIONS WHICH CAUSE STRESS IN FEDERATIONS

These examples of federations which have experienced separatist movements or disintegration may provide us with some understanding of the conditions which lead to stress within federations. While the detailed circumstances have varied among these federations, common to them all has been the polarization of political conflict in such a way that eventually any compromise seemed impossible. Four sorts of conditions have contributed to this pattern: regional divergences of political demands; weaknesses of inter-regional communications; the evaporation of transitional inducements to union; external influences.

Regional divergences of political outlook and demands are typical of all federations: that is usually why they have adopted a federal solution in the first place. But a number of factors may sharpen such differences, and where several of these operate simultaneously, reinforcing each other, the cumulative effect may drive regional cleavages and political conflict to critical proportions.

Among the sharpest divisive forces have been those of language, race, religion, social structure, and cultural tradition. As in Canada, so in Switzerland, India, Pakistan, Malaysia, Nigeria, and Rhodesia and Nyasaland, linguistic, religious, and racial minorities who have feared discrimination at the hands of numerical majorities have defended provincial autonomy as a political way of preserving their own distinct identity and way of life. And in each of these federations, when that provincial autonomy or their cultural distinctiveness has been threatened, the minority groups have turned to advocating secession as the only defence against assimilation. Examples of the impact of cultural, linguistic, or racial forces on separatist movements, parellelling the trend in Quebec, are numerous: the separatism of the conservative Roman Catholic Sonderbund in a liberal Protestant Switzerland; the secession in 1861 from the United States of the Southern states, which felt that their social institutions and way of life were threatened by an abolitionist majority; the insistence of the Muslims of the Indian peninsula upon partition and the creation of Pakistan in 1947 in order to avoid domination by a Hindu majority; the growth in South India during the last decade of the Dravida Munnetra Kazhagam, a party dedicated to the separation of the Dravidian-speaking peoples from the Hindi-speaking majority to the north; the pressure by Bengali-speaking East Pakistanis for greater autonomy or even independence (the Bengalis being a majority of the population of Pakistan but complaining of their treatment by the central government as a minority) ; the complaints of the Singapore Chinese at their second-class status within a Malaysia ruled by Malays, complaints that were cured only by the separation of Singapore in 1965; the attempted secession of Eastern Nigeria because of the fears of the Ibos that unless they established an independent Biafra they would be oppressed in a Hausa-dominated Nigeria; the insistence of black African nationalists in Malawi and Zambia that these territories should break away from a federation in which the white settlers of Southern Rhodesia were dominant.

The political impact of linguistic and cultural cleavages has often been underestimated. Language and other cultural differences are not only barriers to communication but go deeper because they are fundamental to the activities which are distinctively human. It is language, for instance, which provides the individual with a means for expression and for communion with others. It is language which shapes the very way in which men order their thoughts coherently and which makes possible social organization.[1] Thus, a common language is the expression of a community of interests among a group of people. Not surprisingly, then, any community which is governed through the medium of a language other than its own has usually felt itself to some extent disenfranchised, and this feeling has always been a potential focus for political separatism, as in South India, East Pakistan, Singapore, the Bernese Jura in Switzerland, and Quebec. Moreover, like skin colour, language is an identifiable badge for those who wish to take issue with a different group, and thus, in many of these instances, as in Biafra, it has provided a rallying point even for issues which were basically not those of language and race.

While language has provided a basis for cultural cleavages in India, Pakistan, Nigeria and Switzerland, and linguistic and racial differences combined have divided Malaysia and Rhodesia and Nyasaland, we must not underestimate the divisive impact of other cultural factors also. In many instances religious differences have been particularly explosive and even more significant than linguistic divisions. An individual can learn to be bilingual, but to be bi-confessional is a self-contradiction. Thus, in Swiss history political divisions have tended more often to follow confessional lines than linguistic ones. In the newer federations of Asia and Africa the religious differences, such as those on the Indian sub-continent between Hindus and Muslims, or those in Nigeria between the predominantly Muslim North and more Christian or Animist South, have gone much deeper than those between different Christian denominations in Switzerland or Canada.

While regional differences in language, race, religion, social institutions, and culture have been powerful factors in most separatist movements, their influence has been strongest in those situations, such as in Nigeria, Malaysia, and Canada, where these regional differences have reinforced rather than cut across each other. In India and Pakistan, internal linguistic divisions have been moderated by the fact that within each federation a common religion prevails to a large extent. In Switzerland, the religious divisions between Protestants and Catholics are of fundamental significance; but they cut across linguistic ones—unlike the Canadian situation where the distinctive cultural outlook of Quebec is based not only on language, but on a cultural tradition derived from a different faith. In Switzerland, because the German-speaking cantons are divided almost equally between Protestant and Roman Catholic cantons and the French-speaking cantons are divided similarly, the cantonal alignments on political questions have tended to vary according to whether linguistic or religious considerations were most at issue. Thus, the linguistic groups have not been further solidified into unchanging political blocks by reinforcing differences in religious tradition, as in Canada.

In some federations, regional differences in degree of modernization have greatly accentuated regional consciousness. This has especially been the case in some of the newer multicultural federations where modernization and the penetration of Western ideas during the period of colonial rule were often very uneven. Some regions, especially those which had been under indirect rule, usually lagged behind others and were therefore fearful of being dominated after independence by the more modernized regions. In the Northwestern Provinces of pre-partition India and in Northern Nigeria during the early 1950s, these predominantly Muslim regions, influenced by a general Muslim conservatism and by their own educational backwardness, advocated ultra-autonomy or separation for their regions as a means of protecting themselves from exploitation or domination by the more advanced regional groups. The result in India was the partition of 1947 which led to the creation of Pakistan. In Nigeria, extensive regional autonomy was conceded in order that the Northerners, protected politically from the more modernized Southerners, might have a breathing space in which to accelerate their own development and so improve their position relative to the other regions. There are some parallels here to the situation of Quebec which, in the realm of education and technology, lagged behind the English-speaking provinces during the first half of the twentieth century but is now attempting to catch up.

Another contributing factor to the tensions between regional groups within a federation may be differences in the prevailing political orientation and ideology and in the style in which politics is carried on.

This consideration is certainly relevant to the Canadian situation: until the mid-twentieth century Quebec, with its emphasis upon its own traditions, was distinctively more conservative in its political viewpoint than most of the rest of Canada. Since 1960, however, under the impact of the "Quiet Revolution," there are some indications that the situation has been reversed. The gulf now appears to be between an English-speaking Canada which is relatively conservative in political orientation and a Quebec which has thrown up more radical tendencies and movements.

An examination of other federations indicates that in many of them inter-regional tension which was overtly cultural was closely related to differences of political outlook and ideology. Malaysia, Nigeria, and Pakistan present the most obvious examples among the newer federations. The departure of Singapore from the Malaysian Federation resulted not only from a struggle over the relative political roles to be played by the Malays and Chinese within the federation, but also from a clash between the inherently conservative outlook of the Alliance Party, including the commercial Chinese elements supporting it, and Lee Kuan Yew's extreme socialist People's Action Party which governed in Singapore. Indeed, it was the PAP's decision to campaign actively in federal politics, not as a Chinese party, but as a Malaysian socialist party, which triggered off the crisis leading to Singapore's separation. In Nigeria, the Southerners looked upon the political conservatism of the Northerners as a source of frustration and were fearful of what they considered to be the "feudal" outlook of the leaders of the Northern People's Congress. In Pakistan before 1958, the Bengalis, inclined to be more radical in politics, resented the dominance of West Pakistani landlords and businessmen in central politics, while the latter groups, in turn, were fearful that federal elections might result in a shift leftwards in the politics of the country. Indeed, some East Pakistanis have claimed that the imposition of military rule and the suspension of the federal constitution in 1958 was engineered by these West Pakistani groups in order to prevent the impending election and the expected political shift leftwards from occurring. Going further back in history, the nineteenth-century separatist movements in Switzerland in 1847 and the United States in 1861 were both the reactions of conservatively oriented groups who were opposed to the liberalizing, reforming outlook being taken by the majority in each of these federations. Even today, in Switzerland the main divisions between the political parties are not linguistic but ideological or economic, the major parties being the Catholic Conservatives, the Radicals, and the Socialists.

Besides cultural factors such as language, race, religion, social institutions, or ideological orientation, other factors have also contributed to tensions within federations and to separatist movements. For example, although in most federations the economic benefits of the larger political union have been prominently stressed and in some cases have provided a bridge between differing cultural groups, clashing economic interests have often contributed to regional consciousness. Even where federal union brings economic gains to a federation as a whole, there may be specific economic influences preventing certain provinces from sharing the benefits. An economic union may have not only "trade-creation" but "trade-diversion" effects which act adversely on some provinces within the federation. Thus, the operation of natural market factors may provide unequal benefits for different provinces and even increase, rather than reduce, inequalities. This may mean that, unless adequate equalization policies are adopted, some provinces, from their point of view, would be better off outside the federation. Complaints of such effects have contributed to separatist feeling at one time or another in Western Australia, the Southern United States, Nyasaland, Northern Nigeria, and East Pakistan just as they have in certain parts of Canada. In an era when the application of active public monetary and fiscal policies is in vogue, the problem has sometimes been further aggravated by the fact that governmental policies aimed by a central government at the vigorous economic development of the federation as a whole inevitably cannot equally accommodate differing specific interests and degrees of unemployment in particular provinces. Moreover, the very differences in provincial products which contribute towards the exchange of products across provincial boundaries may, at the same time, foster provincial consciousness because of related differences in problems of production, types of exports, sources of foreign capital, and appropriate policies for the promotion of economic development. In federations like Pakistan, Malaysia and Central Africa, distinct regional economies were clearly discernible and contributed to internal political tensions, just as Western Canadians are separated from Quebec not only by distance and language but by the different economic problems with which they are concerned.

Most federations have joined together territories with disparities in economic development and wealth, and where these regional inequalities have been acute they have invariably accentuated separatist pressures. This has especially been the case where the federation has given inadequate financial assistance to the poorer provinces for the provision of services available elsewhere in the federation. Experience in Pakistan and Nigeria suggests that regional disparities in wealth can be one of the most political explosive divisive forces in a federation, especially if they coincide with linguistic and cultural cleavages. Yet, by comparison with Australia, Canadian attempts to meet this problem appear in the past to have been only half-measures. Australia has a long history of positive attempts to deal with this problem. In 1964–65 the per capita income of the wealthiest state in Australia exceeded that of the poorest by but 25 per cent. In Canada we have been less successful for in 1964 Ontario's per capita income exceeded that of Quebec by 38 per cent and that of the Atlantic Provinces by 86 per cent. In Australia, federal unconditional grants, the major form of intergovernmental transfer, have been so adjusted that in 1964–65 the poorest state received on a per capita basis, 63 per cent more than the wealthiest state. In Canada, it is only in the last twenty years or so that we have made any direct attack on the problem of regional disparities, and only in the last ten that effective measures have come to be accepted. Even the equalization approach and the special Atlantic Provinces Adjustment Grants of that period were inadequate, and it was not until 1967 that a policy of bringing provincial revenues up to the national average was adopted. This, along with certain equalized, shared-cost programs and the new special programs of assistance for the under-developed economic regions, has provided a new approach to an old problem. Nevertheless, by contrast with the Australians, who have attempted to consolidate federal unity by a positive emphasis on reducing regional disparities in wealth, Canadians until quite recently appear to have been unwilling to make a serious effort beyond preventing the gaps from becoming wider.

The demand for active public development policies has also invariably aggravated any regional consciousness derived from disparities in wealth, because different fiscal and monetary policies are likely to be appropriate for different stages of delevopment and hence for different provinces. The resulting pressures for regionalization of government policies, or even political independence, have not been unique in Quebec but have been strongly felt in other federations, such as Nigeria, and even the culturally homogeneous West Indies Federation.

Apart from the direct influence of economic factors, many separatist movements which have been ostensibly linguistic, racial, or cultural in motivation have had strong economic undercurrents. The insistence of the Muslim middle class in North-West India upon partition was directly related to the desire of that group to protect themselves from a larger and better-educated Hindu group. The linguistic regionalism and Dravidian separatism which have dominated independent India have been rooted in large measure in the intense struggle for jobs among the different linguistic and caste groups. In Pakistan, Bengali demands for greater autonomy have been derived from discontent with central economic policies which appeared to give all the spoils to the landlords and businessmen of West Pakistan, and with the degree to which the civil services and the armed forces were primarily manned by West Pakistanis. The anti-Ibo feeling in Northern and Western Nigeria owed a good deal to ethnic and religious differences, but accentuating these were the migration of the aggressive, educated Ibos to regions outside their own and the fear that the Ibos would come to dominate the economy, the civil services, and the officer corps of the army. In Malaysia, the three racial communities have been differentiated by sharply different economic roles and, therefore, racial resentments have been closely related to economic ones. The Malays, particularly in the economically backward northeastern states, have resented the dominance of commerce by the energetic Chinese; the Chinese, in turn, have resented the constitutionally guaranteed dominance of the Malays in the federal civil service. In Central Africa, the ostensibly racial cleavage reflected sharp economic disparities between the prosperity of the white settlers in Southern Rhodesia and the copperbelt, and the poverty of Nyasaland and the African areas of Northern Rhodesia. Thus, in many federations, as in Canada, local economic interests and the desire to legitimize a number of local spoils systems have contributed strongly to the overtly linguistic, racial, or cultural demands for increased provincial autonomy or separation. In such circumstances, political solutions aimed at accommodating regional linguistic and cultural demands have achieved little unless they also took into account the closely related economic factors.

Variations among provinces in degree of political influence have also been a factor in interprovincial tensions and demands for greater autonomy or even separation. Important factors bearing on the relative political influence of a province within a federation are its population and wealth in relation to other provinces. The distrust of Ontario by Quebec suggests that this may be a significant element in the Canadian situation. Such a tendency for disparities in the size and wealth of provinces to accentuate tension may be independent of linguistic or cultural divisions. One need only look at the distrust of Ontario by the other English-speaking provinces in Canada or at the distrust of Jamaica among the smaller islands in the West Indies Federation to see this. Similar pressures have been felt in other federations. Examples are the resentment of the smaller states at the dominance of New South Wales and Victoria in Australia, Uttar Pradesh in India, the Northern Region (before it was split up in 1967) in Nigeria, and East Bengal in Pakistan (before the various provinces and states of West Pakistan were amalgamated to counterbalance it). Even in Switzerland, the growth of Zürich as an industrial and commercial centre has been felt in some quarters to be threatening the balance among the cantons. In each of these federations fears of domination by the larger provincial units have exacerbated distrust between provincial groups. In some cases this has been severe enough to produce pressures for the splitting up of the largest units, such as Uttar Pradesh or Northern Nigeria, or for the amalgamation of smaller units into larger ones, such as in West Pakistan (1955–1969). These movements have aimed at reducing the ascendancy of one provincial unit or ethnic group within the federation. It is significant that among the new federations created since 1947, the four that have proved the most unstable—the West Indies, Rhodesia and Nyasaland, Nigeria, and Pakistan—have been those in which a single provincial unit held a majority of the federal electorate. In Canada, no single province occupies quite such a position, but the anxieties of the French Canadians of Quebec have certainly been accentuated by the proximity of the even larger English-speaking province of Ontario beside them, by the location of the federal capital in the largest province, and by the prevailing assumption in Quebec that the nine provinces of English-speaking Canada represent a monolithic political majority.

Weaknesses in inter-regional communications have also contributed to the widening of political cleavages in many federations. Relevant here are geographical, technological, economic, and social factors. The impact of geographical distance and topography has been felt in the remoteness of Western Australia, the mountain barriers in central Switzerland, the continental vastness of India, the separation of East and West Pakistan by a thousand miles of hostile territory, and the scattered islands of the West Indies. These parallel the remoteness from central Canada and the problems of Quebec felt by some of the Atlantic Provinces, the Prairies, and especially British Columbia. In most federations, technological advances in transportation and communications have tended with time to strengthen the interprovincial links, but where, for reasons of cost or technological difficulties, direct rail, road, air, sea, or telecommunications traffic is limited for most of the populace, as has been the case in most of the Asian and African federations and particularly the West Indies, the effect has been marked. It is no accident that federal politics in the early years of the American and Canadian federations were so closely tied to "railway politics." Even today, in the wealthier federations like the United States, Australia, and Canada, the sheer cost of transcontinental travel has continued to place limits on the degree to which people in one region may understand at first hand the problems of people in other regions. The strength of economic links is especially important. The proportion of a province's total trade which is with other provinces within the federation is likely to affect the degree to which the people of that province see their future in continued federation or in "going it alone." To take one dramatic example, it is not surprising that the Jamaicans, with only one per cent of their total exports going to other islands within the West Indies Federation, saw little to discourage them from opting out of that federation. Similarly, in Canada it has been those provinces, such as British Columbia, which depend least on interprovincial trade which have sometimes adopted the most independent stands. Limitations upon social communications, such as contacts between similar classes in different provinces and interprovincial mobility of persons in politically relevant strata, may also contribute to a sharper regional consciousness. Such links have been weakened by the essentially regional character of caste structures in India, the different occupations of racial groups in Malaysia and Central Africa, and the cultural divisions between the regional or provincial élites within Nigeria and Canada.

In most federations, the forces and demands that lead to the original establishment of a federal union have continued to exert pressure and to influence the operation of the federal system after its creation. But in some instances, the influences for the original federal unification included transitional inducements which have evaporated with time, thus changing the balance of pressures within the federation, either in the direction of greater centralization or greater decentralization. Among the transitional unifying inducements of this sort have been the feeling of unity generated in opposition to alien imperial rule, the original agreement to union by some acceding governments as an escape from imminent insolvency, the acceptance of a wider union in order to surmount internal political friction, or the acceptance of union as a desperate immediate necessity at a time when an external aggressor was threatening. A decade or a century later, such motivations for union may have lost their urgency, and in the changed circumstances the weakening of the cement holding the federation together may not be recognized until it is too late.

If we assess the Canadian situation, we see that here, too, there have been transitional inducements to unity operating in 1867 or at certain later periods in our history, which under different circumstances are now weakened or even inoperative. Apart from the changed internal circumstances of each of the provinces a century later, it is clear that the external influences have also changed during that period. In 1867 Canada was a colonial federation. Today Canada is an independent federation in which the external influence of Britain is much reduced. Moreover, with independence assured, the nationalistic pressure for greater self-government which helped to unify Canadians at certain times is no longer an issue.

External influences have had an important impact on the degree of unity within most federations. Indeed, one scholar, W. H. Riker, has suggested that the only necessary condition for the establishment of political federations has been the desire to achieve security against an external military or diplomatic threat.[2] This obviously overstates the case, since in some federations, like Australia, such external threats were clearly not the most influential factor for union. Nevertheless, the desire for security against an external threat was a major motivation for union at the time of federation in Canada, the United States, and Switzerland. But in most of these federations over a century or more, the nature of these external threats has altered radically. The United States no longer sees the return of British intervention as a threat, but instead is concerned with its own role in Europe and Asia. The nations surrounding Switzerland are no longer warring with each other and looking upon Switzerland as a pawn in their struggles. Instead they are united in an Economic Community. Canadians are no longer alarmed at the threat of a Yankee army, victorious over the Confederates, being unleashed across the border. Instead, what threat there is from the United States comes in the beguiling form of American influence upon the economy and the cultural life of Canada. Thus, although the fear of American domination may continue to unify Canadians, the fact that it is no longer a military threat has meant that there is no longer the galvanizing impact for unity which a direct military threat usually stirs. It is significant that among the newer federations, the West Indies and Nigeria, which were both relatively free from any external military or diplomatic threat, each suffered from the lack of a positive urgency for unity.

A divisive form of external influence felt in some federations has been the direct encouragement of a regional separatist movement by a foreign government. Such encouragement may have diplomatic, economic, or cultural motivations. Historically, in Switzerland the threat to unity imposed by interventions from nations related to one of its own cultural groups led to the Swiss adoption of neutrality as a fundamental policy in its relations with all external states. More recently, France, under the leadership of General de Gaulle, overtly encouraged separatist movements not only in Quebec but also in the Jura region of Bern and in Eastern Nigeria. Indeed, because of the French supply of arms to Biafra, de Gaulle's resignation was greeted in one Nigerian newspaper with the headline "Ojukwu's Man de Gaulle Resigns!"

External influences may affect unity within a federation in another way, by the impact which foreign examples and precedents come to have. The Swiss, in creating their constitution of 1848, borrowed heavily but critically from the example of the United States. Canadians, with the experience of the American Civil War before them, created a blend of British and American institutions. The Australians, in turn, took account of both American and Canadian experience, and most of the new federations established in the last twenty-five years have paid a great deal of attention to the experience of preceding federations. But while, in the past, such precedents provided examples in favour of larger political units or federations, the march to political independence and full membership in the United Nations of a large number of relatively small former colonial territories has provided, within the last two decades, a different sort of example. Where twenty years ago the watchword was the need for "viable" political units sufficiently large to maintain genuine independence, separatist movements in Southern India, East Pakistan, Singapore, Malawi, Zambia, Jamaica, Biafra, or Quebec are now able to point to independent member countries of the United Nations which are much smaller than themselves. In Africa alone, there are twenty-five independent states each with a population less than that of Quebec. There may be some question about the real meaning of political or economic independence in many of these countries, but the existence of so many smaller African states provides at least an emotional counter-cry for Separatists against those who would argue that Quebec is too small to be politically independent.

THE ROLE OF FEDERAL POLITICAL INSTITUTIONS

Among the factors which have a crucial bearing on the degree of stress in a federal system is the institutional structure of the federation. The way in which the federal institutions channel the activities of the electorate, political parties, organized interest groups, bureaucracies, and informal élites contributes to the moderation or accentuation of political conflict. Indeed, Robert Dahl, in his analysis of pluralist democracy in the United States, has described the primary function of federal institutions as that of taming power, settling conflicts peacefully, and securing the consent of all.[3] The extent to which the federal system will moderate or polarize internal political conflict depends on the size, number, and internal homogeneity of the provincial units, the distribution of legislative and executive responsibilities and financial resources among the component governments, the machinery facilitating intergovernmental consultation and co-operation, the manner in which regional groups are represented in the institutions of central government, the degree of political security provided for minority groups by constitutional safeguards, and the flexibility of the political institutions enabling them to adapt to changing needs over time.

From federation to federation, there have been striking contrasts in the area and population of their provincial units. India, Pakistan, and Nigeria have each contained individual states in which the population is greater than the total federal population of Canada. At the other end of the scale, half the Malaysian states, eight of the ten West Indian territories, and all but two of the twenty-two Swiss cantons have had individual populations less than half that of Montreal or Toronto. It would appear that the larger provincial units have been able to sustain full governmental responsibilities more effectively and to minimize the costly duplication of administrative machinery. But large units, such as Jamaica, or those in Pakistan, Nigeria, and India, have also tended to assert themselves more at the expense of the central government and have been more prone to contemplate a separate, self-sufficient existence. Furthermore, as noted earlier, where the size of provinces relative to each other within a federation varies sharply, this has nearly always accentuated interprovincial tensions because of anxiety that the larger provinces would dominate federal politics. This has been a particularly contentious issue in the West Indies, Nigeria, and Pakistan. The number of provinces of which a federation is composed also affects the character of politics within the system. It is significant that, in contrast to the United States, with fifty states, or Switzerland, with twenty-two cantons, those federations composed of a smaller number of units, such as Australia (six), Nigeria (three then four), Rhodesia and Nyasaland (three), and Pakistan (two), have experienced the sharpest fears that one or two provinces might dominate. In addition, the position of the individual provincial governments has, in practice, been strengthened at the expense of the central governments, and pressures for provincial self-sufficiency have been encouraged. This has been most severe in Pakistan, where the biprovincial structure contributed to the polarization of most political issues into a struggle between the two provinces. Although Quebec may chafe at being only one of ten provinces, the creation of a bi-provincial federation or confederacy is unlikely, therefore, to provide a stable solution to the problems of Canadian bilingualism.

In the actual distribution of functions and resources between central and state governments, there has been considerable variation from federation to federation.[4] In the interests of both efficient administration and palatable political compromise, each federation has had to strive for its own particular balance between central power and provincial autonomy. But there have been a number of common sources of stress among federations. To begin with, where the distribution of responsibilities and resources has failed to reflect accurately the concurrent aspirations for unity and provincial autonomy, it has led to pressures for a shift in the balance of functions actually exercised by each level of government, as in Switzerland, Australia, India, or Nigeria. In more extreme cases it has even led to the discrediting and collapse of the federal system, as in overcentralized Pakistan and Rhodesia and Nyasaland, or the ineffectual West Indies. This indicates how important, and yet how difficult, it has been in most federations to find the appropriate balance between, on the one hand, adequate central power in order to provide military and diplomatic security and economic development, and, on the other, sufficient provincial autonomy in order to protect vital regional aspirations and interests and avoid discontent and resentment.

Experience also indicates that in the distribution of legislative and executive authority a simple compromise between economic centralization and cultural provincialization has proved, in mid-twentieth century circumstances, to be no longer a realistic possibility. Consequently, in most multicultural federations, as in Canada, regional linguistic or cultural groups have developed a deep-rooted anxiety that centralized fiscal and economic policies aiming at the rapid development of an integrated economy would undermine their cultural distinctiveness and opportunities for employment in culturally congenial conditions. In its cruder form, this feeling has expressed itself, especially in India and Nigeria, in the desire of each regional linguistic or ethnic group for its own local spoils system. In the face of such pressures, most contemporary federations have found it necessary to permit both central and provincial governments an interlocking responsibility over a wide range of functions, including many economic matters.

In almost every federation, the subject of federal finance has been a major source of contention. Financial resources define the limits of what provincial governments may do for their own regional groups, and where taxing powers are centralized and the provinces are heavily dependent upon central financial assistance, provincial governments have invariably chafed at this dependence. Most of the newer federations have attempted to minimize such friction by combining a more centralized control of taxing powers for purposes of co-ordinated economic policy-making than in Canada, together with a more decentralized responsibility for expenditure. To do this and to protect provincial autonomy at the same time, they have followed the Australian example of setting up formal, standing intergovernmental councils and commissions for the purpose of regulating the substantial unconditional financial transfers to the states which are required. But even such machinery has not always eliminated intergovernmental tensions, as the sharpness of the controversies over federal finance in Australia in recent years indicates. A further element which has contributed to tension within federations has been the grievances of poorer provinces when the arrangements for equalization of provincial financial resources have been inadequate. This has been a major source of friction in Pakistan and Nigeria, and, as noted earlier, Canada has lagged behind Australia in tackling this problem effectively.

Some federations such as Malaysia, India, Pakistan, and Rhodesia and Nyasaland, faced with contrasts in the strength of pressures for autonomy in different provinces, have experimented with giving certain provinces more autonomy than others. A similar solution has been proposed for Canada in the form of a "special status" for Quebec with more autonomy than prevails in the other provinces. This has a certain logical attractiveness as a compromise, meeting Quebec's desire for more autonomy while permitting English-speaking Canada a greater degree of reliance upon Ottawa. But such experiments elsewhere suggest that major contrasts within a federation in the degree of provincial autonomy have generally fostered, rather than reduced, tension. Such attempts have usually been followed either by a reduction in the differences in autonomy between provinces, as occurred with the reorganization of states in India in 1956 and the unification of West Pakistan in 1955, or by the eventual secession of the more autonomous states, as in the cases of Malawi and Zambia in 1962 and 1963, and Singapore in 1965. The example of Singapore indicates that where one state is given greater autonomy than others, special care is needed to ensure that its citizens are not restricted in central politics to the point where they cease to feel themselves an integral part of the federation.

Because in practice the interpenetration of the activities of central and provincial governments has been unavoidable, most federations have found it desirable to minimize friction by establishing a variety of intergovernmental councils and commissions to facilitate consultation and co-operation. In this area, most of the new federations have seen the Australian model as the most effective and have established standing commissions and councils to adjust the allocation of financial resources, to co-ordinate public borrowing, and to enable consultation on general economic policies. Some federations, most notably India, have also created intergovernmental councils and conferences whose specific function is to consider ways of fostering federal cohesion. (Examples in India are the National Integration Conference which led to the creation of the National Integration Council, and the Committee on Emotional Integration set up by the conference of Education Ministers.) Most federations have established a variety of commissions, councils, boards, agencies, and conferences, each concerned with specific areas of common concern to both central and provincial governments; but the degree to which intergovernmental tension has been moderated has depended on the relative effectiveness of such bodies.

While an essential feature of any federal system is the autonomy of provincial governments making possible regional distinctiveness, federations which have failed to develop a positive consensus among their different regional groups have almost invariably disintegrated. The ability to generate such a sense of community depends largely on the central institutions: the form of these institutions, the processes by which central decisions are reached, and the participation of the different regional and minority groups in these decisions. Particularly critical is the way in which minority groups are represented in the central legislature, executive, civil service, political parties, and the life of the capital city. Where groups such as the East Pakistanis, the Singapore Chinese, the Jamaicans, or the black Africans of Nyasaland and Northern Rhodesia have been inadequately represented, their resulting alienation has directed itself into movements for separation.

In the United States and Switzerland, the creation of a second federal chamber in which the states are equally represented has provided a check upon the sweeping power in the central legislature that representation by population would give the majority groups. But in Canada, Australia, India, Malaysia, Nigeria, and the West Indies, the adoption of a parliamentary cabinet system, with the cabinet responsible to the lower house, has in each case undermined the effectiveness of the federal second chamber as a guardian of provincial rights, even when, as in most of them, senators are either directly elected or appointed by the provincial governments. In the United States and Switzerland, the central institutions, based on the principle of the separation of powers, have provided a framework of checks and balances which have in most periods encouraged the search by politicians and political parties for compromises because of the variety of points at which minority groups could otherwise block action. But this beneficial influence has been achieved at a price. Solutions often take a long time to emerge, and sometimes there are deadlocks. The result is that some fundamental problems may remain unsolved, and this has contributed in certain critical periods to considerable stress, such as in the United States during the decade before 1861.

The parliamentary federations, on the other hand, have given cabinets with majority legislative support an opportunity for more rapid and effective action, but at the price of vesting complete sovereignty in a parliamentary majority with no institutional checks upon it. This lack of institutional checks upon the majorities in parliamentary federations has put the responsibility for reconciling political conflicts and for aggregating support from diverse regional and cultural groups directly upon the internal organization and processes of the political parties themselves. If the political parties fail in the task, and a fragmented multiparty system develops, or political parties become primarily regional in their bases, then the parliamentary federations have been prone to instability. The experience of Pakistan before 1958, of

Nigeria before 1966, and even of Canada with minority governments between 1962 and 1968 illustrates this danger.

In most multicultural federations it has proved necessary to recognize as official languages the languages of major minority groups and to provide constitutional or political guarantees of justiciable individual rights against linguistic, racial, religious, or regional discrimination. It is noteworthy that where the language of a major regional group has been denied recognition as a federal language, extreme bitterness and tension have resulted. The initial insistence in Pakistan upon Urdu as the sole national language aroused a storm of heated protest, and eventually it proved necessary to give way and recognize Bengali. In India the policy of replacing English by Hindi as the official language for central government has on several occasions provoked widespread demonstrations of protest from the non-Hindi groups, especially those in the South, forcing the central government to stretch out the change-over. In Malaysia language has been one of the issues on which the most extreme positions have been taken, and the continued insistence of the Alliance governments upon Malay as the eventual sole official language has provoked resentment and even riots.

Because the social, economic, political, and external conditions in which a federal system operates inevitably undergo considerable change over time, a constitutional structure which is not flexible and adaptable is likely to experience considerable stress. Most federations face a dilemma here: some constitutional rigidity is necessary to ensure the confidence of minorities in the federal structure as a safeguard for their interests, but if federal institutions are too inflexible they may soon cease to reflect changes in the social and economic conditions of the society. Some federations, such as Switzerland, have managed to achieve flexibility through frequent formal constitutional amendments, while others, like the United States and Australia, in order to avoid stresses arising from inflexibility, have come to rely more heavily on judicial interpretation of the constitution and on direct negotiation and agreement between central and state governments concerning political, administrative, and financial arrangements. Canada, without an accepted formal amendment process has had to rely especially on these latter processes, but it is now open to question whether these means alone will be adequate.

THE PROCESS OF FEDERAL DISINTEGRATION

If the preceding survey has shown anything, it is that there is no single condition or institutional arrangement upon which one can pin the sole responsibility for stress or for the disintegration of federations generally. In each case, crises have been the product of a combination of factors.

The critical conditions appear to be of three kinds. The first is the development of a situation in which various regional demands and interests—cultural, social, and economic—instead of overlapping or cutting across each other, reinforce each other in such a way as to polarize cleavages and conflict between regional groups. The second is the failure of the federal institutions to perform the dual functions of accommodating minority fears through the provision of adequate provincial autonomy and of encouraging federal cohesion through representative and effective central policy-making. Where a federal system has proved inadequate to the task of enabling regional groups to maintain their own distinctiveness, then secession and fragmentation have followed. But the devolution of controversial matters to the provinces in order to avoid conflicts within the central government has by itself never been enough. Equally important in the long-run has been the ability of the central government to generate a positive federation-wide sense of community counterbalancing regionalism. In such federations as the West Indies and Nigeria, when the central institutions failed to produce any consensus, the federal system lacked the cement to hold it together. The third critical condition is usually an outgrowth of the other two. Where a cumulative political polarization has occurred, the federal institutions have proved inadequate in moderating these cleavages, and negotiations have repeatedly failed to produce decisions, there has usually resulted a decline in support for the value of political compromise and the federal solution as ways of solving problems of political conflict. Political conflict has then taken on the character of a contest with very high stakes in which each side becomes convinced that only one side can win and at the expense of the other. Consequently, intransigence, the resort to violence, and secession or oppression have replaced compromise and conciliation as political attitudes considered to be legitimate. Once such a situation has been reached, it has usually taken only a relatively insignificant incident suddenly to trigger off secession, civil war, or disintegration.

One of the stages in this process that has marked the disintegration of several federations, most notably that of the West Indies and Rhodesia and Nyasaland, has been the attempt to halt the disintegration by instituting a formal review of the federal constitution with a view to its total revision. Since Canada is now embarked on such an exercise, one might well consider how such reviews have worked out elsewhere. The evidence is not encouraging. Where intergovernmental conferences for the review of the constitution have been held, they were usually viewed as an occasion on which weaknesses and difficulties revealed over time might be dealt with and the stresses within the federation reduced by new compromises. But in practice such conferences have usually served only to encourage uncertainty and lack of confidence in the future form, or even continued existence, of the federations in which they have been held. Moreover, they have almost always aroused new expectations among different regional groups, and the difficulty of satisfying all these expectations has added further to the difficulty of finding an acceptable compromise. The formal constitutional review conferences in the West Indies in 1961, and Rhodesia and Nyasaland during 1960–61, were marked by the intensification of inter-regional disputes and the rapid growth of secession movements. Within a year or two both federations had disintegrated. There is a stern warning here that once the Canadian central and provincial governments get past the preliminaries and down to the really hard bargaining involved in the review of our federal constitution, Canada may be entering an extremely critical period for her survival as a federation. This is especially so if these conferences, having aroused expectations, fail to produce any results. There is one ray of hope. In 1874 Switzerland undertook a successful general revision of her constitution, but it must be remembered that that review was undertaken in less controversial conditions than those prevailing now in Canada or in 1960–61 in the West Indies and Central Africa.

Most federal constitutions have explicitly or implicitly excluded a unilateral right of secession from the federation. The federal constitutions of the United States, Switzerland, Canada, Australia, India, Pakistan, Malaysia, Nigeria, Rhodesia and Nyasaland, and the West

Indies do not grant to states or provinces any right of unilateral secession. Among quasi-federal constitutions, that of the USSR does include such a right, but in practice this right would appear to mean little. Several arguments have usually been advanced against tolerating secession in a federation. First, it has been feared that the right to secede unilaterally would weaken the whole federal system by placing a weapon of political coercion in the hands of provincial governments. Secondly, there has been an anxiety that the possibility of secession through the unilateral action of one government would introduce an element of uncertainty and lack of confidence seriously handicapping efforts to build up federal unity and economic development. Thirdly, theorists have argued that if a provincial government acting alone is given the right to leave the federation, or if the central government acting alone is given the right to expel a member government, then, in effect, one tier of government would be subordinated to the other, thus violating the federal principle that member governments should be co-ordinate and not subordinate.

But whatever the constitutional restrictions upon unilateral secession, this has not prevented alienated regional groups from taking matters into their own hands. Once a province has declared its own secession, a central government is faced with the dilemma whether it should enforce union upon the unwilling minority or simply accept the secession as a political fact. Most independent federations have chosen the former course, fearing that once the secession of one province is accepted *de facto*, there will be nothing to prevent other provinces from separating whenever they wish, or, at the very least, using such a threat as a lever against the central government in political negotiations. Consequently, in both the United States and Switzerland the central government has actually resorted to military force to prevent secession. On much the same grounds Nigeria turned to military means to resist the attempt to establish a separate Biafra. In Pakistan military rule has three times been imposed, at least in part, in order to avoid the potential threat of Bengali separatism. Among independent federations, only in Malaysia has a central government tolerated the separation of a state, but the separation of Singapore in 1965 was more a case of the expulsion of that state by the central government than a case of unilateral secession.

In colonial federations, secession movements have presented a spe cial problem to the imperial government. In early cases Britain normally rejected requests for secession arising in Commonwealth or colonial federations, such as those from Western Australia in 1934, Penang in Malaya in 1951, and Western Nigeria in 1954. On the other hand, as the creator of the colonial federations, Britain retained the right to dissolve them, and in practice did actually agree in four federations to the secession of territories. These were the partition of India in 1947, the separation of the Southern Cameroons from Nigeria in 1961 following a referendum, the secession of Jamaica and subsequently Trinidad from the West Indies Federation in 1962, and the granting of separate independence to Malawi and Zambia in 1962 and 1963. It is significant that in most of these cases, once the prestigious right of complete independence had been conceded to one state within a federation, other states raised demands which led eventually to further disintegration. It would appear, therefore, that federations which have resisted secession as merely the first step before further disintegration have probably been correct in their assessment of the consequences.

Furthermore, generally speaking the resentments aroused by the circumstances occurring at the time of separation have tended to persist and to discourage the subsequent creation of a looser form of association between the territories concerned. Whenever secession has occurred, it has inevitably been accompanied by sharp political controversies which are not easily forgotten. In addition, the unscrambling of a federation requires the allocation of assets and liabilities among the successor states, and rarely has it been possible to achieve this difficult and complex task without adding further to the resentments felt by one or both sides. An example of the long-lasting impact of the process of separation is the continued hostility between India and Pakistan. In 1947 most of the Congress leaders, Nehru among them, accepted partition with the belief that "Pakistan was not a viable state—politically, economically, geographically or militarily—and that sooner or later the areas which had seceded would be compelled by force of circumstances to return to the fold."[5] Similar views are often expressed in English-speaking Canada concerning Quebec. But it is significant that the trauma of partition has continued to the present day to mark Indian-Pakistani relations with hostility or, at best, distrust. Nor in the West Indies or Central Africa has the creation of a new or alternative form of post-federal, interterritorial political association proved feasible in spite of earlier expectations. It would seem, therefore, that René Lévesque's proposal for the establishment, following political independence, of a new economic association between Quebec and the rest of Canada is based on highly optimistic assumptions. The continued relations between Singapore and the Federation of Malaysia provide the only hopeful precedent. Elsewhere the precedents are distinctly unpromising.

THE CONSEQUENCES OF FEDERAL DISINTEGRATION

Once the disintegration of a federation has gone so far as to be marked by the secession of one of its units, one of three possible consequences has usually followed.

One is simply the general acceptance of permanent separation, as occurred in partitioned India, the shattered West Indies Federation, and the separate independent territories of the former Federation of Rhodesia and Nyasaland. This solution avoids civil war, eliminates the central government as a centre of political controversy, and produces a number of more compact independent political units. But it involves a considerable price, since it entails the loss of the economic and diplomatic benefits associated with the larger political union. The economic difficulties experienced by the remnants of the federations in the West Indies and in Central Africa after their dissolution, and the contemporary general international trend towards larger economic units would suggest that political balkanization is a regressive step. In external relations, whether in the terms of diplomatic influence or of security, smaller political units such as these have proved weak and vulnerable to pressure from larger, more powerful neighbours. Moreover, the legacy of distrust inevitably created by the process of disintegration among the formerly united territories has usually complicated their subsequent relations with each other, an effect most marked on the Indian sub-continent but noticeable elsewhere.

An alternative consequence of federal disintegration is the attempt to establish, as a substitute for the federation, an economic union or confederacy. This solution would avoid the full effects of balkanization and has appealed to supporters of regional autonomy, since it might obtain some of the benefits of economic association while re-taining for the component units their political independence and a veto over all central political decisions. But such a solution is not as simple as at first sight apears. To begin with, and as noted earlier, no federation has actually been succeeded by such an economic union, the resentments aroused at the time of separation making the required goodwill difficult to achieve. Moreover, in practice such systems have found it almost impossible to isolate economic and political matters from each other. Economic unions, therefore, have proved politically unstable and have rarely lasted for long in the contemporary world.[6] The European Economic Community represents an economic confederacy, but after an extremely effective beginning it has experienced some internal stresses. In any case, its main supporters regard it not as a final solution, but merely as a stage on the road to fuller political federalism. Other contemporary examples are the East African Common Services Organization and the Central American Common Market, neither of which has proved a very stable arrangement politically. It is perhaps worth noting that in both the United States and Switzerland a federal system was adopted directly as a result of the deficiencies and difficulties experienced in the looser confederacy which had preceded.

A third pattern of consequences following the declaration of secession by a state has been the resort to military force to maintain the union. This was the policy adopted by the central governments in Switzerland in 1847, in the United States in 1861, and more recently in Nigeria in 1966. The price of this alternative—civil war—may be high indeed in human lives, disruption, and the legacy of bitterness. Much depends, however, on the length and fierceness of the civil war and upon the character of the federal reconstruction which follows. In Switzerland, where the war itself was brief and where the political settlement that was subsequently imposed was generous to the vanquished, the federal reconstruction was remarkably successful. In the United States, on the other hand, the length and ferocity of the Civil War and the Northern dominance which followed it left a much stronger legacy of bitterness.

It is clear, then, that whichever of these patterns has followed, the disintegration of a federation has generally exacted a high price in economic costs, diplomatic and defensive ineffectiveness, bitterness between the groups involved, and sometimes even in human lives.

THE AVOIDANCE OF DISINTEGRATION

When we look at the conditions and processes which have contributed to the disintegration of other federations, the closeness with which the situation in Canada today parallels them is chilling. It would seem that we have reached a critical stage in the cumulative polarization of political cleavages and that unless we are able to arrest this trend the process of disintegration may very soon become irreversible.

If the experience of failures and successes in other federations is any guide, the survival of Canada as a single political entity will depend on the degree to which we are able to moderate political cleavages and to maintain support for the value of the federal solution as a means to the resolution of political conflicts. Much will depend on the extent to which the institutions of our federal system and the political parties, electorates, and public services operating through them, work effectively to encourage the search for compromise and consensus in the interests of federal cohesion rather than political conflict.

NOTES

1. On the function of language for the individual and for society, see especially Robert Brock LePage, *The National Language Question* (London and New York: Oxford University Press, 1964), Chapters 1 and 2.

2. William H. Riker, *Federalism: Origin, Operation, Significance* (Boston: Little, Brown, 1964), p. 12.

3. Robert Alan Dahl, *Pluralist Democracy in the United States: Conflict and Consent* (Chicago: Rand McNally, 1967), p. 24.

4. For detailed analyses see, for instance, Kenneth Clinton Wheare, *Federal Government* 4th ed. (London and New York: Oxford University Press, 1963), Chapters 5–10, and Ronald Lampman Watts, *New Federations: Experiments in the Commonwealth* (Oxford: Clarendon Press, 1966), Chapters 8 and 9.

5. Michael Alan Brecher, *Nehru: A Political Biography* (London and New York: Oxford University Press, 1959), p. 377.

6. See, for instance, Joseph S. Nye Jr., *International Regionalism* (Boston: Little, Brown, 1968), *Pan-Africanism and East African Integration* (Cambridge, Mass: Harvard University Press, 1965), and *Central American Regional Integration* (New York: Carnegie Foundation for International Peace, 1967).

Scenarios for Separation

Richard Simeon

*Regardless of the discords among political
parties, regardless of the often only half-
concealed interests of certain classes of society,
regardless of the deep emotional fear of risk, it
appears indisputable that Quebec is heading
down a one-way street to sovereignty.*

Jean Blain, in the Preface
to René Lévesque, *An Option for Quebec*

LET US ASSUME for the moment that Jean Blain is right. Let us assume
that separation of Quebec from the rest of Canada is inevitable and
the moves towards it irreversible. The question then immediately
arises: How might it come about? How do two complex societies
which have been associated in a federal union for more than a hundred years go about the difficult process of disengagement? Can it be
done peacefully, without bloodshed—or will it inevitably lead to
bitterness, mutual reprisals, or even war? And, since the two societies
will continue to share the northern half of the continent, will they be
able to work out some stable relationship which will govern their
future? These are a few of the central questions which guide this essay.

They are not idle or mischievous questions. Separation is no longer
a remote possibility advocated by a small group of militants. It is a
respectable political movement. It may well succeed. If this is the case,
then English Canadians must begin to ask themselves some difficult
questions and think seriously about how it might happen. Only by

doing this will they be able to retain some control over events. In asking these questions I am not assuming that separation is inevitable, much less that it is desirable. But by thinking about them, perhaps both sides can gain some insight into what is at stake and how relations could be conducted through what would be, at best, a difficult process.

One way to approach the problem is to sketch out some alternative scenarios about disengagement. We cannot predict with any certainty at all what might happen, but we can suggest the range of possible results and reactions, given certain assumptions about reality. The discussion, then, will be hypothetical and speculative. The reader will undoubtedly be able to think of other scenarios and of variations on the ones presented here.

Most broadly, let us consider two scenarios.

1. Separation and sovereign status can be negotiated amicably; English Canada and Quebec will, after separation has been achieved, continue to co-operate and will indeed create a mutually advantageous "Canadian Union," with a common market and joint overall economic policies.

This we will call the optimistic scenario. Its main proponent is the leader of the Parti Québécois, René Lévesque, and it is most fully developed in his book, *An Option for Quebec*.

2. Separation and sovereign status cannot be achieved peaceably. English Canadians will not tolerate it, and are likely to use force to prevent it. Quebec, whether successful or not, is likely to become a Fascist state. If separation is achieved, future relations will be hostile and non-co-operative. Mutual reprisals will replace peaceful negotiation. Economic relations will be similar to those between the United States and Cuba. This is the most pessimistic scenario. It predicts something approaching civil war. Bits and pieces of it have been suggested many times, but it has never been spelled out in complete detail.

Between these two extremes, a range of other possibilities exist. But let us deal with these two, and examine the assumptions that underlie them. Can we say anything at all about the conditions which might make one or the other the more likely scenario? Can we, indeed, suggest strategies by the leaders of either side which will enhance the chances for one or other possibility?

In order to evaluate the optimistic and pessimistic scenarios, a great number of relevant factors must be considered. Few, if any, can at this stage be delineated with any degree of certainty. Broadly, there would be three stages in the disengagement process. The first is the "pre-separation stage"; it includes all events leading up to the decision by Quebec to separate. The second is the separation stage itself; it focuses on the immediate actions and reactions of the participants after the decision has been made. Third is the post-separation phase. Assuming the achievement of separation, this stage involves the working out of a fairly stable set of relationships which will govern the parties for the future. The events at each stage will be greatly affected by the preceding ones; to a great extent each will determine the future ones. As a result, the initial stage leading up to separation is the most crucial: it will set a pattern of expectations by both sides which will likely be difficult to change.

At each step, a slightly different set of factors will be most important. They can be laid out as follows:

In the pre-separation stage, what will be the developments in Quebec leading to separation? Will the final decision result from a long, gradual, cumulative process, or will the break be brief and abrupt? How will the decision to separate be made: by referendum, by an Act of the legislature, by a *coup*, or in some other way? What will be the overall goals of the Separatists: primarily a symbolic disengagement, or a total and complete break with the rest of Canada? Equally important will be the goals and attitudes of the Separatists on a number of other matters, such as treatment of English Canadians and English-Canadian business in the province. It will also be important to know how united the French-Canadian population will be, and how strong the authority of the government is.

Answers to these questions will, in turn, affect the responses of English Canadians to the act of separation. Of particular importance are questions like these: What will be the reactions of ordinary citizens to the event, and what pressures or demands will they make on the government leaders? What will be the reactions of non-governmental élites such as newspapers, businessmen, interest groups, and the like? How will the governmental authorities react?

In the separation stage, we ask what the immediate actions by each side are. How do the French-Canadian leaders conduct themselves, and what reactions does this provoke on the part of English Canadians? Again there are several factors to be considered here. Are there incentives for both sides to take "hard" positions; and, conversely, are there incentives to promote agreement? What kinds of bargaining resources does each side possess? What are the levels of hostility or cooperativeness, trust and distrust between leaders of each side? What are the actual issues to be negotiated? And, finally, how do third parties like the United States or France behave?

Continuing relationships in the post-separation stage will depend primarily on what has gone before; though other immediate factors may well enter into the process—for example, whether there was an economic depression in either of the separated sides, or whether the pressures for disintegration and dismemberment grew within the truncated English-Canadian remainder of the federation.

This is simply a skeleton framework; we need now to put some flesh on it, and attempt to draw out some of the relationships among the various factors involved.

Both the optimistic and pessimistic scenarios make assumptions about the factors mentioned above. Let us first examine the option advocated by the Parti Québécois. René Lévesque believes strongly that independent status for Quebec can be achieved without severe conflict, in a peaceful and orderly way. Moreover, he argues that the achievement of sovereign status for Quebec will be *mutually beneficial* for both sides. This is because, he argues, the present federal system effectively frustrates both Quebec in its aspirations for control over its own destiny, and English Canada in its desire for "simplifying, rationalizing and centralizing." Continuing the existing federal regime makes mounting conflict and hostility inevitable; the two majorities "will inevitably collide with one another repeatedly and with greater and greater force causing hurts that would finally be irreparable." "Tomorrow," he writes, "English Canada would be grateful to Quebec for bringing it [separation] about."

In addition, of course, Mr. Lévesque does not envision a total separation of Quebec from the rest of Canada. Instead, there would be an association of the two countries, which would include common currency and monetary systems, a common market and co-ordination of fiscal policies. A cynic might say that Lévesque's plan is not so very different from the present state of affairs—and certainly no different from many of the projects for *statut particulier*—with the exception that in the future Quebec would possess all the symbols of sovereignty.

The pre-separation phase of the separation process under the Lévesque option would be relatively peaceful and democratic. The decision to separate, itself, would be achieved through legitimate constitutional means. He expects that in a short time Quebec will elect to the *Assemblée nationale* leaders pledged to establish a sovereign Quebec. Once in office, the new government will not immediately declare independence. There would instead be a three-year transition period, during which, presumably, there would be negotiations between Quebec and English Canada. In these discussions, Quebec would combine "unshakeable firmness with a polite insistence on speaking calmly." During this period too, Lévesque expects English Canadians would undergo a period of "psychological development" by which they would come to accept the inevitable and thus be willing to "sit at the same table without too great a gap between us." It would therefore be possible to negotiate peacefully the "contract of Association." Both parties in these negotiations would have an incentive to agree: Quebec would not want to lose the benefits of economic association with Canada; Canada would not want to lose the Quebec market, or risk disruption of its basic economic and monetary system. It also seems clear from Lévesque's arguments that Quebec's economic policy would not greatly threaten existing investments and economic arrangements, thus limiting the danger of major opposition from economic interests. Similarly, Lévesque has made fairly clear that the political form of a sovereign Quebec would not likely be repugnant to most English-Canadian values. Lévesque himself—though there are major differences of opinion within his movement—would also not provoke deep English-Canadian hostility through denying rights of English Canadians and other minorities in Quebec. Thus, Lévesque's "optimistic scenario" can be summed up: The decision to separate is made in an orderly, democratic fashion; it is broadly accepted as a legitimate decision by English-Canadian authorities; the Quebec government would have general support from the population, and would be accepted by it; the goals of the independent government would be moderate, in terms of the degree of separation envisaged, in terms of the kind of political philosophy and institutions which will be developed, and in the tactics used to achieve separation. This scenario also assumes certain patterns of English-Canadian reaction. There may be cries for reprisal and forcible prevention of granting sovereignty, but these will be controlled. Gradually, English Canadians will become reconciled to the idea of an independent Quebec, and, indeed, will even come to see the advantage in it. Thus, governmental authorities will react in a moderate way.

In the second stage, therefore, they will be willing to negotiate with Quebec. Both sides will have strong incentives to reach agreement, on both political and economic grounds. It is assumed there will be few pressures or incentives to take hard or inflexible positions. There will be little overt hostility and much desire to co-operate. There will be many issues to be negotiated; Lévesque dos not spell them out, but does assume they can be negotiated successfully. He assumes no third party involvement by the United States, France, or other countries. As a result, the two independent countries will move into the post-separation phase with a high degree of co-operation in a wide variety of fields, and a stable relationship, beneficial to both sides, will emerge.

This analysis rests on some central assumptions. The most important are those to do with the reaction of English Canadians. According to Lévesque, English Canadians will generally admit the legitimacy and even the desirability of separation, and will therefore accept it with some equanimity and be willing to negotiate peacefully towards some mutually agreeable set of future relationships. The fact that close relations would continue should mean a diminished English-Canadian opposition. The validity of the assumption depends largely on the nature of the blow to English Canadians that separation would pose. It seems likely that at first the blow would be primarily a psychological and symbolic one; it would not immediately (if ever) mean a great lowering of economic well-being among English Canadians; probably few would be materially put out, especially if economic partnership were worked out.

But if one assumes the blow is primarily psychological, what happens materially would not matter much. What would matter is a much more emotional reaction. Thus, even if separation were a symbolic recognition of what Quebec had already achieved, and meant no real change in the *status quo*, it might still be violently objected to. The dilemma in this is that, in a sense, what French Canadians seek most, at least in the Lévesque formulation, is a symbolic freedom— and that may well be the hardest thing for English Canadians to give. The symbolic blow of separation would revolve primarily around the question of failure. National identity in Canada is a tenuous phenomenon, but at least we can assume it means some commitment to an entity, Canada, which is defined as a certain territory; to break up that territory would represent the breaking of one of the few distinctive elements of the national identity. For some other English Canadians the psychological blow might also represent defeat. If one of the defining characteristics of Canada is the attempt to build a binational, bicultural society, it would obviously be almost impossible to accept even a symbolic break.

This symbolic opposition could be especially strong among English-Canadian intellectuals. This is because the evidence seems to suggest that it is the more educated who most tend to think in abstract symbolic terms, and to be concerned with matters like national identity and ideology. The greater concern of the intellectual élites, however, may well be tempered by an equal commitment to non-violence, self-determination, and other abstract values which might lead them to grant greater legitimacy to Quebec's decision. Thus, again, we get back to the importance of the manner in which separation takes place and whether the ground is prepared over a long period.

If the suggestion that opposition to the act of separation would be more psychological than material is right, then Lévesque's assumption that future material-economic relationships could be negotiated with ease is also called into question. This is true even if it is in some hypothetical sense materially to the advantage of the English Canadians to do so. This is because the perception of whether there is something to be gained or not from a negotiation, how the issues are to be defined, and so on, depends only partly on the "real" objective situation. At least, it depends equally on much more subjective considerations. The analysis of whether or not there would be mutual advantages in a common market, common currency, and so on would be, at best, a highly technical exercise with a great many uncertainties and a great many dubious assumptions to be considered. In such an uncertain situation, the role of subjective perceptions becomes even more important. Thus, even if it could be said that "objectively" it would be to English Canada's advantage to negotiate the arrangements that Lévesque contemplates, it may well be that many English Canadians would be unable to perceive the advantages. Or, if a negotiated arrangement would help English Canada a bit and French Canada a lot, there could still be the feeling that discussion would constitute "selling out to the French," even if in formal, rational terms it would still be to English Canada's advantage to negotiate an agreement. It is therefore unlikely that the calculations of gains and benefits from various types of negotiations would take place on purely material-economic grounds.

Opposition based on symbolic factors would probably vary considerably among different groups. For example, it might well be much stronger among intellectuals than, say, among businessmen, with a different set of criteria to consider. The position of economic élites would depend very heavily on what economic policies a sovereign Quebec intended to pursue. Similarly, opposition might be less among government officials who can perceive (because of their perspective and information) more clearly the consequences of non-agreement.

Assuming the decision to separate is made along the lines Lévesque suggests, and English Canadians do indeed decide to negotiate its achievement peacefully, how might these negotiations take place, and with what results? Are they likely to lead to an acceptable outcome, or to breakdown and deadlock? Many difficulties would arise, but there are some strong grounds for believing that arrangements could be worked out, though they would probably not be as advantageous to Free Quebec as M. Lévesque expects. How might they develop?

First, Lévesque correctly asserts that each side would have strong motivations to develop at least some minimally co-operative arrangements. Like it or not, both are, and will continue to be, part of a single economic system, and both share contiguous territory, joint river basins, and so on. The incentives to negotiate in good faith would be of several kinds. Both sides would probably share a moral and cultural desire to avoid armed conflict. Both would probably agree on the desirability of keeping third parties from becoming involved in the dispute, since that would probably threaten the independence of both. English Canadians would have a strong incentive to ensure the equitable treatment of English-speaking minorities in Quebec; Quebeckers would have similar feelings about French-speaking minorities elsewhere. Then there would be economic incentives. English-Canadian capitalists with fixed holdings in Quebec would greatly wish to prevent loss or destruction of their property (the threat to do that would be a powerful bargaining tool for Quebec, and armed intervention would only increase that danger) ; English-Canadian industry, especially in Ontario and the Maritimes, would not wish to threaten markets in Quebec. Even if English Canada could survive economically without Quebec, there would be dislocations and uncertainties which they would want to minimize. English Canadians would also be anxious to maintain rail and water links with the Maritimes.

On the Quebec side, too, there would be even stronger economic motivations to agree. It seems fairly clear that Quebec needs the North American market, more than the North American market needs Quebec. Thus, in federal-provincial relations, the Quebec position has already been moderated somewhat by the harsh imperatives of the investment market. If separation were to come about, the same economic pressures would exist.

The disincentives for negotiating differences would stem primarily from the symbolic problem mentioned earlier. English Canadians might argue that the negotiation was one-sided—that they could only lose. Or, if there were mutual advantages to be gained, as seems likely, they might not admit or perceive them. Similarly, many elements in Quebec might oppose negotiation, since meaningful bargaining implies making concessions. If these concessions were felt to limit significantly the degree of sovereignty achieved, they might be strongly opposed. Certainly a condition for the Quebec negotiators would be a basic acceptance of Quebec sovereignty by English Canadians.

But let us assume that relations between the two sides are not so strained as to make negotiations impossible, and that the incentives to find agreement outweigh pressures to disagree. What issues would have to be negotiated? The list would be very long, including, to mention only a few examples, the rights and guarantees of English-speaking minorities in Quebec, and, to a lesser extent, French-Canadian minorities outside Quebec; the status and future of English-owned corporations located in Quebec; links with the Maritimes; trade relations; monetary arrangements and the machinery for fiscal co-operation; and the disposal of federal property in Quebec. Thus, there would be a great deal on the table; we could expect very lengthy discussions since the process of disengaging, even partially as the Lévesque model implies, would be a complex, lengthy process. However, this very length and complexity might well make agreement easier in the long run. Agreement on some matters at the early stage would undoubtedly make agreement on later issues easier. The large number of issues, with complex variations within each, would allow the possibility of considerable trading of concessions both within and between issues, as Mr. Jordan's paper shows for only one—the future of the St. Lawrence system. In addition, on very complex issues winning and losing become much less clear-cut, with a greater possibility that both sides could feel they have "won" and that conflict on them would be blurred.

Another important factor that would help shape the negotiations is the climate and institutional setting in which they took place. We have already suggested that negotiation at all is possible only when both sides are willing; more broadly, it will probably take place only if the separation process itself is amicable, and only if English Canadians accept the basic premise—that Quebec should be a sovereign state. Presumably that would not be a negotiable issue. Similarly, the more legitimate the goals of the Quebec government in the eyes of English Canadians, the better the climate will be. In any circumstances, the climate of the negotiations is likely to be severely strained; negotiations can still take place, however, as long as both sides perceive possible advantages.

Equally important is the institutional setting. We could expect agreement to be much more difficult if there were no relatively agreed, clear-cut forum and procedures for working it out. It would also be more difficult if either side were disorganized, and did not have a spokesman who was accepted as legitimate both by his own society and by the other side. In fact, of course, existing federal-provincial negotiating machinery suggests a model that could well be followed with very little modification in the negotiations about separation. The recognized form of these negotiations is government-to-government bargaining in a quasi-diplomatic way. The major spokesmen for provincial interests are provincial governments, rather than, say, provincial party activists, federal Senators or federal MPs. In addition, a striking characteristic of ethnic conflict in Canada is that it has usually taken the form of conflict between governments rather than direct conflict between individuals. It may be expected that these precedents would continue in the negotiation of separation, and that they would facilitate finding agreement. There would, of course, be some important problems with the existing machinery—what role, for example, would the English-Canadian provinces wish to play? They have been suspicious of bilateral negotiations between Ottawa and Quebec in the past, but it seems reasonable to believe that in the kind of national crisis that separation implies, provincial governments would rally to the federal government and would consider it the logical spokesman and bargainer for English Canada. Again, however, there could well be some differences among the provinces. Another factor which would affect the chances of a successful negotiation is the degree of unity on each side. If there were wide disagreement about the appropriate attitude toward the Quebec decision and about the most desirable goals and tactics to be used, the authority of the spokesman at the bargaining table might be limited. A likely development would be for the officials of both Quebec and Ottawa to be pressed towards harder positions by extremists—by French Canadians arguing for a more complete break and impatient with protracted negotiations; by English Canadians unwilling to accept the fact of separation itself and pushing for a punitive line. These pressures would, in one sense, strengthen the bargaining power of the participants in the negotiations ("I cannot concede to you because my constituents would revolt"), but, in another sense, they would obviously make agreement much harder, even if the authorities on both sides wished it. Assuming the latter, it then becomes very important to know how effectively the negotiators are able to manage and contain opinion within their respective constituencies.

Recent manifestations of widespread social tensions within Quebec call into question the likelihood that the Quebec government would have complete authority within the province. Separation itself could have the effect of rallying and unifying Quebec opinion. But it could have the opposite effect, too. And disagreements within the population could grow rapidly if wages dropped, unemployment rose, and so on. The social mobilization of recent years which has increased nationalist demands in Quebec has also increased internal cleavages and disagreements. These could well severely complicate negotiations between the two sides. So, of course, would a separation achieved by leaders who are also radical socialists. Such a development might not only preclude any agreement between French and English Canadians, but also lead to great internal conflicts in which some French Canadians might well call on English-Canadian aid to put down the Revolution. There are strong elements of such a scenario in the reactions of the Quebec and Montreal governments to the FLQ kidnappings.

Another factor affecting the course of negotiations once begun is the amount of political resources, or bargaining power, available to each side. Both would have considerable levers to employ, but it seems likely that English Canada would be in a stronger bargaining position. It would always possess the threat of physical violence—even though its use would be costly and probably repugnant to most English Canadians. It could also pose a series of other threats which Quebec would have trouble countering, such as economic blockade. Clearly, English Canada would be in a much stronger position to use these kinds of tactics than Quebec. Paradoxically, indeed, English Canada might find itself in a stronger bargaining position after separation than it is in present negotiations with Quebec.

Today, Quebec's bargaining power is partly based on its being the only province which can make any sort of credible threat to break up the country. Any federal government with maintenance of national unity as a major goal is then motivated to make concessions on many substantive issues. This was clearly evident during the Pearson years. It has been less obvious since 1968, partly because a French-Canadian prime minister can challenge Quebec government leaders' claims to be sole "representatives" of the French Canadians. Nevertheless, even since 1968, it is obvious that a great many federal policies have been modified in advance to accommodate the Quebec position. But with separation already a fact, Quebec's ultimate threat would be removed.

English Canada would also probably have stronger support in the international community, especially from the United States. Probably more important is the fact that in a real bargaining situation French Canada would need to establish "normal" relations and economic partnerships with English Canada more than English Canada would with Quebec. Quebec would have both more to gain from negotiations and more to lose; it would thus be motivated to make many concessions to English-Canadian interests, though always, of course, short of giving up the claim to sovereignty itself. Breaking off the talks might hurt English Canada; it would hurt Quebec more.

Quebec, of course, would not be powerless; its resources would stem from possession of several things desirable to English Canadians, especially control over English minorities, access to the Maritimes, possession of national governmental assets, and English-Canadian industry. This pattern of resource distribution should ensure both that the parties would be motivated to seek agreement and that each would be prepared to make concessions. But it also suggests that, given English Canada's acquiescence on the basic issue of Quebec's sovereignty, and given a willingness on both sides to negotiate, English Canada would be able to negotiate a set of future relationships which would achieve most of its major goals, and which would probably come closer to English Canada's desires than to Quebec's.

What that end-point would be is unclear. For Lévesque it is a common market, common monetary system, and co-operative fiscal policy, with decisions being truly joint. If the analysis above is correct, these mechanisms, while benefiting Quebec, would also operate substantially to the advantage of English Canada, especially Ontario and the Maritimes. With its bargaining strength, English Canada might, for example, retain a preponderant weight in determining the major joint economic policies.

In addition, following the assumption of a peaceful attainment of separation and of a subsequent peaceful and successful negotiation, we could assume that much of the existing economic interdependence between the two countries would be retained. At the governmental policy level, there would be co-ordination. At the private economic level, with free movement of population, goods, and investment, there is no necessary reason why there should be much change from the *status quo*. True, there might be initial flight of capital from Quebec, but a moderate government, coupled with successful negotiations, could presumably recover it. At another level, too, the societies would remain highly interdependent. Just as the Canadian government now is unable to introduce many policies which differ radically from policies within the United States, so the Quebec government would find itself constrained by English Canada. The policies of both countries would continue to have important spill-over effects, though, of course, there would be freedom for some variations in policy. Thus, the likely outcome under Lévesque's scenario is only a very partial disengagement—a disengagement at the political level, without much disengagement in the complex structures of the modern state.

However, one should not use the word "merely" in describing this outcome. The model would be very similar to the existing relation-

ship between Canada and the United States, where Canada's freedom in economic and other policies is strictly limited, and where, in
the private economy, Canada and the U.S. are essentially one. But this
does not necessarily mean that what differences remain are trivial. Indeed, the Canada–United States experience shows that questions of
political sovereignty and economic relationships are only very indi-
rectly related. For example, while a very large majority of Canadians
maintain the desirability of political separation from the U.S., much
smaller numbers argue for a severing of the economic ties. The one
can and does exist without the other. Canadian political sovereignty
is a real, meaningful, and satisfying concept to most Canadians: few
would argue that because we exist interdependently with the United
States in so many other ways, this political distinctiveness should be
abolished, though many of us wish Canada did have more freedom of
action. Indeed, Canadians are even willing to pay a substantial price
in purely material terms to maintain this difference.

I believe exactly the same analysis could apply to Quebec. Maintaining close ties in overall policy-making, as well as in other spheres,
would not render Quebec sovereignty trivial, and need not vitiate its
satisfaction for French Canadians. Symbolic change *is* real change.
If this is true, then a negotiated set of arrangements for future relationships could probably work well for a considerable period. A major
exception could arise if the relationship seemed to work systematically
to the disadvantage of Quebec, with rapidly increasing gaps between
the standards of living in the two societies, for example. The less
existing economic relationships are disturbed, the less likely this is to
happen. Thus, a successful set of negotiations in the immediate post-
separation phase would be crucial. If they set up workable institutions
and left much room for continued economic interdependence, future
relations would likely continue to be amicable, and, indeed, co-operation could well increase. If, on the other hand, the negotiations failed,
or if the outcome were a set of arrangements which systematically
favoured English Canada, the gaps between the two societies would
increase, resentment in Quebec would grow, and so would the likelihood of steadily increasing animosity and increased degree of separation.

To summarize, the Lévesque scenario is a plausible and persuasive
one. It *is* possible to envision a situation in which Quebec's decision to

separate was accepted—albeit with reluctance and with many areas of opposition—by English Canadians. If this is the case, it is also possible to envision a series of negotiations that would be to the advantage of both sides, that would result in some form of "Canadian Association." One can predict with some plausibility how these negotiations might be carried out and what the outcome might be. The separation, in Lévesque's case, would not be total. But it would be a severe blow—psychologically more than materially—to English Canada. The key question, assuming a certain legitimate process leading to a decision to separate by Quebec, is just how strong a blow to English Canada this would be—for that is what would determine the initial and vital reaction.

At the 1968 Constitutional Conference, Prime Minister Pearson suggested it was unrealistic to believe that English Canada would be willing to sit down with a Quebec which had just declared itself independent:

> I should like to say merely two things. The first is a comment on the suggestion that has been made that if Quebec were to secede, it could then enter into negotiations with Ottawa in order to work out a *modus vivendi* with the rest of Canada while acquiring its own independent sovereignty. As someone not without experience in international negotiations, I should like to state frankly my own view that any such proposal rests on an illusion; indeed on a whole set of illusions. Surely it is an illusion to think that a declared intention . . . to seek a disputed divorce can be the basis of amicable and productive negotiations, especially when the parties concerned would still be living in the same house or as next-door neighbours. It may even be an illusion to think that in such circumstances there would necessarily be an "Ottawa" which could speak for the whole of English-speaking Canada.

But the possibility that a *modus vivendi* could emerge does not appear wholly illusory. To pursue Mr. Pearson's analogy, one can imagine an originally disputed divorce in which even the reluctant party decided the costs of continuing the marriage were not worth the effort, and that "for the children's sake" an amicable solution would be preferable. Or the party which wanted the divorce could make life in the family so miserable that the partner would cry "enough!" Lévesque indeed suggests something like this: that Quebec could persuade English Canada of the moral virtue of its desire, and that increasingly severe clashes under present federal-provincial arrangements would make continued federation seem less and less attractive. In addition, one can propose that while the negotiations undoubtedly would not be very amicable, they could be productive if both sides believed that they would gain by avoiding direct conflict. It is precisely because the two entities "live in the same house" that there would be the greatest pressures to arrange an accommodation.

Finally, though the question of the likelihood of disintegration of English Canada is not a central concern of this paper, it seems probable that, for the short-run at least, Ottawa would remain the spokesman for the rest of the country. Again, a desire to keep the country together might be an incentive to work out an agreement with Quebec.

Thus, Mr. Pearson may be right, but not necessarily so. Some of the conditions under which he would be right will become clear as we examine the second scenario.

This one suggests something approaching a civil war if Quebec were to separate. English Canadians, it is suggested, are likely to oppose violently any attempt to separate; they would not accept a Quebec decision as legitimate; if separation were achieved, they would likely adopt punitive policies towards the new state, and so on.

One can easily imagine such developments occurring. If they did, the possibility of a peaceful accommodation would be very small, and the potential for violence great. One could, in such a case, envision a progressive escalation of conflict, a progressive hardening of lines, and a growing likelihood of armed conflict which could be mutually destructive.

Just like the "optimistic scenario," the "pessimistic" one makes certain assumptions which need to be examined. How realistic are they? The primary one, again, is that about English-Canadian reactions: it is alleged they could not tolerate such an action. But in what sense would they not tolerate it? Would they resort to armed repression? This has certainly taken place in other historical contexts, but it seems fairly clear that a very strongly held norm among Canadians is a desire to avoid violence. This desire may well be strongest among those who, on other grounds, would be most opposed to separation.

The experience of civil wars in other settings, from the American Civil War to the Nigerian, might provide strong disincentives for Canadians to carry conflict to that point. But one cannot consider the possibility of this militant reaction of English Canada without considering some of the other factors in the equation. Thus, we can suggest a series of conditions which would make the violent response more likely. Most have to do with the attitudes and goals of the Separatists. The more thorough-going the degree of disengagement sought, the more likely stiff resistance. If the Separatists wanted to win not only symbolic sovereignty, but also wished to disturb all existing economic arrangements and transportation systems, for example, resistance would come from more quarters and be more violent. Similarly, if the Separatists threatened the rights and livelihood of English-Canadian minorities in Quebec, reaction would be angry. At the extreme, outright persecution of non-French-speaking minorities would almost certainly provoke violence.

The ideological make-up of the Separatist movement would also be important. A movement which was not only Separatist, but also Marxist or Fascist, or which threatened to nationalize all industries would be more bitterly opposed, because a wider range of important English-Canadian values would be threatened. Again, the way in which separation would be achieved is vital. The more the decision can be shown to be legitimate and democratic, the more likely English Canadians are to accept the decision, even if unpleasant. But if separation came after some kind of *coup*, or if a referendum showed only a slim majority in favour, demands for intervention would likely grow. Similarly, reaction might be more militant if separation was accomplished quickly rather than being prepared over a longer period.

A crucial factor here is the degree of unanimity and the strength of political organization in Quebec. If Quebeckers themselves were deeply divided, it would be very difficult for English Canadians not to take sides. That might begin on an individual basis, but quickly expand to the governmental level. Instead of a clear-cut Quebec–Canada conflict, there might instead be a complex set of alliances between elements in each area. Negotiations in such a situation could well be impossible. Deep disagreement within Quebec is likely to be associated with some sort of breakdown in social organization. Political leaders could lose their authority and influence. Militant groups like the FLQ would become more active and stronger. If this were the case, it would become extremely difficult for English Canadians to deal with Quebec, the likelihood of threats both to English-Canadian minorities and English-Canadian property would grow, and intervention would be more likely. Therefore, it is in the interests of English Canada to avoid adopting policies which would prompt these developments and threaten Quebec élites which would be more willing to negotiate.

From this we can distil the following summary. If separation is achieved by orderly, legitimate political process, if it poses little threat to English-Canadian political values other than unity itself, and poses little danger to English-Canadian minorities or industries, if it is achieved gradually over time and is guided by political leaders who share a common sense of the most important political rules of the game with English-Canadian leaders and who maintain a fair degree of authority within Quebec, then English-Canadian reaction is likely to be moderate, and English Canadians will ultimately accept the inevitability of separation. In this case, the outlook for maintenance of at least some degree of co-operation is bright. But if separation is achieved through manifestly undemocratic means, such as a *coup,* if it is accompanied by much social disorganization and wide internal dissension within Quebec, if the separatist doctrine is associated with other political doctrines English Canadians find repugnant, or with actions threatening to English-Canadian minorities and property interests, then we can expect a militant reaction from English Canadians, up to and including demands for military repression.

This suggests that the attitudes, goals, and behaviour of the French Canadians would be decisive influences on the English-Canadian reactions. The converse is also true: the ways in which English Canadians react would influence French Canadians. In particular, a threatening posture by English Canada would be likely to produce pressure for more militant Quebec action, for repressive measures against English-speaking minorities, and so on. Similarly, an English-Canadian policy of economic sanctions, if successful, might greatly increase the chances of widespread social disorganization and unemployment in Quebec, thus increasing the chances of the formation of extremist political movements. Thus, one hears it said that a Fascist government in Quebec would be intolerable: to some extent at least, English

Canadian attitudes would determine whether the conditions for such a development existed. Such predictions may become self-fulfilling prophecies.

Hence, the conditions for a spiralling escalation of the conflict could easily exist. Hostility on one side would breed hostility on the other. Such a spiral once started becomes very hard to break, especially with the absence of a third party to intervene. Therefore the initial reactions and behaviour of both sides are crucial.

Factors other than the ways in which separation is achieved would also affect the likelihood of English-Canadian repression. English-Canadian élites would have to be responsive to pressures from their constituents. Undoubtedly, in whatever form separation occurred, there would be demands for armed repression from some voices. The question is how strong would they be and how easily could they be resisted? Hostility to Quebec, and to separation, would not necessarily take the form of "Stop them." It could as plausibly take the form of "Good riddance, and let them go." We might expect great regional variations here: perhaps in the West, where the feeling that Quebec gets too much attention already appears to be widespread, and where a sense that Quebec is really part of Canada seems attenuated, this "good riddance" reaction might be typical. Few might be willing to exert much real effort to keep Quebec in. In the Maritimes, perhaps, with the most at stake if separation occurred, reactions might include far more willingness to force Quebec to remain. But even here, Professor Rawlyk found that when asked what they would do if Quebec separated, "the absence of responses" was more striking than any militance. Perhaps the answer is that it is impossible to predict what attitudes English Canadians both generally and in different regions would take: it would depend on the ways English-Canadian élites defined the issue, and, again, on how and with what objectives Quebec moved. One cannot dismiss the possibility that a political leader could gain power on a platform advocating harsh measures toward Quebec, but it appears unlikely.

Assuming some acceptance of the legitimacy of Quebec's decision, it is probable that most English-Canadian political leaders would oppose armed intervention, again because non-violence is such a strongly held value. In addition, militant intervention would be exceedingly costly in economic and emotional terms. It is hard to imagine what "success" would constitute in such an enterprise. Even the threat of force would be costly, since it would likely only increase Quebec militance. Political leaders, with their superior information, would be most able to perceive such factors and could be expected to counsel actions short of armed intervention.

English Canada could use other forms of reprisal against an independent Quebec, notably economic ones. But again, all would be costly to implement, and the effects would be difficult to predict. It therefore might be more rational for English Canada to hold such reprisals in reserve for use as bargaining counters.

And if that is accepted, then the two sides would again find themselves in a bargaining situation. Since, as I have suggested, English Canada would be in a very strong bargaining position, once it had accepted the fundamental decision to separate, it would then have a very good chance of attaining goals like guarantees of communications with the Maritimes. To the extent that this took place, demands for a militant policy towards Quebec would presumably decline.

Both scenarios we have considered have considerable plausibility; we have been able to visualize situations in which either one could take place. The reality would probably lie somewhere in between—it would not be as painless as the optimists suggest, nor as bloody as the pessimists conclude.

In my view, the actual results would much more closely approximate the optimistic scenario than the pessimistic one. Its assumptions in the current Canadian context are more plausible. In Quebec, the most influential Separatist groups do appear committed to attaining separation in a democratic manner, do have other political goals not widely different from those of English Canadians, and do perceive the need for continued co-operative arrangements after separation. There are, of course, other elements, and these could easily grow—as they have recently appeared to. It is, however, extremely difficult to visualize a militant, violent Separatist group rapidly attaining power in Quebec and leading it abruptly out of confederation. Outside Quebec, there is little evidence of widespread sentiment supporting "sending in the troops" if Quebec were to separate, though separation itself is deplored. Both on practical and moral grounds, one would expect most English-Canadian élites to resist a violent response to Quebec actions. They would certainly try to persuade Quebec to change its course, and would have a variety of sanctions to back them up. But if Quebec went ahead, the incentives for both sides to agree and the sanctions each would have for use against the other would make both likely to be willing to negotiate some kind of *modus vivendi*, though whether it would benefit both sides equally, and whether it would be as happy a *modus vivendi* as M. Lévesque suggests, is definitely open to question.

Separation would be a psychological, economic, and political blow to Canada. It would undoubtedly release dangerous passions, which would be difficult to control. But it is unlikely, given some of the basic attitudes in the country, and some of the existing relationships between the two societies, to result in civil war. In this, perhaps, the degree to which the two societies are already separated, in language, culture, associational life, legal systems, and political institutions, would be important. The two societies already are largely separate. Conflict between them only seldom takes the form of direct interpersonal hostility at the individual level. Rather it takes the form of conflict among organized institutions, which would be well able to bargain with each other under a new arrangement. Relatively few existing arrangements would be irreparably disturbed by separation—unlike, for example, the question of Black separation in the United States, which would imply much greater disruption.

The single most important variable determining the way in which relations between the two societies would develop is, as I have suggested, the attitudes and behaviour on the part of the élites on both sides. This suggests that leaders could engage in activities designed to lessen—or increase—the chances of peaceable disengagement, and that at least partly co-operative relationships could subsequently develop.

To conclude, as I have, that it is possible for Quebec to separate without bloodshed or violent conflict, and that it is also possible to work out a future relationship which approaches that envisioned by René Lévesque is not to argue the desirability of independence for Quebec, or that the future arrangements would be better than current ones. Discussion about benefits and costs of separation, for both sides, belongs elsewhere. What is important is that "separation" has many meanings; it can happen in many ways, in many differing degrees, and with many varying reactions. If Quebec were to decide, democratically, to opt for separation, my own desire would be for English Canadians to recognize the legitimacy of such self-determination, to pursue strategies which would encourage maintenance of relatively friendly authorities within Quebec, and to use the considerable bargaining power available to ensure economic co-operation on beneficial terms, protection of English-Canadian minorities, and maintenance of transportation and other such links with the Maritimes. It would be a period of difficult adjustment. Far better is it to pursue strategies in the present which will avert the need for the Prime Minister of Canada one day to respond to a telegram headed "Quebec's Declaration of Independence."

Sharing the Seaway System

F. J. E. Jordan

AS CANADIANS and Americans joined together in the summer of 1969 to commemorate the tenth anniversary of the completion of the St. Lawrence Seaway system, many optimistic political words were spoken, predicting an even greater future for the deficit-ridden waterway. Less audible voices, however, are raising serious questions concerning the economic viability of the inland seaway. Will the mounting debt of the seaway ever be arrested, let alone retired? Can users of the system bear additional tolls? Can the seaway continue to compete with alternative routes and modes of transportation? Should the lock capacity of the seaway be expanded to accommodate larger vessels? Should tolls be abolished? Should the governments direct their resources to more efficient modes of transportation?

While these and other matters relating to the future of the Great Lakes–St. Lawrence system have become the subject of increasing public debate, one which has not been scrutinized, at least publicly, is the potential impact on the waterway of an independent Quebec. For over 1,000 miles of the seaway's 2,350-mile course, the St. Lawrence River flows entirely within the territory of the Province of Quebec. Consequently, any change in the political status of this part of Canada could have serious implications for all parts of the drainage basin and beyond. It will be apparent that the effective use of the resources of the waterway depends heavily upon co-operation among the various political jurisdictions sharing the system and one more independent state simply complicates the processes of co-operation. Indeed, an entirely new perspective of the future growth and development of the basin may be inevitable in the event of separation by Quebec from the rest of Canada.

This paper seeks to examine some of the problems which might arise if Quebec were to become a sovereign state in North America, straddling as it does a major part of the Great Lakes–St. Lawrence drainage basin. In order to articulate and to assess the situation as it then might be, it is necessary first to describe the basin in present physical, demographic, economic and political terms, to outline the major uses of the waterway for the present and foreseeable future, and to characterize the jurisdictional interdependence of the system. Only then does the potential presence of another sovereign riparian state become significant.

THE GREAT LAKES–ST. LAWRENCE BASIN

As a major part of the St. Lawrence River system, the Great Lakes and their tributary waters are the most important source of the St. Lawrence flow. Thus, in talking about the problems for the seaway system of an independent Quebec, one must consider the entire drainage basin, since what is done in one part of the basin will generally have an impact, both physical and economic, on the other parts. A particular use in one jurisdiction along the waterway may have implications not only for the same use at other points along the system but also for different uses of the water resources. In drafting the model rules governing the uses of international rivers, the International Law Association emphasized the point that "[the] drainage basin is an indivisible hydrological unit which requires comprehensive consideration in order to effect maximum utilization and development of any portion of its waters."[1] Consequently, throughout this paper terms such as seaway, waterway and system will be used, not simply to describe that part of the St. Lawrence and Great Lakes between the Atlantic Ocean and Lake Erie, but to encompass the entire water basin.

The drainage basin of the Great Lakes–St. Lawrence system comprises some 678,000 square miles of territory lying within the American states of Minnesota, Wisconsin, Illinois, Indiana, Michigan, Ohio, Pennsylvania and New York, and the Canadian provinces of Ontario and Quebec. The water surface of the lakes and rivers in the basin, the largest freshwater system in the world, exceeds 100,000 square miles and extends inland from the Atlantic Ocean to the head of Lake Superior—a distance of 2,350 miles. In its flow to the ocean, the water drops from an elevation of 600 feet to sea-level, the main falls occurring in the river reaches between Lake Erie and Lake Ontario (326 feet) and Lake Ontario to Montreal (225 feet). The vast storage basin created by the five lakes provides for a stability of outflow over the year unique among major river basins of the world and extremely beneficial to the users of the system.[2]

This immense tract of navigable fresh water, coupled with an abundance of other natural resources within the basin, provided the ideal setting for communities to establish; and today the population of the basin is approximately thirty-six million persons, with ten million of these living in Canada. A projection for the year 2000 has over sixty million persons resident in the basin.[3] The population of the area is mainly urbanized with major growth centres sprawling along the Canadian and American shorelines. Those concerned with future planning of urban growth in the basin have described the megalopolis which will presently encircle most of the waterway, from Milwaukee to Buffalo and from Windsor to Montreal, and worry that it may become "an ungracious, dehumanized, sometimes tortuous, chaotic sprawl. . . ."[4] Of equal concern must be the unprecedented and often conflicting demands which will increasingly be made by this development on the water resources of the basin.

The Great Lakes–St. Lawrence region is rich in natural resources, and heavy concentrations of industry have developed in the basin to exploit these resources as well as others brought from outside the basin. Many of these resources are consumed within the region; others are exported to other parts of the continent and the world. Agricultural production is intensive in several parts of the basin. The western and northern reaches of the Lakes and the Ottawa and Laurentian valleys yield major timber harvests which are processed into a variety of wood and paper products. Mineral wealth, from the Mesabi range in the west to the Quebec–Labrador boundary in the east, is exploited in vast quantities.

The range of primary and secondary industry which has developed in the basin to manufacture the natural resources of the region and those transplanted from outside defies enumeration. From the belching steel mills of Chicago and the grain elevators of Milwaukee and the Lakehead, through the motor capitals of Detroit and Windsor, and on to the petroleum, aluminum and pulp and paper complexes of Quebec's North Shore, the basin is a hive of industrial activity which provides the bulk of Canada's gross national product and a significant part of the United States'.

The economic progress of the entire region is, and always has been, dependent on the bountiful water resources of the basin. From the earliest days, the river and lakes have provided an important cargo route, and today lakers and ocean vessels navigate the seaway from the Atlantic Ocean to the Lakehead, carrying millions of tons of cargo from one port to another within the basin and to many ports outside the basin. At Niagara Falls, Cornwall–Massena, and Beauharnois as well as on many of the tributaries, massive turbines generate millions of kilowatt-hours of electricity to power the metropolises and industrial complexes in the basin. The same waters are increasingly used in the production of steam and nuclear power.

Another important demand on the water resources of the basin is that levied by cities and industries for consumption and for waste disposal. The latter demand has reached a level in some parts of the basin where the quality of the water imperils uses such as consumption, recreation, and commercial fishing. Increasingly, this conflict and others among the competing uses of the water resources are testing the ability of the various political jurisdictions to co-operate in the utilization of the waterway. For, while the Great Lakes–St. Lawrence basin is a single hydrological system, it is nevertheless politically divided between two sovereign states and several subdivisions of each state.

Some 1,100 miles of international boundary divides four of the Great Lakes and the Upper St. Lawrence River between Canada and the United States. This same boundary delineates the jurisdiction between Ontario and the states of Wisconsin, Minnesota, Michigan, Ohio, Pennsylvania, and New York, as each of these units claims a portion of the waterway as its territory. The provinces of Ontario and Quebec, in turn, share the Ottawa River and a small part of the St. Lawrence as their common boundary. Lake Michigan, wholly in the United States, is shared by the states of Michigan, Wisconsin, Illinois, and Indiana.

In consequence, a waterway impossible of division in a physical sense, is internationally and domestically shared by a number of political divisions, each asserting a degree of ownership and jurisdiction over parts of the basin, and each capable of actions in relation to its part which will have effects, perhaps beneficial or perhaps detrimental, on one or more of the other political parts. For example, a diversion of water by Ontario into Lake Superior will ultimately raise the basin levels from Chicago to Montreal. Likewise, a dam on the international section of the St. Lawrence can have repercussions upstream in the Lake Ontario basin and downstream in Quebec.

This state of affairs has meant that there must be, if the water resources are to be used beneficially by all people in the basin, a high degree of co-operation among the political divisions in the development and management of the system. Unilateral action cannot be tolerated, either domestically or at the international level, for the consequence to the other riparian jurisdictions will usually be disadvantageous.

The method of resolving disputes which arise between the various governments at different levels over the uses of the waters of a drainage basin is complex, and the more so as the number of jurisdictions increases. Nationally, one might assume that the federal constitution would suggest the framework for interjurisdictional co-operation, but such is not necessarily the case. In both Canada and the United States, co-operation among the political subdivisions and between the two levels of government has frequently been achieved only after strenuous bargaining and lengthy delays, rather than by resort to fundamental law.

Internationally, general legal rules have been found wanting, and Canada and the United States have worked out over the years a number of international arrangements regulating the uses of boundary waters in the Great Lakes–St. Lawrence basin. Despite the rules and machinery which have been developed, problems still occur when international, national, and local interests on both sides do not coincide. At these times the national governments seek to find the necessary compromise among their subdivisions and between themselves. This process could be substantially complicated with three rather than two sovereign states sharing the basin, particularly if one of the states did not consider itself obligated by the basic rules which had earlier been established by the other two.

JURISDICTIONAL INTERDEPENDENCE OF THE BASIN

As the population and industrial activity have grown in the Great Lakes–St. Lawrence basin, so too have the demands on the water resources. This has led, in turn, to increased government involvement at all levels in developing the resources and in regulating the uses to resolve conflicts among the multiple and frequently competing users of the waters.

To illustrate the nature of the conflicts which can arise and the methods by which the governments seek to resolve them, three situations will be examined in relation to the major uses of the waterway, all of which have particular significance to Quebec as the downstream riparian state. These are navigation of the waterway, development of hydro-electric power on the system, and control and abatement of water pollution in the basin. Each of these provides a good example of the competing demands on the water and of the need for interjurisdictional co-operation and control in achieving optimum use of the waterway for all parts.

The Seaway: Construction and Operation

In both Canada and the United States, the construction and operation of navigation and shipping facilities rest exclusively within federal jurisdiction, and generally each sovereign state may do what it wishes in its territory in developing and using such facilities. Both countries have long recognized, however, that in relation to the Great Lakes–St. Lawrence waterway, sharing of the resource for such purposes was mutually beneficial, and in 1871[5] and 1909[6] provisions were included in international agreements guaranteeing free navigation rights for commercial purposes to one another throughout the waterway. Thus, when proposals for developing the waterway so that it would be accessible to ocean vessels began to crystallize, it was evident that international co-operation between the two countries in carrying out the project would be desirable, if not essential.

Equally obvious was the fact that the eight American states and two Canadian provinces in the basin had a direct interest in any development of the seaway and their co-operation would have to be secured despite their lack of jurisdiction over matters of navigation and shipping. First, any such development would affect the existing and potential power interests on the waterway. Second, the seaway would have a significant economic impact on the riparian states. Third, property interests in some of the riparian states would be affected by water level variations brought about by the construction.

In consequence, it was necessary in planning a common course of action to devise a means of reconciling the conflicting interests of the various parties at the international and national levels. In the United States, the federal administration, which wished to proceed with the development, was for many years faced with a Congress hostile to the project (reflecting the opposition of railroads, East Coast ports, and supporters of alternate canal systems) and several state governments which favoured power development but not seaway construction. The Canadian government, which generally favoured the undertaking on a joint basis, was subject to vigorous opposition from Quebec, whose ports enjoyed an advantage without the seaway and who opposed upstream power development, and at times from Ontario as well. In both countries disputes arose over who should develop the power, what interests would be adversely affected, and how these interests should be protected.

Despite the desire of the national governments to proceed with joint development of the seaway according to plans devised by the International Joint Commission in 1922,[7] opposition by various interest groups in both countries, including state and provincial governments, thwarted every attempt for thirty years.[8]

Finally in 1951, the Canadian government determined that the national interests could no longer tolerate delay in constructing the navigation and power facilities, so vital to economic development. Assuring Quebec that its particular interests would be protected, Ottawa advised the United States government that it could no longer await co-operative action by the United States and proposed to proceed with an all-Canadian seaway. Both governments still preferred a joint undertaking, but the President agreed to support the unilateral Canadian action if domestic barriers prevailed.[9]

On 21 December 1951 Parliament enacted legislation constituting a federal agency to construct and operate seaway facilities between Lake Erie and Montreal, either alone or in co-operation with an appropriate American agency if the United States decided to participate.[10] In operating the system, the agency was authorized to levy tolls sufficient to meet construction and operation costs.[11]

This unilateral action, supported by the United States government in an exchange of notes on 30 June 1952,[12] plus the joint application by the two governments on the same date to the International Joint Commission for approval of joint power facilities to be built in the International Rapids, resolved the opposition in Congress and the state administrations. Canada agreed to renew plans for construction of an international seaway,[13] and on 13 May 1954 Congress enacted legislation creating a federal authority empowered to construct and operate navigation facilities in co-ordination with those being built by the Canadian agency and the power entities.[14]

With the subsequent exchange of notes on 17 August 1954, incorporating plans for United States participation in the seaway,[15] the last hurdle to joint, co-operative development of the waterway for navigation was overcome. The power interests of the provinces and states upstream and downstream were preserved, competing seaports and transportation facilities were protected by the imposition of tolls on the seaway, and property owners on the waterway were to be protected against varying water levels and compensated for property injured or taken. Canada had reserved its right to develop in the future an all-Canadian channel through the International Rapids, but not without first consulting with the United States, and both nations agreed not to undertake any unilateral action concerning their parts of the seaway which would adversely affect the shipping interests of the other or a third country trading with either.[16] In addition, tolls on the seaway were to be fixed by agreement between the two governments in a single structure and to be imposed unilaterally only if the parties failed to reach agreement.

For Quebec, in particular, the following benefits were to accrue from the co-operative action. Tolls would preserve the interests of the Quebec seaports and the federal government would keep the river up to Quebec City open during the winter. All costs of construction of the seaway in Quebec, including bridges in the Montreal harbour, would be borne by Ottawa. Construction of the navigation facilities in the Lachine section would be undertaken so as to facilitate future power development. Power generation upstream would be regulated to ensure a stable water level in the Montreal harbour and to avoid flooding of downstream properties during spring run-off.

From earliest times, the Great Lakes–St. Lawrence waterway has been a vital transportation route in North America and, since 1958, when the twenty-seven foot channel was completed throughout the system, its importance has grown even more. With the increased capacity of the seaway, cargo traffic has risen substantially from 20.5 million tons on the St. Lawrence section and 27.5 million tons on the Welland section in 1959[17] to 48 million tons and 58 million tons respectively in 1968.[18]

Of the cargo passing through the St. Lawrence section in 1968, 30 per cent was agricultural produce, mainly wheat and corn, shipped from Lakehead ports either to St. Lawrence River ports for overseas transshipment or directly to foreign ports; 38 per cent was iron ore mined in the Quebec–Labrador area and transported from Sept Iles to Ohio ports; and 24 per cent was manufactured goods, largely upward bound to inland ports.[19] The great bulk of the commodity trade through the St. Lawrence section remains intra-basin, with 27 per cent of the traffic moving between Canadian ports, 41 per cent between Canadian and American ports, and 30 per cent between basin and foreign ports.[20]

While the growth of commercial traffic on the seaway has not reached the projected levels nor produced the toll revenues necessary to liquidate the capital investments of Canada and the United States, the waterway remains an important link in the North American transportation network. Indeed, despite the arguments of those who foresee the time when containerized ocean carriers and unit trains will make the seaway obsolete,[21] government plans are presently under way for expanding the seaway capacity to accommodate more and larger vessels.

The seaway facilities were built by public agencies created by federal laws in Canada and the United States[22] and financed entirely (exclusive of the integrated hydro-electric facilities) out of funds appropriated by the federal legislatures.[23] Today it is operated exclusively by the two federal agencies under the direction of their respective governments. In Canada the St. Lawrence Seaway Authority administers the parts of the seaway owned by the Dominion, controlling assets valued in excess of $500 million, 60 per cent of this amount being the Canadian investment in the St. Lawrence section.[24] The United States counterpart, the St. Lawrence Seaway Development Corporation, administers assets worth $130 million.[25]

In addition to the seaway facilities, the Government of Canada, through the National Harbours Board, maintains port facilities in a number of basin ports including Chicoutimi, Quebec City, Three Rivers, and Montreal, and owns two bridges crossing the St. Lawrence at Montreal. These assets in Quebec are valued at $265 million.[26]

Beyond this, the federal Department of Transport operates and maintains those navigable parts of the waterways not under the control of the Seaway Authority and, in the St. Lawrence River below Montreal, provides extensive dredging and ice-breaking services along with other navigational aids. Ensuring that water levels adequate for navigation are maintained throughout the system—a matter of particular concern in the port of Montreal—is also a responsibility of the federal government, performed in the case of the St. Lawrence River by the International Joint Commission.

Thus, the Canadian government, in co-operation with the United States government through the aegis of international machinery, has full responsibility for navigation, and shipping facilities on the waterway and future development will be undertaken, in Quebec and elsewhere, with national revenues and in the national interest.

Power Development

Power development in the Great Lakes–St. Lawrence basin has often been a source of controversy among the various jurisdictions in the basin as, on the one hand, it has been in conflict with other uses of the waters and, on the other, as development in one jurisdiction has tended to interfere with development in another part. The Chicago diversion, for example, has long been a source of conflict between the federal governments and among several of the states. So too has development at Niagara Falls caused interjurisdictional controversy.

When proposals were made for development of the hydro-electric potential at the International Rapids, several factors had to be taken into account. First, it must be done in conjunction with the navigation facilities or at least in a fashion which did not conflict with navigation interests in the section. Second, it must be built in a way which did not impair the present and future hydro-electric developments downstream in Quebec. Third, it must not cause adverse effects on harbour and channel water levels downstream. Fourth, it must be regulated so as to mitigate the dangers to downstream property owners from flooding and level fluctuations. Finally, the water levels upstream must be regulated in the interests of navigation and riparian property owners.

In addition to resolving all of these competing interjurisdictional and multiple use claims and ensuring maximum development of the power potential, the federal governments had to decide how the power was to be developed (under the Boundary Waters Treaty, it must be divided equally between the two countries) and, in particular, the level of government to be charged with the responsibility.

In both Canada and the United States, ownership and jurisdiction over water resources for power development lies generally with the provinces and states. However, when these waters are navigable, interstate or international, the federal governments have a clear interest and jurisdiction. In the United States in such cases, the federal government may build the power facilities itself as it has done in several instances.[27] In Canada, a positive federal power is not so clear, but Parliament certainly may exercise a negative power by requiring a federal licence before such works are undertaken.[28] In boundary waters, no authority may undertake construction which affects the water levels on the other side without first obtaining the approval of the International Joint Commission.[29] Thus, whatever the course of development followed, co-operation at all levels of government is necessary.

Quebec, obviously concerned as a downstream riparian province, voiced early objection to development of the International Rapids power for the benefit of the United States and Ontario.[30] Premier Duplessis reminded Ottawa that no works could be undertaken in the St. Lawrence without the consent of Quebec.[31] Even when Quebec later came to favour construction of the seaway facilities, its government continued to resist the upstream power development, contending before the International Joint Commission that it had no authority to pass upon power applications.[32] In his statement before the International Joint Commission, the Hon. Paul Sauvé insisted that any approval must fully protect Quebec's constitutional interests.[33]

Although Ottawa had some difficulties in reaching agreement with the recalcitrant Premier Hepburn of Ontario on development of the power at the International Rapids, there was never any real doubt that Ontario should be responsible for developing the Canadian power.[34] The operative agreement signed in December 1951 provided that Ontario build and operate all the Canadian power facilities in co-operation with the American agency to be designated and in conformity with all conditions which might be laid down by the International Joint Commission or the Governor General-in-Council for the protection of other interests.[35]

In the United States a fundamental difference of opinion existed on the question of jurisdiction over power development at the International Rapids. New York insisted that, as riparian owner of this section of the St. Lawrence, it alone had the authority to develop the power and, in 1931, Governor Roosevelt created the public Power Authority of the State of New York to plan development of the state's interests.[36] Washington, on the other hand, believed that water power in this case was a federal responsibility and that therefore the federal government would decide who should develop the power and in what manner.[37] Some New England states were opposed to a New York "power grab."

New York, to force the issue, applied to the Federal Power Commission in 1950 for a development licence, but this was rejected by the federal agency on grounds that power development, along with the navigation facilities, should be undertaken by the federal government.[38] Even when the federal government agreed to support the New York plan in the joint application to the International Joint Commission in 1952, other states insisted that any licence granted to New York must provide for making available to adjacent states power from the International Rapids.[39]

New York finally received approval of the Federal Power Commission in 1953 to undertake the power development, subject to building and operating the facilities in a manner which did not hamper navigation and other uses of the waters, in co-operation with the Canadian agency.[40]

The domestic conflicts finally resolved, or at least compromised, in both countries, the federal governments had also to comply with the international obligations imposed by Article III of the Boundary Waters Treaty. In 1952 the two governments made joint applications to the International Joint Commission for approval of their plan to designate public agencies of Ontario and New York to undertake construction and operation of the power facilities.[41] The commission's consent set out the conditions under which the works would be built and operated.[42] Essentially these were designed to protect other users of the waters and, in particular, to guard the downstream interests.[43] To ensure the observance of these conditions by the agencies, the Commission authorized establishment by Canada and the United States of the Joint Board of Engineers "to review and co-ordinate, and, if both Governments so authorize, approve the plans and specifications of the works and programs of construction . . ."[44] To provide overall supervision by the Commission, it established the International St. Lawrence River Board of Control to ensure that water levels above and below the installations complied with the regime of regulation approved by the Commission.[45]

Fluctuations in the water levels of the Great Lakes–St. Lawrence basin, a matter of great concern in hydro-electric power generation as well as to shipping, property owners, and consumers of the water, have caused major problems including substantial property damage in the basin from time to time. The extremely high levels in 1952 caused flood damage estimated in the United States at over $60 million.[46] Low levels from 1963 to 1966 created serious shipping problems, particularly in the Montreal harbour. And now, once again, high level extremes are posing a threat.[47]

To alleviate the injuries to interests occasioned by fluctuating levels, the two governments directed the International Joint Commission in 1952 to attempt to devise the most effective method of regulating the levels of Lake Ontario to minimize the extremes of stage.[48] This the Commission has sought to do, in particular seeking to protect the shipping, hydro, and property interests downstream from the International Rapids. With the low levels experienced in the sixties, the federal governments directed the Commission to consider the wider problems of regulating water levels throughout the Great Lakes.[49] This is a major task which will take a number of years to complete and will require the co-operation of all jurisdictions sharing the basin for the adverse effects are felt everywhere,[50] but particularly so in the vicinity of Montreal. Since all of the regulation of water levels is presently done through control structures in St. Mary's River at the Lake Superior outlet and in the International Rapids, the International Joint Commission and the federal governments must maintain constant surveillance to ensure that the power interests which operate the structures do so, not only in their own interests, but as well in the interests of all other riparian neighbours.

Maintenance of Water Quality

The potential for conflict between Canada and the United States in relation to water quality in the Great Lakes–St. Lawrence basin was recognized as early as 1909 when the Boundary Waters Treaty was signed.[51] The actual existence of the problem was drawn to the attention of the two governments in 1918.[52] However, it is only in the last two decades that the seriousness and complexity, both scientific and jurisdictional, of water pollution in the basin has been recognized and co-operative remedial action taken to combat the problem.

Perhaps no use of the basin waters provides a greater threat of conflict and requires greater co-operation among the political jurisdictions sharing the system than that for industrial and domestic purposes. It is not the quantity of water consumed which is the problem, but rather the quality of water which flows through the system after it is used in industrial operations and as a carrier for sewage disposal. Urban growth and industrial expansion place severe demands on the water, and careful planning plus effective controls are essential to ensure that water contaminated in one jurisdiction is not passed on in that condition to another.

That serious water pollution exists in various parts of the lakes and river basin is in no doubt. Both the International Joint Commission and the Federal Water Pollution Control Administration of the United States have illustrated the extent of the problem and the magnitude of the necessary remedial measures.[53] The major sources of pollution in these waters are the industrial and municipal wastes, although agriculture, shipping, thermal power production, harbour dredging, and shore erosion contribute their share. The adverse effects are felt directly by other water users in the basin as well as by the self-same users. Water supplies must be treated, industrial costs are raised, fishing is impaired, and recreational activities are curtailed.

Were the adverse effects of water pollution confined to the vicinity in which the offence occurred, the problem would be serious enough. However, as water travels the course of the currents, the deleterious substances are carried to other areas, frequently into other political jurisdictions. In extreme cases, such as Lake Erie, an entire body of water is affected. Powerless to take effective action against offenders in another jurisdiction, the various political units are compelled to seek co-operative action in the interests of all.

Until recently in both Canada and the United States—particularly in the former—the control and abatement of water pollution has been considered essentially a local matter to be dealt with by the provinces and states. With each of the ten basin jurisdictions free to establish its own standards of water quality, particularly over the basin waters, the protection afforded these waters has generally been less than adequate. While some jurisdictions have been very concerned with the growing pollution problem in the basin, there is little incentive for rigorous control standards in one part when other jurisdictions sharing the same body of water are not showing similar concern for action.

Most riparian states and provinces have now enacted legislation establishing standards for water quality in their respective parts of the basin, but the standards and their degree of enforcement vary considerably. Because of this diversity and the size of the basin, inevitably participation by the federal governments both at the national level and the international level is required. In the United States, Congress has already sought to achieve a measure of uniformity in the quality control of interstate and navigable waters, giving the federal government the means to force action by the states if necessary.[54] Canada has recently enacted similar legislation empowering the federal government to protect the quality of interjurisdictional waters.[55]

Beyond this, the federal governments have for some time engaged in limited co-operative action on pollution control in the Great Lakes–St. Lawrence basin through the machinery of the International Joint Commission. This agency has been empowered by the two governments from time to time to investigate water quality conditions in various parts of the basin and to report to the governments on measures necessary to prevent trans-boundary pollution of these waters. While the Commission has done some valuable research and recommended steps for remedial action, it has no powers itself to give effect to its recommendations, and the federal governments have left to the local jurisdictions the task of implementing the Commission's recommendations. In consequence, persuasion rather than compulsion has been the only device for obtaining action to remedy the effects of pollution in the basin.

By and large, the downstream user and jurisdiction is the party which suffers the consequence of continuing activities in the basin which cause pollution. While Quebec does not yet appear to be suffering any serious pollution caused by users of the St. Lawrence in the upstream jurisdictions,[56] such will not remain the case as concentrations of population and industry upstream increase, unless effective remedial actions are taken by these upper riparian parties. This in turn will depend upon the effectiveness of international and national co-operation among the basin jurisdictions.

In all of the foregoing illustrations of water uses in the Great Lakes–St. Lawrence basin, co-operation among the political jurisdictions is the keynote to meaningful sharing of the water resources. Unilateral action by any one jurisdiction, national or local, generally has implications for the water users in other jurisdictions and, in most cases, the lower riparian party is the one most adversely affected. While it may be in a position to take some action adverse to the interests of the upper jurisdictions, more often it must rely upon assertion of legal rights which it may possess and the goodwill of the other basin jurisdictions.

A SOVEREIGN STATE OF QUEBEC

One can only speculate whether Quebec will actually move to a sovereign status in North America and, if so, by what means and on what terms. We have heard the bomb blasts of those who would employ violence to achieve a total independence for Quebec. We have heard the proposals of others who would simply declare Quebec an independent state and then negotiate an accommodation with the rest of North America. Others, again, have advocated the course of negotiating a limited independence from Canada which would gradually be transformed to a full and recognized sovereignty.

Not only is the path to independence unknown, but also speculative is the nature of an independent Quebec government. Would it be totalitarian and hostile, or democratic and conciliatory? This would depend in large part, no doubt, on the method of separation which occurred.

Equally conjectural in the several possibilities is the reaction of the rest of Canada and the United States to a move by Quebec for independence. Would there be armed resistance or lesser forms of hostility and retaliation? Would the inclination be for conciliation and mutual accommodation? Again, much would depend on the course and attitude chosen by Quebec.

In this paper the following scenario is suggested for purposes of attempting an assessment of the consequences for the Great Lakes–St. Lawrence waterway of an independent Quebec. First, the separation declared by the Quebec government will be a complete one in which the independent state asserts all sovereign rights over the St. Lawrence River in Quebec. This claim will include ownership by Quebec of all seaway and shipping assets on the river and will include a renunciation of any treaty obligations existing in relation to uses of the river. Such action will be taken in order to make Quebec's independent status clear to all and to provide a future bargaining position. Second, the separation will be peaceful but decisive and will engender, at the outset, ill-will on both sides with little hope for compromise or co-operation. This will be so because the United States and Canada, though reluctant to resort to armed force, will be prepared to employ other forms of pressure to restore the *status quo* or, at least, to preserve their existing rights in the waterway.

In asserting its sovereign rights over the St. Lawrence, the state of Quebec would be claiming it by virtue of a status equal to that of Canada and the United States and, like any other nation, would be seeking the maximum concessions obtainable. Clearly, the strongest position of Quebec would relate to the rights of navigation on the St. Lawrence River. In this matter, Quebec would be free of any restrictions imposed by the B.N.A. Act and would be subject only to those limitations imposed by international law to the extent that these might be respected.

First, as sovereign owner of the St. Lawrence from Lake St. Francis to the Gulf, Quebec would possess the port and navigation facilities now owned and operated by the Government of Canada in this part of the waterway. The ownership of these assets, valued in excess of $500 million, would be a matter of dispute. Canada would undoubtedly call for compensation in the full amount, in accordance with international law, but the new state might not be prepared to concede this. Financially, it would likely be unable to afford such a payment. Politically, it might be argued that these facilities were initially financed from federal revenues derived from Quebec and, therefore, actually the property of the citizens of that country. In any case, Quebec would want some concessions from Canada in return for any promise to pay for the assets in its territory.

Beyond this, the government of an independent Quebec would be in a position to lay down the conditions under which Canada, the United States, and third states would be permitted to navigate the river to and from the sea. As noted earlier, the United States' right to navigate the St. Lawrence for commercial purposes rests on a provision in the Treaty of Washington and is classed as a perpetual privilege, while the passage of naval vessels appears to be by informal leave of Canada. Canada's navigation rights flow, of course, from its present ownership of the territory. Third states possess the right only by virtue of commercial treaties existing between Canada and third states. With regard to the United States and third countries, the question is whether Quebec would be prepared to honour the existing treaty obligations of Canada. International law on the matter of state succession is unsettled, and it is by no means clear that the new state would assume present treaty commitments. Rather, it would prefer to negotiate new transit arrangements for United States and third state vessels on terms most advantageous to Quebec. As for military vessels of the United States, it is unlikely that they would be permitted to enter the waterway.

No doubt the federal government of Canada (and likely the United States government) would claim a right of passage as a riparian state on an international waterway. Such a right has been asserted as the governing international law by the International Law Association,[57] although this right expressly excludes naval vessels.[58] But this rule would not necessarily prevail since similar arguments advanced at an earlier time by the United States were summarily rejected by Great Britain.[59]

Even if Quebec were, in its own interests, to recognize or to grant transit rights in the St. Lawrence to Canadian and American commercial vessels, the government would still be in a position to establish a toll structure on the seaway facilities and promulgate shipping regulations which encouraged the use of port facilities in the lower St. Lawrence rather than carrying cargo through to upper lake ports. Tolls are presently set for the seaway jointly by Canada and the United States under international agreement,[60] but Quebec might not feel obligated to honour this arrangement.

If Quebec refused a co-operative approach to sharing the seaway for navigation purposes, Canada and the United States, apart from other actions to be considered later, would be obliged to seek alternative transportation routes. In this respect, the United States would be better situated than Canada. With its East Coast ports and connecting rail system, and its southern rail and water routes for moving agricultural produce through the Gulf of Mexico to overseas markets, the United States could readily divert the bulk of the seaway cargoes to other, only slightly more expensive, routes. Canada is not so advantaged. The alternative seaports all present problems of accessibility and transportation costs. The Pacific Coast ports are too remote from the production centres of eastern Canada, and shipments from there to Atlantic markets are not feasible.[61] Churchill, which could be expanded to handle more traffic, is accessible only during the short ice-free season. The Maritime region with its ports would be physically separated from the rest of Canada, since all connecting rail and road lines pass through Quebec. Canada would be forced to rely heavily upon transportation routes through the United States to the East Coast.

Finally, depending on the character of the government in an independent Quebec and its attitude toward the rest of North America, it is possible that Quebec might permit the waterway in its territory to be used by naval vessels of one or more foreign powers to establish a base or bases in the Gulf or inland. This could be the case if the Quebec government were fearful of a threat to its independence from Canada or the United States. What response this might evoke from the latter two countries is uncertain; the United States action in relation to Cuba might offer a clue.

Having looked at some of the actions which might be taken by an independent Quebec adverse to the interests of Canada and the United States, it is necessary to consider the disadvantages which might accrue to Quebec if it were to assert sovereign jurisdiction over the St. Lawrence River without consideration for the interests of other parties.

In the first place, Canada would remain the upper and lower riparian state on the St. Lawrence system and consequently would be in a position to impede or prevent commercial or naval navigation by Quebec or its partners both to and from the ocean and between

Montreal and the upper lakes. Canada might, for example, refuse to permit passage of vessels from the St. Lawrence to the Atlantic through the Strait of Belle Isle and Cabot Strait, and even though Quebec could assert that its vessels had a right of passage under international law, it could not make such a right effective in the absence of force. Similarly, in the event that Quebec established trading relations with the United States, Canada could deny the vessels carrying iron ore from Sept Iles passage through the Canadian St. Lawrence above Montreal.

As noted earlier, the water levels of the lower St. Lawrence River are extremely susceptible to fluctuations occasioned by changes in regulation upstream. Low flows, for example, have a significantly adverse effect on navigation downstream, particularly in the Montreal harbour. Such a situation occurs when upstream diversions are increased at Chicago, Niagara Falls, or the International Rapids for the benefit of power, domestic, or industrial users in these areas. The upstream uses of the water are quite legitimate interests, but at present their activities are regulated by the federal governments of Canada and the United States in a manner which takes into account other competing interests throughout the basin, including those in Quebec

If, however, Quebec is an independent state, its navigation interests are no longer a part of Canada's national interest, and the downstream protection now afforded by international agreement or by Canadian law would no longer prevail for Quebec. If Chicago wished to increase its diversion rate from Lake Michigan and Canada were agreeable, Quebec's only recourse would be to protest to Washington. Equally, if Canada and the United States agreed to a proposal by Ontario and New York to increase the hydro-electric generation at the International Rapids by further storage in Lake Ontario, St. Lawrence water levels downstream would be impaired. But no longer would the International Joint Commission be acting as statutory guardian of the downstream interests as it now does to ensure that upstream uses do not impair navigation downstream.

It might also be noted at this point in relation to navigation that an independent Quebec would, in the absence of other arrangements, be obliged to carry the full financial burden of servicing the navigation channels and facilities through its part of the St. Lawrence. Channel and harbour dredging, lock servicing and operation, ice-breaking, and many other activities necessary to maintain the seaway are all provided at federal expense, but these would fall to Quebec at substantial cost.

As with navigation in the lower St. Lawrence River, so too with power generation, the water flows and levels are critical and dependent for their consistency on activities upstream. Quebec, as noted earlier, has sizeable hydro-electric installations on the St. Lawrence at Beauharnois and Cedar Rapids above Montreal, and a large potential development in the Lachine Rapids. At present, the upstream power interests at the International Rapids are required, under the watchful eye of the International Joint Commission, to operate the control structures not in their own greatest interest but in a manner which protects the power interests downstream. Were Quebec no longer under the protection afforded by the Boundary Waters Treaty, the upstream facilities could be operated solely in the interests of New York and Ontario.

Property interests downstream are also presently protected from damage caused by flooding in the Montreal basin during ice-breakup and high-water periods. Waters which could otherwise pass downstream in quantities injurious to property in Quebec are controlled by facilities in both the St. Lawrence and Ottawa Rivers operated by Ontario. Again, in the event of a sovereign state in Quebec, it might no longer be in the national interest of Canada to give equal consideration to the property interests downstream from Ontario.

Of all the situations where actions by upstream riparian jurisdictions may cause serious consequences to the downstream users, none is potentially more serious than water pollution. Whereas changes in water flow and levels have obvious impacts downstream which can be readily predicted, science cannot yet provide an accurate assessment of the total impact of discharging wastes and other deleterious substances into lakes and rivers.

While the present upstream discharges of pollutants into the Great Lakes, St. Lawrence River, and Ottawa River do not appear to be contributing too heavily to the impairment of water quality in the river in Quebec, there is no guarantee that the situation will remain so in the future as population and industry grow in the basin. Protection of the downstream water quality will depend largely on the stringency of the controls imposed by the upstream jurisdictions, both federal and local. And even then, we have seen recently on the Rhine River the consequences for a downstream state of an accidental industrial spill of lethal material upstream.

At present, Canada and the United States are both attempting to ensure that the local jurisdictions take effective action to control water pollution, particularly that which has a trans-boundary impact. Beyond this, the two countries have been moving to make meaningful their mutual obligation under the Boundary Waters Treaty to prevent international water pollution. Quebec, as a part of Canada, will enjoy whatever protection is afforded a downstream riparian partner under this federal and treaty law.

As an independent state, however, Quebec will no longer be able to invoke such rights. As a sovereign state, it may claim a right under international law to receive water from the upper riparian neighbours in a reasonable quality, but legal claims at the international level are meaningful only to the extent that they may be realized in practice. The United States and Canada will control pollution activities by persons in New York and Ontario who may impair the water quality downstream only to the extent that it lies in their respective national interests to do so.

CONCLUSION

The lesson to be taken from the various situations described above is obvious. The waterway is now a cohesive force in Canadian unity, and neither Quebec nor Canada stands to gain anything in dividing the Great Lakes–St. Lawrence basin further among sovereign jurisdictions. Quebec as a sovereign state probably stands to lose more than the rest of Canada or the United States if a separation occurs. Regardless of the number of jurisdictions which share the basin, it remains physically a single, hydrological unit which requires close and continuing co-operation among the parts. And it is a truism that the greater the number of independent parties free to engage in unilateral action on a question, the greater the delay in reaching agreement on the matter. For example, Canada and the United States may reach agreement on a revision of the toll structure for the seaway but, with Quebec a separate state identifying its own national interest on the matter as different from that of the other two, agreement might be delayed indefinitely.

Canada and the United States have worked out within the framework of a number of international agreements relating to the basin a surprising degree of common accord on uses of the shared water resources, designed to mitigate conflicts between jurisdictions. In doing so, they have also been able to reconcile, by national legislation if necessary, the domestic conflicts among the basin jurisdictions within the federal state. The importance of this international co-operation is particularly evident when one considers the difficulties, and, indeed, hostilities which have occurred amongst some other nations sharing a common waterway: the Rio de la Plata whose basin is shared by Argentina, Paraguay, Uruguay, Bolivia, and Brazil; the Indus River shared by India and Pakistan; and the Jordan River shared by Israel, Jordan, and Syria. Adding another sovereign state with complete jurisdiction over a substantial portion of the Great Lakes–St. Lawrence waterway merely complicates relations, particularly if the new party is more concerned with a question of national identity than it is with economic realities.

If, however, Quebec opts for an independent status with sovereign rights over the St. Lawrence River in its territory, it will be essential for its government to seek an agreement with Canada and the United States which will provide for that protection in relation to the uses of the waterway which it is now afforded within the federal system. In return, Canada and the United States will seek to preserve their particular interests which might be impaired by a third independent state within the basin.

The agreement would have to provide for reciprocal rights of navigation for all parties throughout the basin, including rights for vessels of trading partners of the three states. Presumably Quebec would become a party to the seaway agreements now existing between Canada and the United States concerning toll structures and operation of facilities. In addition, Quebec would have to agree to maintain the waterway throughout the state in satisfactory condition and to compensate Canada for the assets acquired at the date of independence. With regard to naval vessels, presumably the two upper riparian states would want access to the Great Lakes and Quebec would want access to the sea.

As for the matters of hydro-electric power development and water quality, Quebec is in the weaker bargaining position, and in return for a guarantee from Canada and the United States to ensure that an adequate flow and acceptable quality of water was delivered downstream to Quebec, the new state would have to be prepared to make further concessions. As to what these might be, no answer is attempted.

Whatever the arrangement may be, one important point to be borne in mind throughout is the fact that the parties, whatever their own aspirations, share a common resource which can never be treated as other than a single unit if it is to be used to the optimum advantage by all. Unilateral action by one jurisdiction will ultimately lead to a lessened value of the waterway for all. On the other hand, cooperative development and use will usually enhance its value for all.

NOTES

1. International Law Association, *Helsinki Rules on the Uses of the Waters of International Rivers* (London, 1967), p. 8. Adopted by the International Law Association at the 52nd conference, held in Helsinki, 20 August 1966. The international drainage basin is defined as a "geographical area extending to or over the territory of two or more states and bounded by the watershed extremities of the system of waters, including surface and underground waters, all of which flow into a common terminus." See Albert Henry Garretson, ed., *The Law of International Drainage Basins* (Dobbs Ferry, N.Y.: Oceana Publications, 1967), p. 4. The importance of the basin approach has now been recognized by the Canadian Government: see Hon. Otto Lang, *Policy Statement on Proposed Federal Legislation for the Management of Water Resources in Canada* (Ottawa: Department of Energy, Mines and Resources, Public Relations and Information, Press Release 25 August 1969).

2. For a detailed description of the hydrology of the Great Lakes–St. Lawrence basin, see MacNish and Lawhead, "History of the Development of Use of the Great Lakes and Present Problems" in Great Lakes Water Resources Conference, Toronto, 24–26 June 1968, *Proceedings* (Toronto: Engineering Institute of Canada, 1968), pp. 5–11; and *Canada Year Book, 1968*, p. 9.

3. MacNish and Lawhead, "Great Lakes and Present Problems," p. 19. Note that the figures provided in this table do not include the Quebec population located within the drainage basin.

4. "Planner Warns of 'Sprawl' in Great Lakes Basin," *Kingston Whig-Standard*, 6 May 1969.

5. *Treaty of Washington* (1871), Art. XXVI.

6. *Boundary Waters Treaty* (1909), Art. I.

7. International Joint Commission (U.S. and Canada), Docket 17, *St. Lawrence River Navigation and Power Reference* for terms of reference and report of the Commission.

8. U.S. Department of State, Publication No. 347, *Great Lakes–St. Lawrence Deep Waterway Treaty* (Washington, 1932); and Richard Reeve Baxter, ed., *Documents on the St. Lawrence Seaway* (London: Stevens; New York: Praeger, 1960), pp. 11–17 for texts of international agreements on joint development signed in 1932 and 1941 but rejected each time by the United States Congress.

9. Baxter, *Documents*, pp. 17–18.

10. *The St. Lawrence Seaway Authority Act,* R.S.C. 1952, c. 242, secs. 3 and 10.

11. Ibid., secs. 15 and 16.

12. Baxter, *Documents*, pp. 50–54.

13. William R. Willoughby, *The St. Lawrence Seaway: A Study in Politics and Diplomacy* (Madison: University of Wisconsin Press, 1961), p. 246.

14. *St. Lawrence Seaway Act* (Wiley-Dondero Act), 1954, 33 U.S.C., 981 et seq.

15. Baxter, *Documents*, pp. 54–57.

16. Ibid., p. 56.

17. St. Lawrence Seaway Authority, *Annual Report, 1959* (Ottawa: Queen's Printer), p. 7.

18. Ibid. *1968*, p. 5; also *Financial Post*, 31 May 1969, p. 1.

19. St. Lawrence Seaway Authority and St. Lawrence Seaway Development Corporation, *Traffic Report of the St. Lawrence Seaway, 1968* (Ottawa: Queen's Printer, 1968), pp. 24–25.

20. Ibid., p. 19. The export-import figure does not, of course, include goods which are transshipped at Montreal or other St. Lawrence ports downstream.

21. See, for example, "Statement Sinks the Seaway 'Magic'," *Globe and Mail*, 17 July 1969.

22. *Wiley-Dondero Act*, 981 et seq.; and *St. Lawrence Seaway Authority Act*, c. 242.

23. In Canada, $340 million; in the United States, $130 million.

24. St. Lawrence Seaway Authority, *Annual Report, 1968*, p. 31. The remaining 40 per cent is the investment in the Welland Canal section. On 31 December 1968 the Authority reported total assets on the St. Lawrence section valued at $322 million, of which approximately $220 million are located in the Quebec portion of the river.

25. St. Lawrence Seaway Development Corporation, *Annual Report, 1967*, pp. 7–8.

26. Canada, National Harbours Board, *1968 Annual Report* (Ottawa: Queen's Printer, 1968), pp. 29–43.

27. Charles Herman Pritchett, *The American Constitution*, 2nd ed. (New York: McGraw-Hill, 1968), p. 275.

28. See *The Navigable Waters Protection Act*, R.S.C. 1952, c. 193, and *The International River Improvements Act*, S.C. 1955, c. 47, for examples of the exercise of this power.

29. *Boundary Waters Treaty* (1909), Art. III.

30. Willoughby, *St. Lawrence Seaway*, pp. 139–40.

31. Ibid., p. 178.

32. Ibid., p. 242.

33. I.J.C. Docket 68, *St. Lawrence Power Application*. Transcript of hearing in Montreal, 8 September 1952.

34. Willoughby, *St. Lawrence Seaway*, p. 187.

35. Baxter, *Documents*, pp. 61–65.

36. Willoughby, *St. Lawrence Seaway*, p. 141.

37. Ibid.

38. Ibid., p. 225.

39. Ibid., p. 243.

40. United States Senate Document No. 165, 83rd Congress, 2nd Session, *St. Lawrence Seaway Manual* (Washington: Government Printing Office, 1955), pp. 150–56.

41. I.J.C. Docket 68, *St. Lawrence Power Application*.

42. Ibid., Order of Approval, 29 October 1952.

43. Ibid., Conditions (a), (b), (c), and (d).

44. Ibid., Condition (g).

45. Ibid., Conditions (h), (i), and (j).

46. "Rising Lakes Pose Threat for 1970," *Detroit Free Press*, 16 August 1969.

47. Ibid.

48. I.J.C. Docket 67, *Lake Ontario Levels Reference*. Terms of Reference, 25 June 1952.

49. I.J.C. Docket 82, *Great Lakes Levels Reference*. Terms of Reference, 7 October 1964.

50. See "Rising Lakes Pose Threat for 1970."

51. See Article IV, paragraph 2.

52. I.J.C. Docket 4, *Pollution of Boundary Waters*. Final Report on Pollution of Boundary Waters (1918).

53. See U.S. Department of the Interior, Federal Water Pollution Control Administration, *Lake Erie Report: A Plan for Water Pollution Control* (August 1968); *Lake Ontario and the St. Lawrence River Basins: Water Pollution Problems and Improvement Needs* (June 1968); *An Appraisal of Water Pollution in the Lake Superior Basin* (April 1969); I.J.C., *Interim Report on the Pollution of Lake Erie, Lake Ontario and the International Section of the St. Lawrence River* (December 1965) and *Second Interim Report* (August 1968); I.J.C. Advisory Board, *Summary Report on Pollution of the St. Mary's River, St. Clair River and Detroit River* (September 1968).

54. *Federal Water Pollution Control Act*, 466 et seq.

55. *Canada Water Act*, S.C. 1969–70, c. 52.

56. Such is not the case, however, with regard to the Ottawa River. See *Pollution—Everybody's Business*, pp. 17–22 (Reprint from *Montreal Star*, February 1969).

57. *Helsinki Rules*.

58. Ibid., Art. XIX.

59. Don Courtney Piper, *The International Law of the Great Lakes: A Study of Canadian–United States Co-operation* (Durham, N.C.: Duke University Press, 1967), pp. 53–54.

60. Exchange of Notes, 9 March 1959.

61. It should be noted, however, that recent statistics indicate that 45 per cent of Canadian grain exports now move through West Coast ports. See "Integrated Plan for Shipping Grain," *Globe and Mail*, 3 October 1969, p. B5.

English-Speaking Quebeckers
in a Separate Quebec

J. R. Mallory

THE EMERGENCE OF QUEBEC as a separate state is a possibility which must be faced. It may not happen. But we live in a world in which national self-determination has become a major engine of political change. Self-determination creates new boundaries in which state and nation in fact rarely coincide. Thus, movements of national liberation create at the same time new national minorities for whom the air of liberty blowing through the new state may be less than exhilarating. Such a drastic environmental change threatens the English-speaking population of Quebec in the event of the break-up of the Canadian federal state.

We now commonly think of the Province of Quebec as the political embodiment of the French-Canadian nation, and indeed the phrase "French-Canadian state" is slipping into common use. But the identity of state and nation is by no means complete. In 1961 some four and a quarter millions of the population of Quebec claimed French as their mother tongue. About three-quarters of a million Canadians living outside Quebec were also francophone, while an almost equal number of residents of the Province of Quebec were anglophone. As a consequence, the emergence of Quebec as the independent home of the French nation would not only involve the abandonment of a large number of French Canadians, but the initial inclusion of nearly an equal number of English-speaking Canadians in the new state. From the time of the Conquest there has been a significant English-speaking population in what is now the Province of Quebec, and there are strong economic reasons for believing that this minority will persist without regard to political change.

THE CONSTITUTIONAL BACKGROUND

The English presence in Quebec, apart from a small group involved in civil government and the inevitable garrison, was attracted by economic motives. They were merchants and traders and, in new areas opened for settlement with the coming of peace, farmers. The end of the Revolutionary War brought many exiles from the revolted colonies. In the nineteenth century the flow of immigration from the British Isles developed as a by-product of the timber trade.

They came, they stayed. As British subjects in a British colony they enjoyed the protection and privilege which went with their status. The problem for the British authorities was to devise necessary constitutional arrangements which would protect the Crown's French-speaking subjects. Among the first of these was the continuation of the system of French civil law and the gradual emergence of the French language in the courts and the administration. Because the Roman Catholic religion, for historical and dynastic reasons, was virtually outlawed in the British Empire, it became necessary to introduce local modifications to give a special place to the Catholic religion in the colony. Otherwise the majority of the inhabitants could not have held any office, civil or military, and much of their community life would have been impossible.

It is well known that the grant of representative institutions was delayed, first by administrative foot-dragging and later by the Quebec Act, to prevent the French-speaking inhabitants from falling completely under the domination of a small English-speaking minority. How far the shape of these measures was influenced by the events leading up to the American Revolution is still a matter of debate, but the effect of the end of the Revolutionary War was to increase the importance of the colony in what remained of British North America. The creation, coincident with the grant of representative government, of two separate Canadian colonies so divided that the Lower Province was predominantly French and the Upper essentially English-speaking created a situation in which the inhabitants of the Lower Province could be gradually assimilated to British political institutions. But, as Lord Durham was to testify, this did not remove racial tensions from the political arena. The reunion of the two Canadas in 1841 must be regarded as an attempt to solve the problem of assimilation of the French Canadians, although the provision for equal legislative representation of the two former provinces may be seen as a safeguard against the extremes of majority rule.

By the middle of the century it became clear that the union was unlikely to work. Since self-government had greatly advanced in the period before Confederation, it became obvious that the new political structure must contain effective protection of minorities against majority domination. This was accomplished in two ways. A federal system, rather than a legislative union, protected the French Canadians in Quebec from ultimate domination in the matters most closely linked with their survival. It was this principle of the distribution of power which accounts for the kind of matters which were placed under provincial jurisdiction.

While the protection of minority rights in Quebec and Ontario was uppermost in the minds of the framers of the constitution, such safeguards as there were had a general application to provincial governments. This, in part, was the reason for the preservation of certain powers in the new federal government which enabled it (through disallowance and the veto powers of the Lieutenant-Governor) to exercise a kind of "imperial" dominance over the provinces. It also explains the compromise settlement over education to safeguard the rights of sectarian minorities which had existed before union.

There were, in addition, certain peculiarities of the constitution of the Province of Quebec contained in the British North America Act which were aimed at providing further safeguards for the position of the English-speaking minority in the province. While Ontario was given a unicameral legislature, Quebec was provided with a second chamber in the form of the Legislative Council. Furthermore, the seats in the Council were territorially assigned to ensure adequate English representation in it. Similarly, the Legislative Assembly contained a number of seats which were in effect assigned to the English-speaking population, for these were in areas of predominantly English settlement. The boundaries of these constituencies were protected by the provision, in section 80 of the British North America Act, that no redistribution could be made affecting them without the agreement of a majority of the members representing them, and the passage of an Address of the Assembly confirming that this requirement had been met. In fact, this requirement appears to have been ignored in successive Territorial Division Acts, and its effect in the long run was further nullified by population shifts which made these named districts predominantly francophone. The provision did, however, remain as a serious obstacle to any thorough redistribution of seats to redress the over-representation of underpopulated rural counties. In the end, the difficulty was overcome in 1970 by the simple expedient of repealing, by virtue of the Legislative Assembly's power to enact constitutional amendments, section 80 altogether. In any event, the effect of this provision, as a safeguard of English minority rights, was no longer of any importance. Similarly, there is little evidence to suggest that the Legislative Council ever seriously conceived its role as that of protecting the rights of the anglophone minority.

Furthermore, evolutionary change in the Canadian federal system has led to the falling into desuetude of the federal reserve powers of disallowance and reservation, so that very few of the constitutional provisions of 1867 can now be regarded as effective impediments to the erosion of legally protected rights of minorities in the provincial constitution. The only exception to this is the position of the English language itself, which remains in the constitution, although it may be doubted how far even this is an effective barrier to the will of a determined majority. The political system in Quebec, however, developed a number of conventional practices which effectively retained a decisive English presence in the process of government. At the same time, there grew up between the two communities in Quebec a tradition of non-interference in one another's affairs.

Given the fact that the English-speaking group was a minority too small directly to affect the major course of politics through political means, this arrangement could be regarded as civilized and defensible. In many ways it was. In others it was not, for it concealed the fact that the English minority, though superficially politically impotent, was in fact the major centre of power on matters of significant importance to the business élite. Many writers have described how the system worked, and none more eloquently than Pierre Elliott Trudeau in "Some Obstacles to Democracy in Quebec."[1] The facts speak for themselves, and do not need to be repeated. While the English minority (and the English-language press) played such a passive role in Quebec politics that they seldom even discussed it, the financial base of Quebec political parties (and in particular the Union Nationale in the Duplessis era) was so closely dependent on the contributions of corporate wealth that effective veto existed on any policy which was deemed to be inimical to the interests of big business. Since this clandestine power was so effective, the English minority allowed its direct political role to atrophy, and after a century of disuse it could only be revived effectively in conditions of political calm. For reasons which need little elaboration, the old defences have fallen and there is little ground upon which to build new ones.

The point can be illustrated by a glance at one area of government where separate but equal administrative arrangements over a long period had taken the whole matter out of the political sphere—the field of education. It will be recalled that section 93 of the BNA Act, which conferred exclusive jurisdiction over education on the provinces, contained safeguards of the rights to denominational schools which existed at the time of Confederation. After a brief experiment with a single Minister of Education, the province—for most of the century since Confederation—confided the administration of schools to two essentially autonomous committees, one Protestant and the other Catholic, each with the power to control curriculum and, through local school boards, to assess ratepayers of each faith for the cost of education. In practice the Catholic Committee was dominated by the hierarchy of the Church and devoted the bulk of its energy and resources to a system of education which was both French and Catholic. On the other hand, the Protestant Committee evolved into an English and almost secular system very similar in its administration to the secular systems in other provinces.

The odd-men-out in this division—the English-speaking Catholics and the miniscule French-speaking Protestant group—suffered more or less silently from this division. The latter group was almost entirely ignored by the Protestant authorities, while the English-speaking Catholics, imprisoned in a school tax system based on religious affiliation, were never able to command the financial resources to keep their schools up to the standard of the Protestant schools. But for the majority of each language group the system worked well, and they operated in splendid isolation from one another. One bizarre consequence, as a result of an administrative ruling of dubious provenance, was that neither system felt able to employ teachers of the other faith. As a result, instruction in English schools in the French language had to be entrusted to anglophone teachers. French language schools suffered from a reciprocal difficulty. This absurd situation summarizes the extent of the two solitudes.

Whatever the effectiveness of these arrangements may have been in enabling two quite distinct cultural and linguistic groups to exist side by side, the direction of change in political institutions alters profoundly the structures that existed before. The Legislative Council clung to life in spite of the great efforts of Mr. Lesage either to curb its powers along the lines of the British Parliament Act or to abolish it altogether. To neither of these proposals would the Council itself agree. To implement the second, the Lesage government hit upon the expedient of seeking an amendment to the British North America Act. This proposal was in fact, though not without some visible embarrassment, transmitted by the Government of Canada to Buckingham Palace in order that the British Government could put before Parliament the necessary amendment. The implementation of this no doubt unwelcome proposal was prevented by the defeat of the Quebec Liberals at the polls in 1966. The Legislative Council, however, reached a surprisingly peaceful end under Lesage's successors. Daniel Johnson had inherited a Union Nationale majority in the Council, patiently built up in the Duplessis years, and the mysterious processes of intra-party decision-making were sufficient for the Legislative Council to concur in a bill bringing about its own demise.

The unwillingness of the electorate to support anglophone spokesmen in the Union Nationale has made it impossible for either Mr. Johnson or Mr. Bertrand to accord them representation in the cabinet. It is only reasonable to suppose that the government of a separate Quebec would be hard put to achieve credible and effective English representation, even if they wished it.

Furthermore, the day is not far off when whatever duality remains in the Quebec educational system will be on a linguistic basis, and not one of religion. However rational this may be, it suffers from one significant disadvantage which has not been lost on certain sections of the anglophone minority. Under the constitution as it now exists, separate school rights are protected on a denominational, and not a linguistic basis. This heritage of the past politics of the Province of Canada and of judicial decisions of an earlier age is one for which there are now additional reasons for regret.

The Parent Report[2] found sound rational grounds of public and educational policy for reorganizing the system on linguistic grounds. In addition, since the revival of the office of Minister of Education and the growing self-confidence of that burgeoning department, it is clear that educational policy (particularly in the schools), which was left in the past to the private objectives of the Catholic hierarchy and the English establishment which controlled the Protestant schools, will become more and more an instrument of *national* policy as conceived by the majority.

POSSIBLE CONSTITUTIONAL CHANGES WITHIN QUEBEC

It is well known that while parts of the Canadian constitution in its federal aspects are entrenched and can only be amended by special procedures, no such restraint is imposed on provincial constitutions, except those safeguarding the position of the Lieutenant-Governor (and possibly the parliamentary system itself). While there have been assertions that an independent Quebec would have a new constitution embodying safeguards to minority rights, there is no certainty that these would involve the preservation of existing rights as such. There is little inhibition now on changes in the constitution of Quebec, and in the initial stages of independence the atmosphere would not be conducive to the invention of restraints on majority rule. In fact, it appears that a belief in parliamentary sovereignty is deeply embedded in the political culture of Quebec. When Mr. Lesage objected strenuously to a bill of rights which would impose restraints on the powers of the federal parliament and the provincial legislatures, he opposed it as a restriction on provincial autonomy. But behind this, one suspects, lurked a fundamental belief in legislative sovereignty which is probably shared by most French-Canadian politicians.

There is now a widespread and apparently growing disillusionment within the French-Canadian élite with the British-type parliamentary system, with its cabinet system and monarchical overtones. As far as the monarchy itself is concerned, it is well known that this feeling is by no means confined to Quebec. A Gallup Poll in 1968 revealed that only about half the people of Canada favoured retention of the monarchy, while one third wished a republic, and the rest were insufficiently exercised by the issue to have any opinion at all. In Quebec itself, 46 per cent opted for a republican form of government.

It is more than likely this response understates the situation among the groups who are now, or are likely to be, politically influential.

The reasons for this verdict are two-fold. The first is the immense impact of de Gaulle on the consciousness of French Canadians. While in the past it is doubtful if even major convulsions of French politics had any but the slightest impact in Quebec, this is not the case with the Gaullist phenomenon. Not only was the symbolic *person* of the General an embodiment of francophone weight and authority in a world in which only the Russians and the Americans seemed previously to matter, but the effect of Gaullism in France in apparently re-energizing a futile parliamentary system of squabbling politicians has had its effect. It is now possible, by the strong emotive appeal to a rejuvenated French political system, to articulate doubts about cabinet government and to see a way to reorganize political institutions to give strong leadership and effective government.

Furthermore, the monarchical principle is widely believed by French Canadians to be little more than conclusive evidence of the "colonial" complex of English Canadians. In addition, there has long been a distaste in French Canada for the office of Lieutenant-Governor. In spite of the emasculated character of the office, it looks formidable on paper. On logical grounds the notion of a head of state of a "provincial State" appointed and paid by Ottawa is to them indefensible. Most French Canadians, one suspects, would like to do away with the Lieutenant-Governor and most of the symbolism that surrounds his role. Until the day when he can be eradicated, symptomatic pinpricks abound. It is well known that Maurice Duplessis (perhaps inspired more by political malice than democratic sentiment) treated the holders of the office with embarrassing contempt and rudeness. The recent transformation of the provincial legislature into the National Assembly has been accompanied by the abandonment of the ceremony of the Speech from the Throne—a step which hardly anyone thought worthy even of comment.

This is symbolism and may be dismissed as unimportant and understandable. But a deeper point remains. A switch to presidential government, particularly if it were accompanied by the introduction of the American congressional system, has graver implications. As Jean-Charles Bonenfant pointed out to the Constitutional Committee of the Assembly, both the Legislative Council and the office of Lieutenant-

Governor are instruments of *limited* government.[3] They are curbs on the power of the majority and a protection of the minority. Mr. Bonenfant, in his sturdy conservatism, no doubt exaggerates the extent to which, under modern conditions, these ancient restraints would work. But they might as long as they were there, and to sweep them away may be more than a need to strengthen democratic symbolism.

There is another point which needs to be considered. A presidential system would focus majority politics more surely on a single leader. Countries engaged in political mobilization—from the United States in the eighteenth century to Ghana in the twentieth—have consciously evolved on the presidential pattern, and rejected the muddle and compromise which is one of the liberal virtues of the cabinet system. A congressional committee system, which Mr. Paul Gérin-Lajoie urged on the Liberal Party in 1967 for the best of democratic reasons, contains serious hazards in a plural community. While it would open up politics, increase participation, and create a more genuinely democratic regime, it would widen the opportunities for militants to generate policies harmful to relatively helpless minorities.

Where compromise is essential and minority interests must be protected by negotiation and a certain amount of pious flummery, it is arguable that the comparative secrecy of the cabinet system, where discussions in the cabinet room and the party caucus are not open, make accommodations feasible which would be utterly impossible if democratic leaders had to carry on their discussions in public.

THE PEOPLE INVOLVED

If one looks back over the history of North America since the American Revolution, one can see that one of its most noticeable characteristics has been an uninhibited flow of people over political boundaries in response to economic stimuli. In this movement, because of the similarities between Canada and the United States, questions of political allegiance seem not to have exerted a very strong pull. From generation to generation, people have moved back and forth across the border, intermarried, and sought new homes without much regard to changes in citizenship. This movement of peoples has affected people of French stock almost as much as those of other origins. In the case of migrants of French stock there has been one important difference. Migration to the United States, and even to other parts of Canada, has led to a rapid attrition of the French language and to assimilation into a dominant English-language culture. From this cultural annihilation there has seldom been any return. For those who opt for the anglophone culture, freedom of movement remains—within that cultural matrix. For the francophone there can seldom be any return in later generations to the culture of the original mother tongue. This explains the near-panic of many French Canadians when they look around them. It leads them to postulate only one solution for cultural survival—the construction of a cultural fortress in which the French language can survive in an essentially French community. In such a community, could an anglophone minority be allowed to survive? Would it be able to survive, or must it make the choice of migration or assimilation? These are questions which must be faced.

To answer the question requires some generalizations about the nature of the two communities. It is, of course, obvious that generalizations about "the English" in Quebec—or any other group—are dangerously lacking in rigour. Any large collection of citizens is not the same from one generation to the next. Their actual composition changes as a result of birth, death, and migration. Within the group, political attitudes change for a variety of reasons, such as maturation, socialization, and changes in the external environment. Nevertheless, patterns of behaviour do exist. Both the behaviour and the institutions which contain it will change in time, but the change is a good deal slower than is nowadays thought by many students of politics.

Historically, the English-speaking population of Quebec appeared to play a rather passive role in politics while maintaining a strong and effective influence on what happened because the normal dialogue at the top was conducted in private, not in public. One does not, for example, carry on open negotiations with bishops, but arrangements can be made. The political élite of French Canada developed an effective role as brokers between the open forces of government and the closed bodies such as big business and the clergy, and worked a political system in which many important political issues were kept firmly beneath the surface.

For the kind of plural community Quebec was in the nineteenth century, this system was perhaps politically defensible. Anyway, it worked, and it worked in a fashion that kept the really divisive issues, such as religion and language, out of politics much of the time. It is perhaps worth saying that Quebec had the appearance, and the reality, of a much more civil community than Ireland. But this system is now dead. The inhibitions are gone: all the issues are out in the open. The francophone four-fifths of the population of Quebec is being pushed, by the logic of present political trends, into open confrontation with the remaining fifth, which is anglophone. From this open confrontation there may emerge accommodation. That remains to be seen. The answer lies to some degree in the character of the two groups.

Who are the anglophones, and how deeply are they rooted in Quebec? The last census tells us that by far the largest group of them described themselves as of "British" ethnic origin; the next largest are described as "Jewish," followed by "Other Europeans." This does not tell us much. It is necessary to see if it is possible to identify subgroups whose political behaviour might vary as the political environment changes. Common observation suggests that such different groups exist.

First there are the "indigenous English," who in turn are composed of at least two distinct groups. There are the middle- and upper-class families, whose ancestry in some cases goes back to the fur trade and the related commercial undertakings of Montreal at the beginning of the nineteenth century. They are generally well educated, mostly bilingual, and to an extent intermarried with a comparable francophone social group. Their roots are deep in Quebec and their offspring will no doubt continue entry into the professions and the world of business.

There is a complementary group, the product of generations of accommodation with their francophone neighbours, adequately bilingual and mainly made up of skilled workers in Montreal and the declining small town and farm populations of the Eastern Townships and certain areas of the Ottawa Valley. Many of them would have small disposition to move away from an independent and separate Quebec; indeed from generation to generation a number of them are absorbed into the francophone group.

The remaining groups, of diverse origins, are less deeply rooted in the province and their reactions to finding themselves in a "foreign" state would, in general, be somewhat different from that of the "indigenous" groups. One would expect little change in the habits of the migrant business class who are the managers and other experts of large American and Canadian businesses. For them a tour of duty in Quebec is part of the pattern of upward mobility in the corporate world. Like their counterparts in Latin America and elsewhere, they can be expected to come and go at the behest of their masters. It is possible that life would become sufficiently demanding for their wives and children that they would be less likely to move jobs laterally and more inclined to await the inevitable transfer to another posting. This would depend on whether the English-language schools retained their strength and quality, although it should be noted that Quebec has a large and flourishing private sector in education which already serves the children of the migrant executive class.

Another distinct group are the many professional and skilled workers attracted by the immense gravitational pull of the Montreal metropolis. It must be remembered that for the Maritime Provinces as a whole Montreal has been, for at least half a century, the natural metropolitan centre. How far this group, once established, would adapt and remain under the presumed conditions of an independent francophone state, is uncertain. While it is true that the heartening revival of the Acadian community in New Brunswick will produce in future a significant flow of French-speaking migrants of this type, the large majority of them are, and doubtless will remain, monoglot anglophones. To them the prospect of really learning the French language and using it as a normal working tongue would in itself be sufficient to divert a large part of succeeding generations of internal migrants to Toronto.

Of the immigrants proper (mostly congregated in the Montreal area) one can be less certain. Most of the postwar wave of middle-class professionals from central Europe were already multilingual. While they have tended to group themselves socially with the anglophone community they have adapted naturally to a bilingual environment. Furthermore, they lack the strong sentimental attachment to "British" institutions which is still strong in the Maritime Provinces. The only members of the group who might be sufficiently perturbed by the atmosphere of the new state of Quebec to emigrate in large numbers are the Jews. Their history reminds them acutely that racially exclusive societies have the smell of danger.

Lastly, there is the late wave of immigrants from southern Europe, many of whom have moved into the bottom of the occupational scale, moving up slowly as newer groups come in to displace them in much the same way as successive waves of migrants moved upwards in the great cities of the United States. For them to be impelled into the francophone group would place them several steps down the scale of social and economic ascent, given the present hierarchy of such groups in the income scale. To become anglophone puts them on the road to the North American standard of prosperity. The main weight of educating the children of this group has fallen on the Roman Catholic School Commission, whose financial resources are already gravely strained, and who could hardly have welcomed this uncovenated increase in their responsibilities. As recent events have shown, these school commissions in crowded suburban areas are readily responsive, or at least vulnerable, to extreme nationalist pressures. Hence the new immigrants, who are Catholic and who mainly wish to have their children educated in English schools, have become the centre of a new schools question. The argument which is now commonly used is that while "established" anglophone groups may have an acquired right to their schools, the new immigrant groups have no such right and should be compelled to accept French-language schools for their children.

The plight of the Italian parents of St. Léonard is, of course, the consequence of what is conceived to be a demographic threat to French-Canadian survival. Urbanization already has produced a noticeable decline in the French-Canadian birth rate. While the birth rate of the anglophone minority is lower still, this is visibly offset by the tendency of the overwhelming majority of immigrants to assimilate into the anglophone group for reasons too obvious to need elaboration.

In spite of government efforts to develop a more "positive" immigration policy which might restore the balance, the prospects for francophone immigration remain poor. France, it seems, does not produce emigrants. The prospects from former French territories, such as North Africa, have not been particularly good. Thus, to every French Canadian who cares to think about it a spectre looms: if present trends continue, then French Canadians could easily be a minority even in Quebec by the end of the century.

THE ANGLOPHONE RESPONSE

"For the English-speaking people the pursuit of prosperity has long been a substitute activity for politics." This statement appears in *The*

Times of 27 October 1969, describing South Africa. It might, until recently, have been said about their counterparts in Quebec. However, it would be wrong to think that the response to the resurgence of French-Canadian self-awareness has been one of Bourbon silence and unruffled calm. There is wide recognition that behind the insults, threats, and denunciations are genuine grievances that can and must be met, and that mere aloofness will not do.

The English-language newspapers now seriously report the affairs of provincial politics. There is widespread willingness to enlarge the scope of the French language and to face up to the needs of living in a bilingual society. One could say that there is widespread acceptance and sympathy for a modification of the federal constitution which gives effect to the unique aspirations of the "new Quebec." If the political situation can be stabilized in a way that meets these aspirations within a Canadian federal system, there can be little doubt that English-speaking Quebeckers in the future can be expected to abandon their politically passive role in exchange for one of fuller political participation.

The difficulties in the way of such a new role will be formidable. Effective participation implies the opportunity to be adequately represented, not only on the bench and in the legislature, but also within the bureaucratic élite and in other centres of executive power. The greatly expanded higher bureaucracy which controls the executive departments and the public corporations does not now reflect even the 20 per cent participation which would accord with the population figures. This may well be the result of rapid expansion and selective recruitment. It may be that in time the public service will develop a more balanced intake in a service based on career and merit.

Similarly, major political parties, desperately trying to find an accommodating balance between their more youthful extremists and a realistic policy, may find it increasingly difficult to accommodate their anglophone minorities. One does not expect to find significant English-speaking representation in the Parti Québécois or in the various emanations of Social Credit, but there is a tendency for the English members of party conventions to look like sad little groups on the sidelines. If this happens it may not be easy for the brave declarations of intent of recent years to be honoured.

Such declarations have been numerous. The English-speaking universities have striven manfully to live up to the spirit of the briefs presented by McGill University to the Parent Commission and the Royal Commission on Bilingualism and Biculturalism that it was their duty to enter whole-heartedly into meeting the needs of the "new Quebec" in both higher education and research. The whole English-speaking educational sector has, with little complaint, endeavoured to fit itself into the new pattern of education which is centred on the polyvalent general college interposed between school and university. In all of this it must be said that they have not been greatly encouraged by the fact that severe stringency in provincial finance has made it difficult for them to withstand a starvation of resources which makes effective planning difficult and threatens a severe attrition of quality in education.

Other responses which are evidence of goodwill among the political and economic élite can be found. The strenuous efforts of the Canada Committee to promote the cause, both inside and outside Quebec, of a more bicultural and binational Canada are not without effect.

But these efforts may fail. They may fail through discouragement and lack of success. They may also fail because extremism always begets extremism. There is yet no large sign of the development in Quebec of an anti-French reaction strong enough to rupture the politics of co-operation, which in a new and healthier form is still strong in the anglophone community. But that may come. And it is more likely to appear if a marked decline in investment and a growth of hardship have the effect of driving away significant numbers of the anglophone community, leaving many of the rest fearful and exposed to the economic storm. The flowering of "For Sale" signs on residential streets in Westmount and other similar areas may be simply the result of a downturn in business, but it may be a portent of what is to come.

THE SHAPE OF THE NEW SOCIETY

What happens, and how it is apprehended by anglophone Quebec, is intimately bound up with the kind of new society which is emerging in Quebec. This new society is the result of a radical change in the French-Canadian community which is leading ineluctably to an urban, secular, and collectivist society.

It is not the purpose of this paper to trace the dramatic change in the dominant themes of French-Canadian nationalism from one of survival through isolation and the preservation at all costs of rural and Catholic values, to one based on a strong national state as the custodian of a new and secular nationalism. Nevertheless, the process cannot be understood without some consideration of what has happened.

The direction of this change was not fully visible until the end of the Duplessis era, when changes long beneath the surface suddenly erupted into the open. What has happened is that French-Canadian society, which had hitherto been content merely to reject modern industrial society, now found itself faced with a challenge to all its own authority patterns and assumptions. The authority of the Church and the social values of the past have been questioned as searchingly as have the values of anglophone North America. From this questioning has emerged a new strategy, based on the conviction that the only weapon for effective survival is the state itself. We thus find in the new French-Canadian nationalist an unlimited faith in the efficacy of government in all spheres of life—a socialism for national ends (for obvious reasons it would be wrong to cloud the issue by calling it national socialism).

Underlying this change is a rapid shift in the composition of the élite groups who are now coming to power. Education, in response to the demands of industrialization, has created a new bourgeois class— self-conscious, insecure, impatient, and hungry for change. These are the technicians of the new society—the teachers, the engineers, the scientists, the managers, the university-trained leaders of the trade union movement, the writers, the journalists, and the other new professions in advertising and communications. Most of them, by the nature of their professions, are interested in ideas, irreverent of the past, frighteningly certain that they can remake their world the way they want it. They are learning that much can be achieved by syndicalist means, and it is fascinating to see that even such individualistic and pragmatic professions as the engineers' are effectively and aggressively syndicalized.

This development is only in part because they have been motivated by the old-fashioned economic drive of "bettering oneself." Their lot lies largely in the world of the highly organized work of the corporate world, one in which in the past a fluent command of English was a *sine qua non* of success. Because in many cases they lacked the education of the narrowly-based élites of the past, this requirement must have been both more difficult and more galling. A sense of injustice is the dynamic of social action, and it is not surprising that the struggle for place in the new society has made of this rising bourgeoisie a turbulent nationalist élite.

The experience of the last ten years is leading many of them to the inescapable conclusion that the only way to ensure the survival of a francophone world in which they can live comfortably is one in which the "levers of power" are controlled by French Canadians. While they cannot aspire to gain control of the great international corporations which loom so large in resource-based industries like mining and forest products, they can at least achieve adequate control, partly through nationalization of utilities on which these industries depend, and partly through bureaucratic controls of the economy. In no other way, it is urged by economists like Jacques Parizeau, will it be possible to achieve adequate economic growth and reduce regional disparities.

One can therefore expect in Quebec—whether inside or outside the Canadian federation—the steady, inexorable growth of a far more collectivized economy than is likely to be found anywhere else in North America. While this development is intelligible, and indeed defensible, it has an important implication in the event of the separation of Quebec from the union.

Where political power exists, the rules tend to be subtly and often unconsciously bent in favour of the values and interests of the possessors of power. In a fairly collectivized society, therefore, the opportunities for equal development of an anglophone community would be far less than in a pluralist economy with a number of alternative outlets. Thus, the conclusion is inescapable that an independent Quebec in the 1970s or 1980s would be a far less receptive environment for a culturally distinct minority than, say, Quebec in 1910.

This would be true even if the transition were peaceful and amicable. If separation comes, it is more than possible that it will not be. If it is preceded by several years of terror in the streets and political extremism, then attitudes will be formed and hostilities generated which cannot easily be calmed down. The consequences may be even more ominous if the first years of independence are characterized by economic hardships or mistakes in planning, and the normal confusion attendant on the launching of a new state.

It would be wrong to conclude without making it plain that it is much more likely, should the ultimate break come, that the damage would be minimized and the affair conducted with good temper and good sense. There are a number of reasons why this might happen.

It must not be forgotten that French Canadians in Quebec constitute a mature, politically sophisticated, and balanced society by any standard of comparison with countries new to independence in the twentieth century. There exists a long-established party system and an experience of political activity which is certainly high on a relative scale. There is a competent bureaucracy to support the expanding functions of government.

Nor should one underestimate the politically stabilizing effect of *embourgeoisement*. The new middle class, and the army of organized trade unionists, have a sizeable stake in political and economic stability. Quebec may not be the most affluent society in North America, but it is certainly not the least.

The heart of the matter, however, is the reaction of English-speaking Canadians to the Quebec phenomenon. Even a generation ago, a sullen and bigoted distaste for the survival of the French language and culture in Canada was unhappily common among English-speaking Canadians. It is difficult not to believe that the events of the last decade have brought about much more understanding and sympathy for French-Canadian aspirations. While there are tensions and fears within the English-speaking community in Quebec, there is also understanding and realism. This liberal and generous spirit is the most likely bulwark against the ultimate separation of Quebec. It could well, though somewhat attenuated, survive the shock of separation. If it does it will be bound to affect the mood of both parties.

NOTES

1. Pierre Elliott Trudeau, *Federalism and the French Canadians* (Toronto: Macmillan of Canada, 1968), especially pp. 107–110; 120–122.

2. Royal Commission of Enquiry on Education in the Province of Quebec, *Report*, 1963.

3. *Le Devoir*, 15 août 1969, p. 3.

"Cancel Out and Pass On": A View of Canada's Present Options

John Meisel

THIS PAPER, like the others in this volume, makes no claim to providing an exhaustive survey of its topic. It is, rather, a personal statement on a subject which is of the greatest importance to me, in the light both of my training as a social scientist and of my reactions as a personally concerned individual.

My argument follows from the axiom that when two or more groups of people have it in their power to survive within independent political entities, the only workable basis on which they can arrange the political relations between them is compromise. If they are to cohabit one country then each side must be satisfied that its interests are served best by this arrangement and, consequently, that no other realizable arrangement will serve better.

The respective interests of the groups concerned are often the subject of acute debate. In the final analysis their nature is effectively defined by those members of each group who can exercise political power. The opinion of academic observers, or even of the majority of the group's members, is less important in this context than that of those who control the political apparatus available to each group.

The following friends have commented on an earlier draft of this chapter: Léon Dion, Paul Fox, Peter Leslie, Hans Lovink, and Hugh Thorburn. I am indebted to them for their many suggestions. I agree with, and have responded to, quite a few (although not all) of their criticisms, but failed to expunge all the inconsistencies and unsupported generalizations. The paper was written "off the cuff," and I decided to leave it substantially in this state of nature. There are, therefore, some major blemishes and minor pimples: for all of these I accept sole responsibility.

It is also important to note that while constitutional and historical antecedents affect a group's attitudes, they are less important than current views. When conflicts develop between national groups politically sharing a given territory, those who advocate change tend to stress contemporary opinion and to soft-pedal historical precedents, whereas the more conservatively minded defenders of the *status quo* usually value the older arrangements more highly than what they deem to be more ephemeral recent whims. When differences of this sort develop, it is virtually impossible to resort to any common philosophically or religiously sanctioned values according to which the differences can be resolved; none tends to be shared, at least none to which both sides are prepared to subjugate their *national* interests. It is for this reason that political power, possibly in its extreme form —force—is the only final determinant of the arrangements to be made.

In my view, only a lunatic would resort to force in settling the differences between French and English Canada, and the sole basis on which the accommodation between the two communities can rest is an agreement acceptable to both. To be acceptable, it must be compatible with those things which are most highly prized by the politically effective spokesmen of each group. In the event that no mutually satisfactory basis can be found for their continued political coexistence in one country, they will have to separate, even though, in my view, this would lead to neither group's effectively furthering its interests as they are now conceived.

THE FRENCH-CANADIAN POSITION:
FROM A NATIONALISM OF WITHDRAWAL
TO A NATIONALISM OF PARTICIPATION

It is much easier to give an account of "what French Canada wants," to use the tired cliché, than to expound the interests of English Canada.

Quebec, while more homogeneous than English Canada, does not, of course, speak with one voice. To generalize about its view is, in a sense, an act of monumental folly. And to assume that what may be a consensus in Quebec is shared by French-speaking Canadians in the other provinces dwarfs even this colossal blunder. And yet, one can make some valid generalizations about opinion in Quebec and one can maintain that the interests of all of French Canada are, in a sense, championed by, and identified with, that opinion and some of the policies of the Government of Quebec. In this essay, I shall speak primarily of the views held by Quebec intellectuals and by the nationalists who have tended to dominate current discussions about Quebec's place in Canada and the world.

It is highly questionable whether a people often consciously pursues a goal over long stretches of its history. With the benefit of hindsight, we can nevertheless sometimes detect patterns in historical development which indicate that, generation after generation, a consistent course was followed by a group in a manner which has enabled it to pursue an identifiable goal and which has ultimately entered the consciousness of at least its intellectuals and leaders. When this happens, the goal is articulated and becomes part of the group's self-image and rhetoric. The goal which had heretofore been pursued more or less like the acquisition of Britain's Empire—in a fit of absent-mindedness—then really does become a guideline towards which many efforts of the group are consciously directed.

French-speaking Quebeckers have adopted as such a goal the survival of their group as a group. By this is meant, of course, the continued existence and flourishing of the culture which evolved on Canadian soil among the descendants of the original settlers. The two critical components of this cultural tradition have been the French language and the Roman Catholic religion. Together they, and institutions like the Church and a highly traditional social system, have succeeded in assuring not only the survival of the small number of French-speaking immigrants who came to Canada during the hundred and thirty years before the Conquest, estimated at no more than ten thousand, but, amazingly, their growth to the present population exceeding five and a half million Canadians of French origin.

This phenomenal increase in numbers, achieved with virtually no additional immigration from France, indicates that one of the major techniques in the struggle for survival was a magnificent level of fertility, although I find it difficult to come to terms with the notion that the idea in the minds of the busy fathers and mothers, as they went about the business of increasing their families, was *la revanche de la crèche.*

The major technique, one partially related to the high birth rate, was the isolation of French Canada from many of the dominant trends and developments of North American life. Turning inward, preserving a traditional form of social structure, and being spared the disturbing consequences of having to absorb waves of immigrants, not to mention the menacing presence of an alien North American environment, all combined to create an identifiable and self-conscious French-Canadian culture and a strongly felt sense of national identity. Anyone who has even the scantiest acquaintance with life in Montreal and Toronto, say, or Vancouver, cannot miss the rich consequence of this cultural identity for the French Canadian, as contrasted with the relative absence of an indigenous and unique culture of English Canada. Whether it be the simultaneously lyrical and angry songs of the Quebec *chansonniers*, the particular intellectual universe and flavour of *Le Devoir*, the frequent staging of works by the prolific Quebec playwrights, or the massive output of the poets, novelists, pamphleteers, and other polemicists who have created a veritable sea of little magazines and books, these phenomena all attest to the existence of a French-Canadian identity which constantly finds expression in a vigorous cultural life and an articulate national consciousness missing in English Canada. The intensity and extent of these Quebec activities exceed similar efforts elsewhere in Canada so strikingly that they constitute a kind of critical mass which differentiates Quebec qualitatively and establishes its culture as being *sui generis*—something which cannot be said about the culture of the English-speaking cities mentioned above.

The historical development which has enabled the *Canadiens* to maintain their identity as a nation in the sociological, cultural, and linguistic senses, as distinct from a merely political Canadianism which tends to characterize so much of the rest of the country, has, however, also exacted its costs. French Canada was able in very large measure to isolate *itself*, but it was unable to *be* isolated. This seeming paradox explains much of what has recently been happening in Quebec, and it points to some of the realities which will continue to confront Quebec in the future. French-Canadian society evolved into its present form by successfully cutting itself off from the mainstream of American life, but the isolation was inevitably only partial. While French Canada pursued its traditional mode of life, the world around it was changing, and particularly the economic conditions of Quebec were responding to Canadian, North American, and world developments.

The response came largely from English-speaking Quebeckers or from English-speaking "immigrants" from the other provinces, Britain, or the United States. The innovators, most of whom were financiers, industrialists, entrepreneurs, and merchants, brought with them a large number of people who had the taste and technical training for activities which did not hold much attraction for many members of the more traditionally orientated French-Canadian middle class. And it was these alone who, among their people, had the educational background needed for the full participation in the newer kinds of activities. Many of the large-scale commercial, mining, and industrial enterprises were also fully integrated with similar ventures elsewhere, and like their successors—the present multinational corporations—they did not provide full scope for people reluctant to move frequently from one place to another and to spend their entire working lives in the English language.

Economically, therefore, French Canadians tended to provide the less-skilled and consequently the lower-paid services required by a modern industrial and, more recently, post-industrial economy, and one of the concomitants of their isolation was, therefore, that as a group they suffered a lower standard of living than other Canadians. This was true not only throughout Canada but even in Quebec itself, where most of the commercial, financial, and industrial power was in the hands of English Quebeckers or outsiders.

The reasons for the generally disadvantaged position of francophones in Canada, so depressingly but convincingly documented by the studies of the Royal Commission on Bilingualism and Biculturalism, are exceedingly complex. Only one set of responsible factors has been touched upon here. Without going into additional detail, however, it is possible to assert that some of the factors were self-inflicted (these are invariably noted by francophobic anglophones) and others were imposed by outsiders, usually quite unwittingly. The external causes are most frequently invoked by French-Canadian nationalists deploring the place occupied by their ethnic group in our confederation.

Whatever the reasons, there are penalties attached to being French in Canada, and these normally take at least two forms. French Canadians have traditionally been considered less suitable for the most responsible positions in many spheres of activity and have therefore only seldom followed the promotion patterns common to anglophones. But even where opportunities might appear to be equal, the knowledge of English is considered essential, whereas ability to speak French has traditionally been deemed of lesser importance. This penalty has serious consequences for the francophone. At one of its hearings, the Royal Commission on Bilingualism and Biculturalism was given a telling description of this problem: "Everyone knows that here [Chicoutimi], where the population is 98 per cent French Canadian, big business has made English the working language and anyone who wants to work his way up the plant has to use English. . . . When there are two people with the same level of education, entering one of our factories in Quebec, the English-speaking one has no need to learn a second language to earn his living, whereas the other person has to spend hours, even years, mastering the second language. . . . The first one can go ahead and improve himself in the technological field and take advantage of the first promotion that comes up, whereas the other one loses time learning a second language."[1]

The other penalty concerns the constraint felt by most people who have to use a second language. Since English clearly is the language in which the most important decisions in Canada are made, whether they be in the scientific, economic, or political spheres, French-Canadian participants are inevitably at a disadvantage in the freedom with which they can express themselves, and no doubt also with respect to the effectiveness with which they can do so. Even in those situations in which they are given every opportunity to join Canadian decision-making (and there are many worlds from which they have been and, to a lesser extent, still are excluded), they are less able than their English-speaking colleagues to translate their views and values into action. French Canadians have thus maintained their national identity at considerable cost: that of being backward, as a group, in the sense of not being fully capable of participating in the highly technological, industrialized, and commercialized world of the mid-twentieth century; being worse off than their English-speaking fellow Canadians, enjoying comparable opportunities; and having their own province largely run by "outsiders," and this not only in the economic sphere but in others as well.

Until the advent of the so-called Quiet Revolution, these costs were largely unperceived or, if perceived, condoned by those who benefited from them personally either in a narrowly material sense or in having the gratification of seeing the fulfilment of the ethnically and religiously "pure" role they assigned to French Canada. The single most significant aspect of the Quiet Revolution manifested itself in the minds of French-Canadian leaders who rejected the traditional form of Quebec nationalism: for a nationalism of withdrawal and rejection, they substituted a nationalism of participation. What they sought and still seek to participate in, however, is not necessarily a Canadian political unit but the world which provides the new rewards and opportunities made possible by the current state of scientific, technological, and organizational know-how.

Two elements give this desire for the new kind of participation an enormously powerful thrust: first, the realization that the old protective mechanisms of the French-Canadian identity are no longer effective; second, the sense of dynamic self-consciousness and awareness which has filled French Canada with an unprecedented optimism and confidence in its capacity to "do its own thing" and to achieve greatness. A few words about each of these elements are in order.

The birth rate in Quebec has levelled off dramatically; it is now lower than in many other parts of Canada and *la revanche de la crèche* has become an obsolete weapon. To survive, French Canada must, therefore, find other means than simple population growth to offset losses through geographical and cultural emigration. Furthermore, it has become obvious that the old isolationist nationalism was a potent deterrent to the full *épanouissement* of French Canada's culture and that if the latter was to flourish, and if it was to benefit from contemporary developments, it had to break out of the protective cocoon in which it had enveloped itself in the past. To continue the old way would have led to French Canada's shrivelling into a quaint and picturesque folk society increasingly clinging to *dépassé* formulas out of lassitude or a desire to attract tourists seeking an escape from the monotony of North American industrial society.

The impetus for change, now so vibrantly manifested by French

Canada, is not inspired only by the negative realization that the old ways have become outmoded or that they have perhaps never really worked. There is now a flexing of muscles in Quebec because the renaissance, which became apparent after the death of M. Duplessis, has given most Quebec leaders the sense that their society has within it the ability to participate fully in the contemporary world and to do so in a manner which can preserve their own values and contribute something unique to it as well.

It is usually assumed that French-Canadian values, having evolved somewhat in isolation of the major developments in North America, can add a less materialistic and more humane and aesthetic dimension to the post-industrial society.

There is a quixotic element of messianism in this view, held by many French-Canadian nationalists—an element which I find unconvincing and unacceptable. But the presence of different values in Quebec clearly does add a significant and enriching dimension to North American ways. There *is* a French-Canadian style which differs from the predominant North American mode of doing things and which endows whatever it touches with a quality all its own. A comparison of the Toronto Subway and the Montreal Métro makes the point, as did many of the best features of Expo. The preservation and growth of French-Canadian culture and its lively interaction with the dominant strains of North American and English-Canadian culture are consequently important and creative goals not only for French Canadians but for Canada as a whole.

Be this as it may (and I shall return to the point later), French Canadians, in defining themselves and their role in North America, do not think of themselves primarily as Canadians but as French Canadians or Quebeckers. The whole notion of Canadianism and of being Canadian has very little resonance among a large and politically powerful group of them. They do not feel themselves to be Canadians as much as *Québécois* and they are convinced, not without reason, that the rest of Canada has been quite uninterested in helping them maintain their culture. English Canadians as a whole are to them a nationally faceless group, ever willing to give up their own identity and Canadian national interests for the material advantages of becoming part of the American economy and the Pax Americana. And while French Canada might understand and forgive the past lack of concern of the rest of the country for the survival and flourishing of French culture in Quebec, it has been keenly aware of the degree to which the other provinces have pursued policies which have inevitably led to the anglicization of their French-Canadian minorities. And, as we shall see a little later, whatever the attitude was towards *past* indifference of English Canada with respect to the survival of French-Canadian culture in Quebec, right now Quebec has become passionately involved with the survival of its own cultural values at home (in Quebec) and it will do everything in its power to stop further anglicization. It is in this context that one must look at efforts by the Quebec Government to protect the French language through educational, immigration, and other policies.

In the strong commitment of French Canadians to their own culture, and in their relative unconcern for the rest of Canada, there is not necessarily any anti-Canadian sentiment. There is usually very little animosity towards the rest of the country, but rather indifference. This may be more irritating to English Canadians than outward hostility since, as is well known, nothing is as discouraging to the wooer as apathy. For many Quebeckers, the greatest, if not the only, attraction in the survival of Canada as we now know it is the possibility that within the Canadian framework Quebec might better resist American encroachments on its culture and economy.

To English Canadians, the idea of Canada existing without Quebec has until recently been quite unthinkable, whereas many Quebeckers can tolerate the thought of their province becoming an independent state. To a growing number the possibility is in fact quite challenging and inviting. To put it at its lowest level, the idea of an independent Quebec is not appalling to a great many people in French Canada and is considered a possible alternative to the *status quo* because of the faith of many French Canadians in the feasibility of an independent Quebec state.

The two paramount questions about the Separatist solution are whether French-Canadian culture would gain or lose if Quebec were independent, and whether the economic life of French Canadians could be maintained at least at the present level. Neither question can be answered without engaging in prodigious guesswork, in which one's own wishes inevitably become the mother of invention and the enemy of proof. No one has, to my satisfaction at any rate, come up with anything like convincing evidence which would lead one to make confident predictions about the likely future of French-Canadian culture and of an independent Quebec's economic well-being.

No matter what the long-run cultural and economic consequences of separation for the broad masses in Quebec (to which I turn later), there can be little doubt that the leaders of an aggressive nationalism and of Separatism have benefited personally from the cultural, political, and economic developments which have followed the Quiet Revolution and that they would do so even more in an independent Quebec. Writers and other intellectuals, musicians, artists, politicians, technocrats and civil servants, people in the communications industry —these are the individuals who not only make nationalist revolutions but also, to some extent, live off them. I am not suggesting that their nationalist commitment is insincere or that their idealism is tainted by a mercenary careerism, but merely that in forecasting the future their vision and perceptions cannot but be influenced by self-interest and, more important, by the environment in which they function daily and which they unwittingly come to believe resembles the larger world more closely than is likely to be the case.

I have gone to considerable length in pursuing some of the aspects associated with the idea of a separate Quebec because the limits within which compromise between English Canada and Quebec is to be reached are immensely important to the nature of the solution to be found. And it is essential that English Canadians, who tend for their own reasons to exaggerate the evil consequences of separation, be fully aware of the degree of sanguineness with which rupture with Canada is contemplated by many Quebeckers pursuing their national aims. These will increasingly be pressed with the vigour and self-confidence which comes from believing that a genuine, if drastic, alternative is available.

The aims to be pursued, with the Separatist alternative at the back of many Quebeckers' minds, can now be restated. They are closely related to one another, since they are merely different aspects of the same basic goal, survival of French-Canadian culture.

First, French Canadians as a group wish to enjoy equal economic and career opportunities with other Canadians. Particularly in bilingual areas like, say, Ottawa or Montreal, they are no longer satisfied with providing primarily the night shift—the cleaners of buildings or the operators of elevators—with the sop of seeing a small number of their group occupying the dubious role of the negro king.[2]

Second, they wish to develop the economy of Quebec in a manner which will reflect their own priorities and their own concern for survival. One of the practical consequences of this aim is that in many spheres where the federal government has some responsibility (the location of airports, to take a recent controversial example) they resent Ottawa's decisions, which may have far-reaching consequences for their own plans, and, while perhaps eminently sensible from the all-Canadian point of view, may conflict with policies whose aims are not merely to be efficient *per se*, but to serve French-Canadian *national* purposes. The effect of such aims on the demands Quebec is likely to make for constitutional change in Canada is that the Quebec definition of the country is certain to be a much more decentralized federalism, resting largely on an agreement among the constituent provinces rather than on an overwhelmingly powerful central government.

Finally, French Canada insists on being *maître chez nous*. This resolve to wrest control from outsiders over important parts of Quebec extends not only to the areas just mentioned, like economic planning and governmental policies generally, but also to such vital areas as language use in the province of Quebec. There is no question in my mind that, if it does not opt for French unilingualism, to make bilingualism a two-way street in Canada, Quebec will at least do everything in its power to make *itself* reasonably bilingual, in the sense that English Canadians will have to be able to speak French if they wish to enjoy full citizenship, just as Franco-Ontarians must now be able to manage well in English if they are to compete on an equal footing with their anglophone fellow Ontarians. The present privileged position of the English minority is therefore going to be challenged by various measures designed to strengthen and widen the use of French in Quebec. At the heart of this assertion of French culture lies nothing as crude as revenge against the haughty and arrogant manner of some English-speaking individuals and companies, but rather the stark necessity of preventing the eventual anglicization of Montreal and, with it, all Quebec.

The measures intending to protect the French language, which are occasionally undertaken awkwardly and foolishly, must be understood by non-Quebeckers as a desperate means of coping with new demographic realities in Quebec. In wishing to become a franco-phonic or genuinely bilingual province, and in depriving English of its monopoly position in some sectors of Quebec life, the province is defending the core, or heartland, of French Canada. The dramatic and highly emotional reaction of many even moderate French-Canadian nationalists to the language question must be understood in these terms. For the handling of this question, more even than the problem of constitutional revision in Canada as a whole, and more than the economic aspects of French-Canadian nationalism, will determine whether French culture can survive in Canada, or whether, as in Louisiana, it is largely to become a colourful folk memory to be celebrated annually by a crassly commercial Mardi Gras.

FOUR PERSPECTIVES OF ENGLISH CANADA

The aims of English-speaking Canadians are much less homogeneous than those of Quebeckers, and in a large measure they remain vir-tually unstated and perhaps even unperceived. One of the purposes of this book is to present some of them, and several of its chapters do precisely that. At the risk of repeating arguments to be found else-where in these pages, I must, however, isolate certain aspects of the non-French view and, in particular, describe its response to some of the French-Canadian ideas summarized above.

Some Canadians have a strongly British conception of Canada, not only in the sense that they themselves value the British connection and its heritage but, much more important, in that they believe that the whole country should share these values. The tendency to play down these links and the gradual removal of British heraldry and of the representation of the monarch from public places are viewed by this group as a betrayal indicative of the transformation of Canada in-to a rootless, polyglot entity. To many (but certainly not all) of those holding this view, the presence of French-speaking Canadians is the result of their conquest by the British. The French are tolerated so long as they accept the essentially British nature of the country, and so long as they do not prevent the non-French majority from pur-suing its ends. Most Canadians belonging to this school of thought see nothing wrong in, and often even welcome, the anglicization of

French Canadians. And while they deplore the loss of British elements in Canadian life, and particularly in its political culture, they do not lament the possible or actual decline of French-Canadian culture.

According to a different, more widely held concept, Canada is a country based on its indisputable pluralism. Those who hold this view see themselves as part of a community composed of many ethnic and cultural groups which, for better or for worse, share certain political institutions and certain problems and opportunities. There is a good deal of variation among the members of this group with respect to the degree of Canadian nationalism they display. In this they resemble the next group to be mentioned, and it will save time to discuss this aspect of the two groups together later. Other divergencies of opinion to be found among the "pluralists" concern their ideas about the place to be occupied in the Canadian mosaic by the French-speaking members and the degree to which the members of each of its components should be prepared to abandon their original culture. There are many Scandinavians, Slavs, and others whose families have lost their language and cultural traditions who do not see why French Canadians should accept this kind of metamorphosis any less willingly than they did themselves, as the price of leading a safe and reasonably prosperous North American existence. This position obviously affects the way in which they react to Quebec demands for conditions required for the survival of the French language in Canada. Some do not distinguish between the French and other minorities, whereas others ascribe a special position to the descendants of the earliest *habitants*. This group resembles the third identifiable English-Canadian school of thought about the nature of the country.

Like the terms of reference given the Royal Commission on Bilingualism and Biculturalism and like the commissioners themselves, the Canadians who make this distinction assume that Canada is a partnership between two language groups. These language groups constitute two societies which share one political union. It follows from this position that both English and French occupy a special place in the life of Canada and that both languages must be accorded special and equal status in clearly identified areas. In recognizing the two principal language groups in Canada, the adherents to the country's essential dualism recognize, as I am doing throughout this essay, that people of various origins, in the process of their Canadianization, become part of one or the other of the two language groups and members of one or the other of the two societies. According to this view—and it is one I accept—I am an English Canadian, despite the fact that so far as I know I cannot boast a single ancestor hailing from England.

A fourth fairly common definition of Canada by English-speaking people is more vague even than the three enumerated so far. Unlike these, it does not distinguish between various specific ethnic and cultural traditions but takes a general view of the country by seeing it as somehow different from all others. It tends not to identify anything positive which makes Canada different but is based on its holders' belief that in numerous small ways Canada is different from other countries and that these differences give us our particular national identity. The argument, though extremely vague, is reasonably convincing, since, if casual personal observation is to be trusted, a large number of Canadians share the impression that, as a people, "we just are different" from our neighbours and from other nationalities. The fourth definition gives Canada its character by comparing it with certain *external* phenomena, while the first three I have identified focus entirely on *internal* factors—the ethnic composition of the population.

It is useful to distinguish between the four groups, even though they are not mutually exclusive, by determining where the priorities of various English Canadians lie. People who have *primarily* an internal, demographic perception of the country belong to one of the first three groups. The others are placed in the fourth if they subscribe to its differently based position. The view one has of Canada's population and cultural tradition may of course affect the definition one has of the country when one compares it with others.

The schools of thought identified here can be labelled the British-Canadian, the pluralist, the dualist, and the "Canada just is different" positions. The labels, like the categories themselves, are only very rough-and-ready identification points for four general perspectives which vary greatly from individual to individual. Their usefulness lies in permitting us to make a few comments about English Canadians who share a certain cluster of ideas about the nature of their country.

It is almost inescapable, in view of our history and origins, that Canadians should tend to define their country not so much by reference to characteristics which it possesses, as by those in which it differs from other countries. And the reference points are normally Britain and the United States with, perhaps, an occasional nod in the direction of France. Our British Canadians, ever mindful of the historical development of Canada, tend to define the country still very much in the terms which bind us to Britain, and they are generally disposed to be the most active and jealous guardians of Canada's identity *vis-à-vis* the United States.

They are usually more nationalist than the pluralists and more strongly anti-American. In this latter trait they resemble the dualists and the "Canada just is different" group, who also tend to be fairly actively afraid of American influences, but the groups differ from one another in the means they find most congenial to combat them. The British Canadians wish to preserve the British links, traditions, and institutions. The dualists, on the other hand, are disposed to seek in the French presence in Canada a countervailing force likely to keep the Americans at bay. More precisely, they believe that a close and conscious alliance of French- and English-speaking Canadians wishing to create out of their partnership a different kind of North American society here in Canada can best protect us from the inroads of American culture.[3]

The pluralists are, as a rule, the least concerned about American influences on Canada. They admire the pluralism of American society, and normally seeing no great inherent virtue in preserving British patterns in a North American setting which is radically different from the United Kingdom, and not being greatly impressed by the argument that what makes Canada unique is the French presence, they tend to think of Canada as being like the United States. As a result they are also somewhat less dismayed than the other groups by the prospect of Canada's falling apart because of its inability to resolve the differences between the demands of anglophones and francophones. There are many among the pluralists who would, in these circumstances, consider without extreme anguish the possibility of their province or region becoming part of the United States. This is not to say that they would particularly welcome this development but merely that they would find it somewhat less intolerable and unthinkable than the British Canadians, the dualists, and the "Canada just is different" school. The consequence of this difference, from the point of view of this analysis, is that the pluralists are less disposed than the other groups to compromise with the spokesmen for French Canada for the sake of preserving the realm.

The generalizations I have been making about the four main strands of opinion among English Canadians are, of course, scandalously broad and crude and need to be carefully tested. I would want to subject them to a most rigorous scientific examination before committing myself irrevocably to them. They are, however, plausible, suggestive, and useful in the present context. They are compatible with regional historical and demographic differences in Canada, and they also help explain variations in regional attitudes towards the nature of the country. The so-called British-Canadian view is associated most closely with Ontario (particularly some of the rural areas), with the Atlantic provinces, and with parts of British Columbia, especially Victoria. The pluralist position is evident particularly in the Prairies, most notably among Canadians whose origin is neither British nor French, among the less British parts of British Columbia, and probably also among the inhabitants of the large metropolitan areas. Dualists are probably concentrated geographically in Ontario and overwhelmingly in Quebec; they are to be found in large numbers among young people and also, so far as I can tell, among leaders of national voluntary associations who have had some experience in working out compromises with articulate colleagues from French Canada. The Canadian self-consciousness which leads to an awareness that this country differs from others and therefore to a nationalism not necessarily related to the country's ethnic composition is not localized in any particular region. It is most noticeable among journalists, artists, teachers and intellectuals generally—those, in short, whose occupations encourage them to define the nature of their community and to reflect upon its characteristics and problems. It is my guess that generally (and I readily concede that there must be many exceptions) nationalism among English-speaking Canadians is a middle-class phenomenon. If this is so, then *taking the group as a whole*, one would find those whom I have identified as the "Canada just is different" school among the better educated, the better paid, and those with higher-ranking occupations than the average for the entire English-speaking group. For reasons which I have indicated above, I think that they would be particularly numerous among those with the most years of schooling and those who make their living primarily through symbolic communication. It is, incidentally, in precisely the same stratum of society that I expect to find the most numerous and most active French-Canadian nationalists.

I have devoted a fair amount of space to a somewhat hypothetical exploration of the anatomy of English-speaking opinion about the nature of the country, the place in it of French Canadians, and the possible total Americanization of Canada. The detailed look at this aspect of our main problem was a necessary prelude to a consideration of the degree to which English Canadians can accommodate themselves to the needs of their French-speaking fellow citizens.

Before we turn to this question, however, it is necessary to stress two other points: one deals with the more narrowly political federal-provincial dimension; the other concerns the overall attitude of English-speaking Canadians to their country, for I believe that at least some general statements can, and indeed must, be made about it.

The four approaches to Canada noted above are essentially different clusters of opinion which are not, as such, related to any particular political option, although each predisposes the holder towards certain specific postures *vis-à-vis* the crisis now confronting the country. The latter has a specifically political aspect which brought into being various well-defined positions advocating how we should settle our problems at the constitutional and governmental levels. The most immediate and concrete form of these political choices concerns the relations which should prevail between the federal government and the provinces, and to some extent also among the provinces themselves. What to do about revising the constitution is one important aspect of this side of our problem, as is also the appropriate fiscal relationship between the various levels of government and the means to be employed when governments at either of the two senior levels make decisions which have consequences beyond their own jurisdictions.

Whereas the four groups of definitions of Canada are largely entertained by individuals, it is primarily governments which must take political positions with respect to the nature of the country. Hence, the political options are championed by spokesmen for "Ottawa" or the various provinces, who cannot but endow their formulas and arguments with an aura of official formality. These official formulations, while unquestionably coloured by the four schools of thought considered above, tend to reflect not so much the tastes and inclinations of individuals as the harsh economic realities interpreted by the officials and politicians serving their respective levels of government.

By and large, the poorer provinces favour a strong central government, in the hopes that the latter will engage in an extensive national redistribution of income, whereas the more affluent parts of the country, feeling their potential or actual strength and capable of greater independent effort tend to support a more decentralized arrangement which would enhance the powers of the provincial governments.

The position taken as the result of the economic situation of a province is either reinforced or contradicted by the views on the nature of the country prevailing among its inhabitants. Generally, the pluralists are the most centralizing group, and the dualists the most strongly committed to the idea of a system based on decentralized government by powerful, largely autonomous provinces. The British Canadians, like the pluralists, include a large proportion of centralists. The group of mild nationalists whom we have dubbed the adherents of the "Canada just is different" school also tends to pursue a strongly centralist line.

As for the general attitude of English-speaking Canadians to their country, there is no gainsaying the assertion often made by francophones that it has been influenced by their concern for the economic well-being of the population. This concern for maintaining a high standard of living, comparable to the maximum attained in the United States, has led most English Canadians to adopt an attitude of tolerance towards, and even encouragement of, American encroachments on Canadian sovereignty and, more important, the Canadian mind. For American interests are allowed to permeate Canada's economy, its institutions of learning, its mass media, its world of entertainment, its voluntary associations—all its life, in short —to a degree which suggests that whatever they may *say,* most English Canadians really do not care whether their country becomes indistinguishable from its neighbour.

French-Canadian intellectuals, who, as we have seen, are themselves enormously concerned about the survival of their identity and nation, tend to conclude that the materialistic pursuits of their English-speaking compatriots have deprived the latter of a will to have their country survive as an independent entity. This doubt focuses on several aspects of French–English relations in Canada, at least in so far as the intellectuals of the nationalist movement are concerned. In its general manifestation, it questions whether two groups whose actions are motivated by such divergent sets of priorities as appear to be dividing French- and English-speaking Canadians can, in fact, continue successfully to coexist in one state. More specifically, it questions whether a unified country, even a federal one, can function effectively when part of its population appears disinclined to resist its takeover, in all but the most formal sense, by its powerful neighbour, while another important part of the population prizes its national survival more than anything else in the world. And finally, French-Canadian scepticism is directed at the unwillingness of English Canadians (given their tendency to value everything in economic terms) to sacrifice anything tangible for the development and growth of a country which would afford equal opportunities to French- and English-speaking Canadians. In other words, French Canadians wonder whether English Canadians, who appear so reluctant to make the economic sacrifices required to prevent Canada from substantial Americanization, are going to be willing to make the economic sacrifices necessary to protect their country from the disaffection of a large linguistic minority.

I find it most difficult to resist sharing these doubts, despite the recently increasing concern in English Canada over domination by the U.S.A. I like diversity among people, and while I see many dangers in nationalism, I do believe that Canada has been altogether too ready to permit its neighbour to make inroads into an essentially Canadian way of doing things. We have been largely unconcerned witnesses to the gradual attrition of Canada's dissimilarity to the United States, and our attachment to an ever rising standard of living may prevent us from adopting changes—which may be necessary for the political survival of Canada as we know it. Those of us who take this view resemble, in this particular at least, many Quebec nationalists. Nevertheless, I believe that a dangerously large number of French-speaking Canadians misread the way in which English Canadians view their country.

It is all too often assumed in Quebec that English Canadians are so mesmerized by the alluring dollar that nothing else matters to them and that for a high standard of living they are prepared to give up everything, including their country. This view is understandable in the light of what I have just been saying, but it overlooks a point of the most critical importance: the choice before most Canadians as they make decisions compromising the country's independence and identity is not between gaining an economic advantage and preserving Canada's independence. The implications for national survival of many economic and other decisions are rarely perceived at all, and it is probably correct to say that, in the past at least, most of the inroads into Canadian sovereignty resulted from individual or corporate decisions in which no thought was given to the consequences for the country as a whole. If, in the same decisions, an alternative were presented in which a choice would have to be made between damaging Canada for the sake of some material advantage and not damaging it, the chances are that a great many Canadians would opt for the latter.

In other words, it is quite misleading to assume that, despite the absence of a strong national consciousness and of an aggressive nationalism, English-speaking Canadians are devoid of loyalty to their country. This loyalty, often quite vigorous, is not evident in decisions affecting the Americanization of the country, because so many Canadians have not seen the latter as a threat to national survival. On the other hand, events like de Gaulle's *Québec libre* speech, Quebec initiatives in diplomacy, and Separatist agitation are conceived as genuine threats and provoke violent responses on the part of large numbers of English Canadians, as the perusal of even the moderate (in this context) English-language press reveals at a glance.

A realistic assessment of English-Canadian opinion must distinguish sharply between postures taken *vis-à-vis* the United States and those adopted in relation to what is often considered to be an internal attempt to break up the country. For many English Canadians the internal threat to the continuation of Canada is emotionally and in every other way the equivalent of the challenge to their own survival experienced by most French-Canadian nationalists. An excessively inward-looking and self-centred parochialism prevents many Quebec leaders from realizing this and also from perceiving that the seventies will witness a major effort on the part of English Canadians towards reasserting Canadian interests in the face of the American challenge.

Outright separatism is only the most extreme form in which English Canadians see their country's survival threatened by Quebec nationalism. There are others, and although they are less dramatic and provocative, they nevertheless arouse deep concern and anxiety among the large majority of English Canadians who worry about the future of their country. The most acute and controversial "threat" results from the desire of Quebec to make its own decisions in a wide variety of fields, many of which cannot be confined to the provincial sphere alone. Although English Canada's nationalism is not nearly so well defined and vigorously articulated as Quebec's, it is real enough for all that, and it takes at least two clearly recognizable forms: it is based on considerable pride in Canada as a country and as a member of the international community; and it assumes that there are certain Canada-wide standards and procedures which should be common to, and shared by, all parts of the country. Quebec's occasional encouragement of, and connivance in, the slighting of Canada in the international sphere, particularly by the government of France, evokes bitter resentment in English Canada.

Secondly, and I think much more seriously, the wish of Quebec to make its own decisions in fields which have ramifications far beyond education and the other areas normally under provincial jurisdiction is sometimes seen as a threat to the survival of Canadian standards. It is held that the Quebec demands for autonomous decision-making would, if conceded without qualification, cripple the power of the central government to make decisions affecting Canadians in fields in which the interests of all parts of the country are engaged. Some of the demands of Quebec are thus held to be impediments to the federal government's taking steps necessary for the well-being and equitable development of all Canadians. Even those English Canadians who strongly sympathize with the national aspirations of French Canada sometimes wonder whether the most extreme political demands arising from them may not, unwittingly perhaps, destroy Canada as a viable country by paralysing all attempts to make decisions in the common interests of all. No one has seriously suggested that Canada has reached the stage at which the decision-making powers of the federal government have been seriously frustrated by Quebec demands, but the fear that they may be in danger will quite certainly impose one of the limits on the compromises some English-speaking provinces will be prepared to make in future negotiations about constitutional revisions and particularly the re-allocation of responsibilities between the federal and provincial governments.

Our discussion has now reached the point where we can begin to look at the motivation for, and the content of, the compromise which will have to be reached between French- and English-speaking Canadians if their country is to survive as a political entity. It will be recalled that the major premise of my argument has been that the only acceptable solution to Canada's current national dilemma is one which proves equally acceptable to both major language groups.

THE CONDITIONS NECESSARY FOR AN ACCEPTABLE COMPROMISE

We have seen that essentially both groups are seeking their survival —one in terms of its cultural identity now at last beginning to find political expression—and the other in terms of a political unit which also displays certain national characteristics. Since in each instance it is actually survival which is at stake, the clash of wills is animated by a profound and intense force which cannot easily be moderated and which may, in the end, sweep everything aside, including reason and enlightened self-interest.

And yet, it seems to me that accommodation between the two groups is possible if each believes that its objectives can be reached within the framework of Canada. At the present time English-speaking Canadians overwhelmingly think that this is possible, but they are not yet particularly aware of the adjustments they will have to make to accommodate the interests of French Canada. Franco-phones, on the other hand, probably understand the problems some-what better, at least those aspects of them touching on their own sur-vival. But many of their most articulate leaders are less convinced that their aims can be met without a drastic political realignment, possibly necessitating the disruption of Canada. The most encourag-ing feature of the present impasse is that substantial majorities on both sides have still not rejected a Canadian solution and that the impulse for separation is confined on both sides to numerically unim-pressive minorities.[4] It is nevertheless disquieting to note that a signi-ficant minority is not opposed strongly to the separation of Quebec. The 1970 Quebec election must give serious pause to anyone hoping for the survival of Canada. In my own survey, roughly 70 per cent of those whose background is British, 63 per cent of those whose origin is neither British nor French, and only 59 per cent of French Canadians *strongly* opposed separation.

The situation is fluid, and although I believe that there is still the necessary degree of will required among Canadians to make it possible for us to stay together, there is also much uncertainty which makes the outcome unpredictable. One of the aspects which must be considered is the cost, to each group, of the disappearance of Canada as we know it. So far the emphasis in our discussion has largely been on the costs of staying together. We must now briefly examine the other side: how would the "departure" of Quebec affect the aims of the two language groups?

Canada would, of course, cease to exist in its present form, and to some extent the traditional way of perceiving the world, the loyalty, pride, and ambition of many English-speaking Canadians would consequently be seriously impaired. The often-heard bogey that the succession state would eventually be absorbed by the United States does not strike me as particularly convincing. There would be many very serious communication problems and much economic dislocation, but on the whole it seems likely that the trauma of this experience and the exigencies of adjusting to new conditions might produce a sense of national cohesion among the English-speaking Canadians and the *élan* required to create a new state. The tragic and searing experiences which would almost certainly accompany its birth could easily generate precisely the kind of vigorous and active nationalism which is at present not very much in evidence in Canada (an absence, incidentally, which in the eyes of many who have elsewhere experienced the parochialism and inhumanity of chauvinism bestows on Canada one of its most endearing characteristics). Such a revitalized nationalism would enable the truncated new country to overcome both the internal centrifugal forces and the pull of the United States which would inevitably threaten it. In any event, the United States might not wish to absorb all, or even part, of her northern neighbour.

The consequence of the split might, therefore, in a paradoxical way, make English Canada come to resemble present French Canada in some respects by giving its members a greater sense of national community and by making them more conscious of the need for intensifying the efforts required to resist the ubiquitous influences of the United States. There is little doubt that economically the English remnant could become a viable state and that the standard of living of its members would not, in the long run, be affected adversely by the new political conditions.

This speculation may, of course, be no more than a Pollyanna-like escape from reality. The various far-flung fragments of the new state might find the attraction of the United States too great to resist, and the new Canada might ultimately disappear. I nevertheless believe that many of the important goals of English Canadians—a high standard of living, a peaceful and free society in the liberal democratic sense, and a high level of toleration of diversity—would survive the break-up of their present-day Canada. What would, alas, not survive is the presence in one country of two major language groups constantly interacting on one another and so creating a dynamism and cultural mix of which more homogeneous states are deprived. This would be a grievous loss to me and many other Canadians, but it would not prevent most English Canadians from achieving their major goals in the new state.

I am not nearly as confident about the chances of a "free" Quebec realizing the goals currently pursued by most of the Separatist leaders. This is not to say that I doubt the capacity of an independent state of Quebec to survive as a political unit in North America—I am sure that it could. What it might find exceedingly difficult to achieve is the fulfilment of the high aims pursued by virtually all French-Canadian nationalists, namely, the survival and flourishing of their culture and the opportunity of creating a life of dignity in French without the corroding influences of the English North American culture.

There are many reasons for my pessimism. Three strike me as particularly compelling and I shall mention them without examining them in detail. They are no more than guesswork, possibly induced by constant exposure to English media of communication. The first concerns the capacity of a new small state, beset by many problems resulting from the dislocation of long-established economic, political, and social patterns, to resist the overpowering influence of the United States. Servan-Schreiber, in *The American Challenge*, has admirably portrayed the pressure exercised by the American economy, and he has shown how difficult it is even for all of Western Europe to resist it. Is it likely that an independent Quebec might succeed where Europe has so far failed?

It is, of course, possible to minimize American cultural and economic influence, as Mexico, Castro's Cuba and Mao's China have shown. Conditions in these countries and those prevailing in Quebec, however, are so staggeringly different that the parallel is totally meaningless. It is most improbable that the majority of the population in Quebec, or even a significant minority, would be prepared to pay the price required to eradicate or seriously to reduce the contamination which is said to threaten the survival of French culture. The policies almost certain to be adopted by an independent Quebec to offset foreign influences would be no less inimical to Quebec nationalism than what can, if the will is there, be achieved within the present Canadian framework.

In fact it is quite possible—and this is my second reason for pessimism—that even fairly mild nationalistic economic and linguistic policies in an independent Quebec might lead to serious economic difficulties. Even at the time of writing (Summer 1970), the economic conditions in Quebec are discouraging, in part quite evidently as the result of the political climate, and it is a valid question to ask oneself whether the most numerous economic groups in Quebec—those with the least skills and lowest incomes—would not be hardest hit by economic adversity following separation, at least temporarily, and if so, whether they would be compelled to seek work wherever they could find it, say, in Ontario, British Columbia, or the United States. The goal of strengthening French-Canadian culture would hardly be furthered by this emigration. The lowering of living standards in Quebec would probably also compel some of the most skilled individuals to seek employment elsewhere in Canada or abroad. This exodus would lead to an even further lowering of living standards in Quebec and could do much to defeat the lofty motives and plausible arguments of the Separatists.

Thirdly, I am uneasy about the political reaction in an independent Quebec to the inevitable difficulties and hardships associated with starting a new, breakaway state. Dangerous illiberal elements exist in all liberal democracies and, for a great many reasons, the possibility cannot lightly be discounted that an authoritarianism of the Right or of the Left might develop following serious social and economic dislocation in Quebec. It is easy to overdramatize this kind of argument, and it has often been used in differing contexts by opponents of innovation. This unappetizing precedent notwithstanding, only an ostrich would fail to detect elements in Quebec society and politics which lead one to fear that under conditions of stress, even well-meaning leaders might be driven to exceedingly dangerous means in an effort to achieve their goals, and that if this were to happen the cause of a dynamic and liberating Quebec nationalism would suffer. The creative society expected from an independent Quebec by its proponents would not be likely to emerge from an oppressive regime dedicated to compelling its people to like the controls deemed necessary by the rulers. The emergence of such a regime, while by no means inevitable, is a possibility which no one, I believe, can seriously ignore, particularly those of us—whether French-speaking Canadians or others—who value the richness of Quebec culture and hope to continue enjoying it in the future.

It is perhaps futile to try to predict how separation would affect each of the two groups. The critical point is that, apart from depriving each of the other, it would present quite fearful perils to both French and English Canadians and that, in trying to find a settlement of their present differences, each should be acutely conscious of these. An acceptable compromise will require that the adherents of each side have a reasonably accurate and complete understanding of the position of the other and that they are fully aware of its implications for day-to-day negotiations and bargaining which nowadays occur continually between French and English Canada.

In the present essay it is, of course, impossible to be specific about the position that the two groups should take on every particular issue under discussion. The details have to be worked out in each case, which will dictate their nature, but the accommodation has to occur within certain general guidelines which can be stated. Their generality and simplicity should not lead the reader to reject them too quickly: many profounds truths are simple and may appear both trite and obvious.

For the French-Canadian nationalist the main points to remember, as he redefines his relationships with English Canada, is that he cannot have it all his way and still remain part of Canada. In a partnership the aims and objectives, but particularly the *modi operandi*, of the participants cannot be defined in absolute terms pleasing to one group or the other. Each side must be prepared to accept a little less than it would really like, and compromise is therefore essential. French Canada, if it feels that its long-term aims can best be achieved within a Canadian state, will have to be prepared to bear in mind some of the deeply felt ideas and strongly held values of the anglophones and will therefore have to be content with accepting, *in some areas at least*, somewhat less than it might really want.

Quebec would, I believe, accept this watering of its nationalist wine if English Canadians showed a comparable willingness to be satisfied with less than they really want, if French-Canadian leaders took a really serious and realistic view of the Separatist alternative, and if they had an awareness of the constraints on the freedom of action which would inescapably affect the domestic and foreign policies of an independent Quebec.

The principal guideline for English Canada is to realize that in the past French Canada has benefited substantially less than the English-speaking population from participating in the Canadian state and that, whatever the complex reasons, French Canada's underdog status is in part the result of English Canada's ethnocentrism. Secondly, English Canada will have to accept the idea that in several important areas of Canadian life, and particularly in the political one, there will have to be substantial changes made which will alter the character of Canada in some important ways. There is a widespread presumption, even among some learned experts, that there is only one "real" federal state and that Canada is its most magnificent and perfect expression. They fail to see that there are many possible federal arrangements and that Canada may have to depart quite substantially from the present formula and move toward a new one. In defining the "national" Canadian interest, the pre-eminence of the central government may have to be greatly diminished to make way for a complex scheme in which the provinces, enjoying greater autonomy than they do now, may have to reach agreement among themselves, at the same time as they deal as more or less equals with the federal government. English Canadians will have to recognize, as one of their basic guidelines, that although this may make for a less effective governmental system in some ways, the alternative might be the break-up of the country.

Accepting these guidelines, and the consequences which follow from this acceptance, would require that both sides make efforts of quite uncommon difficulty for the sake of finding a mutually satisfactory solution to their problems. Each group would have to swallow a great deal of pride; each would have to show a degree of realism scarcely ever achieved in the controversies concerning issues of nationalism and of the density of states; each would have to suppress a driving impetus towards being vindictive and malicious under extremely provocative conditions.

The key question in guessing the outcome of the present crisis is whether the leaders on both sides will have the wisdom and courage to make the adjustments to one another required to achieve the accommodation and compromise which, as I have argued, can be the only acceptable way of reaching a solution. It is my guess, admittedly based only on very general, untested, and unsubstantiated observations, that on the French side the general population is able and prepared to make the necessary adjustment in its aims and in its methods of achieving them, but that a substantial number of leaders are incapable and unwilling to take a posture leading to a Canadian solution. The reverse situation seems to exist in English Canada. Here an important number of leaders at the federal and provincial levels have shown the necessary insight and understanding, but the general population appears to be lagging behind.

The outcome will depend on whether spokesmen will be able to take enlightened and far-sighted actions which, in the first instance, at least, may not have the support of the English majority. There is much food for thought in this observation for anyone interested in the working and virtue of liberal democratic political systems, but this is a topic too removed from our present problem to warrant discussion here.

In Strindberg's *The Dance of Death*, as in Albee's better-known *Who's Afraid of Virginia Woolf?*, the protagonists—a married couple—discover that while their life together is full of excruciating tensions and hostilities, they have become dependent on one another and cannot really live separately. Strindberg's Edgar and Alice, realizing their mutual dependence, achieve a partial reconciliation after having inflicted awesome humiliations on one another—a reconciliation which they express by agreeing to "Cancel out and pass on!" Since seeing this play for the first time in Stratford (interestingly in the present context, with Jean Gascon and Denise Pelletier, two of French Canada's finest actors, giving superb performances), I have often wondered whether this modest program could not usefully be kept in mind by French and English Canadians trying to reconcile the differences now separating them. I realize, of course, that Quebec's motto is *Je me souviens*, and that there are many aspects of this country's past which neither ethnic group would wish to forget or cancel out. But in exploiting the many things which Canadians have going for them, as the current saying has it, it would often be highly desirable if both groups could learn to make light of some of the ways of the past in favour of passing on to what strikes me as a *potentially* exciting and highly promising future.

NOTES

1. *A Preliminary Report of the Royal Commission on Bilingualism and Biculturalism* (Ottawa: Queen's Printer, 1965), p. 77.

2. The image of *le roi nègre* is frequently invoked by French-Canadian nationalists. He is the native colonial ruler who receives rewards and honours as compensation for doing the bidding of the imperialist interests.

3. See Maxwell Cohen, "Canada and Quebec in North America: A Pattern of Fulfilment," *Queen's Quarterly*, 75:3 (Autumn 1968) 389–400.

4. Respondents interviewed in a very large national survey I conducted late in 1968 overwhelmingly rejected the idea of separation. Fewer than 3 per cent of the 2,767 Canadians interviewed were strongly in favour, and under 5 per cent said they were slightly in favour. Almost 14 per cent were undecided. Ten per cent of the respondents of French origin supported separation (4 per cent strongly and 6 per cent mildly) but 18 per cent were undecided, as compared with only 11 per cent "undecideds" among those whose origin is British, and 14 per cent among those whose ancestors are neither French nor British.

Ontario's Quiet Revolution

A Study of Change in the Position of the Franco-Ontarian Community

T. H. B. Symons

WHEN THE QUIET REVOLUTION took office in the Province of Quebec with the election of the Government of Jean Lesage on 22 June 1960, another quiet revolution of parallel and of possible comparable significance was already under way in the sister Province of Ontario. This concerned changes in the laws and practices relating to, and the attitudes which prevailed towards, the province's French-speaking population. The decade of the 1960s was to see reforms and innovations so numerous and so profound that they constituted a revolution in regard to the position of Ontario's francophone citizens and the rights and opportunities available to them. These developments in Ontario had, in turn, a wider meaning for Canada as well as the more particular meaning for the people immediately concerned within the province.

The most significant area in which these changes took place was that of education, the key to the survival of any cultural group. The major part of this paper will be devoted, therefore, to a study of the changes in the extent and nature of the educational opportunities provided for Franco-Ontarians. However, it will also examine some of the other major changes in attitudes and policies towards French Canada which were a part of this quiet revolution in Ontario.

THE FRANCO-ONTARIAN COMMUNITY

The French presence in Ontario is both substantial and widespread. Over 10 per cent of the province's population, approximately 650,000 people of a total of 6,236,000, were of French origin in 1961.[1] Indications are that in 1970 this figure approached three-quarters of a million. While this francophone population has areas of concentration in the Ottawa Valley, the mid-north and far north of the province, and in southwestern Ontario, it is present in every region of the province and represented in almost every community of any size. Of the fifty-four counties and districts of Ontario, sixteen have populations which are more than 10 per cent French-speaking in origin. In ten of these, the population of French-speaking origin exceeds 20 per cent, and in three of these it exceeds 50 per cent by very substantial margins. In a further twelve counties and districts, the French-speaking-by-origin population exceeds 5 per cent. In only eleven counties is it less than 3 per cent, and in no county is it less than 1 per cent.[2]

The force of these figures is, however, diminished by the fact that French was, in 1961, the language used by only 425,000 Franco-Ontarians, approximately, or some 7 per cent of the province's population, as opposed to the higher figure of over 10 per cent who were of French-speaking origin.[3] This discrepancy arose in part from a perhaps natural tendency to linguistic assimilation in a province with a vast English-speaking majority. It was also, however, a consequence of the severe limitation upon opportunities for education and development within their own tongue and culture which had been available to Franco-Ontarians through successive generations.

The pressures upon the Franco-Ontarians to assimilate were heavy and real, and an assumption that such an assimilation was both desirable and possible had underlain the thinking, spoken or unspoken, of virtually every provincial administration, regardless of party, from the time of Confederation. The concept of linguistic duality was neither understood nor accepted in Ontario, and the school system of the province (with the important special exception, on religious grounds, of the Roman Catholic separate schools) was usually conceived of as a single centralized entity concerned with uniform standards, textbooks, and curriculum. The possibility of developing two language streams within one educational framework was never seriously considered. In fairness to the educators and politicians alike, it must be recognized that the climate of public opinion was generally such that it could not be otherwise.

POST-CONFEDERATION PRESSURES

The pressure upon Franco-Ontarians to conform to and be assimilated in the provincial English-language school system did not take shape until some time after Confederation, and, when this pressure came, it was a break from the practice and spirit which had to a substantial extent prevailed in such matters in the years preceding 1867. The use of French as a language of instruction in Ontario can, in fact, be traced to the early French settlements, and for many years primary schools in which classes were conducted in the French tongue were established readily and naturally, as the need arose, and without acrimony or debate. Indeed, Dr. Egerton Ryerson, the Chief Superintendent of Education in the province for more than thirty years and in many ways the founder of Ontario's school system, took the view that French was, as well as English, one of the recognized languages of the province and that children could therefore be taught in either language. This view was put clearly by Dr. Ryerson in a letter of 24 April 1857 to the Trustees of School Number 3, in Charlottenburg Township, near Cornwall:

I have the honour to state in reply to your letter of the 16th that as French is the recognized language of the country, as well as English, it is quite proper and lawful for the trustees to allow both languages to be taught in their school to children whose parents may desire them to learn both.[4]

In a letter to the Secretary to the Governor General on an earlier occasion, Ryerson had noted the demand for French and expressed his opinion that its study "independent of its being regarded as a valuable literary accomplishment, is, I think, very important to all Canadian youth who are likely to take a part in the public affairs of United Canada." His own actions as the first Principal of Victoria College were in keeping with this opinion where, his biographer concludes, his "desire to launch out into what was then a new field in university work, the teaching of modern languages, probably was suggested quite as much on national as on cultural grounds."[5]

Ironically, it was probably in part at least because there was so little difficulty or debate surrounding the use of French as a language of instruction in schools in Ontario prior to Confederation that the question was not specifically dealt with when the British North America Act was drafted.

While there were thus a number of so-called "bilingual" schools in the province at the time of Confederation, their right to existence was based upon custom and history and they lacked any specific statutory authority or guarantee. During the next half-century, the implication tended more and more to be drawn that these were—or should be—simply English-language schools in which French might be used in the earlier years and where it could be taught as a supplementary subject. In 1885, the first regulation in regard to language instruction in Ontario stated that English was to be taught in all provincial schools, and required a knowledge of English grammar for future teaching certificates. Many a capable teacher, with much to contribute within a French-language context, was discouraged or excluded from the Ontario school system by this stipulation. An inhibiting sequence of regulations was thus begun which was to restrict severely the opportunity of Franco-Ontarian students to learn from teachers of and in their own tongue. Moreover, this sequence was also to deny to English-speaking students the opportunity, which might have been developed with imagination, of studying French with French-speaking teachers. Instead, a pattern was set for the next three or four generations whereby most English-speaking school children were taught a kind of lifeless, desiccated French by English-speaking teachers for most of whom it was a foreign or dead language rather than a modern, living tongue. The teaching of French was handled as a "subject," akin to Euclid or Greek, rather than as a contemporary language which might provide the means of communication between peoples who shared a common country. It was a wretched and depressing ordeal for countless thousands of Ontario school children and it is remarkable that any sympathetic feeling for French Canada survived the experience.

A further tightening of the departmental regulations occurred in 1890 when it was ruled that bilingual schools were to follow the regular programme of the English public schools, using English-language textbooks. Six years later a revision of the Public Schools Act stated that English was to be the language of instruction and communication in Ontario's schools "except so far as this is impracticable by reason of the pupil not understanding English."[6] Unfortunately, many of the teachers and administrators who set out to enforce these new regulations managed to convey at least some impression that those students who did not understand English were either retarded or blockheads.

These developments in Ontario were parallelled by many similar movements elsewhere in English-speaking Canada, intended to restrict or to eliminate altogether the use of the French tongue. Despite the opposition of many leading representatives of English-speaking Canada, the campaign to suppress the French language in English-speaking Canada gained strength and momentum in the last decades of the nineteenth century and the first decades of the twentieth. No one spoke out with more force or passion against this movement than the chief architect of Confederation, Sir John A. Macdonald. In 1890, fighting for the survival of his Confederation and the vision of Canada which he and Cartier had shared, Sir John A. denounced the objectives of this campaign in the House of Commons in the strongest terms:

> I have no accord with the desire expressed in some quarters that by any mode whatever there should be any attempt made to oppress the one language or to render it inferior to the other; I believe it would be impossible if it were tried, and that it would be foolish and wicked if it were possible. . . . Why, Mr. Speaker, if there is one act of oppression more than another which would come home to a man's breast, it is that he should be deprived of the consolation of hearing and speaking and reading the language his mother taught him. It is cruel. It is seething the kid in its mother's milk.[7]

On this occasion, Macdonald was speaking against a resolution to establish English as the sole official language of the Assembly of the Northwest Territories. However, two years later the Assembly took this step on its own, in an action which expressed the dominant mood of a good deal of English-speaking Canada at the time.

In Ontario, demands mounted for still greater pressures to be placed upon the French-speaking inhabitants aimed frankly at the elimination of the French language from the school system and, indeed, from the province. These demands came from many and diverse sources, and not least from English-speaking Roman Catholics. Irish Catholic clergymen in particular feared that any development of French-language schools would threaten the separate schools of the province. In 1910 Bishop Fallon of London declared that he wanted "to wipe out every vestige of bilingual teaching in the public schools of this Diocese."[8] In the same year, the *Orange Sentinel*, pressing hard from another corner of the ring, declared that "it is this refusal to assimilate that makes the French Canadian so difficult to get along with"![9]

These various pressures reached their culmination in 1912 with the promulgation—against the advice of Dr. John Seath, the provincial Superintendent of Education—of Regulation 17, which virtually forbade the use of French as a language of instruction after Form I. Moreover, the study of French as a subject was to be limited to one hour a day. For the school year, 1912–1913, and for that year only, French could be used as the language of instruction in the case of pupils who, "owing to previous defective training," as it was so felicitously put by the Department, "are unable to speak and understand the English language."[10] A system of inspection was instituted to ensure that the Regulation was observed. Despite the determined opposition of Franco-Ontarians, the Regulation was officially supported by both political parties, and perhaps most vehemently by the Irish Catholic community of that day. Indeed, the only notable exceptions were those, to be found in each party, who wished to go further and to prohibit any recognition at all of the French fact in Ontario's schools.[11]

However, the French fact would not go away. Despite some degree of assimilation, the French-speaking population of the province continued to grow. The realities of the situation were recognized, slowly and in modest ways, in the years between the two World Wars. While Regulation 17, with some modifications, remained technically in force throughout this period, a more conciliatory and understanding posture was adopted by departmental officials and others. By practice and by *ad hoc*ery, the position of French-language pupils in the province improved appreciably. In particular, the publication in 1927 of a report prepared by a committee under the chairmanship of Dr. F. W. Merchant, Chief Director of Education for Ontario, and the acceptance of its main recommendations, marked the beginning of a new and happier phase for bilingual primary schools in Ontario. The supervision of the bilingual schools was gradually turned over to francophone inspectors. Special courses were prepared for the teaching of French as a subject and some textbooks in the French tongue were prepared for use in the early grades. The opening of a Normal School by the University of Ottawa in 1927 to train teachers for the bilingual schools was a development of the greatest importance. While the use of French was still limited as the language of instruction officially to Form I, it became in practice not uncommon for it to be used throughout all grades in the bilingual elementary schools.

However, the essential issue in regard to the educational opportunities and, indeed, the civil liberties of French-speaking Ontarians was not faced or resolved by this approach. What resulted from it was aptly described in 1968 by the Royal Commissioners on Bilingualism and Biculturalism as "a non-system of education for Franco-Ontarians."[12] Their schools operated without adequate resources of equipment or staff. Neither their teachers nor their pupils were in a helpful relationship with the English-language schools of the jurisdictions around them or with the provincial educational system as a whole. There were often inevitable and serious problems in regard to academic standards which placed Franco-Ontarians under a severe handicap in their native province. This "non-system" of bilingual schools lacked the overall planning and the co-ordination, both amongst its own members and with the provincial Department of Education, which were essential for the development of consistently high standards of instruction.

Although the years after the Second World War brought some further amelioration of the position of French-language pupils and of bilingual schools in Ontario, it was still chiefly the result of administrative changes by sympathetic education officials rather than of any overt or formal political action. Their educational rights and opportunities were not, in law, fundamentally different in 1960 from what they had been some forty years before. In fact, the steady growth in the number of French-speaking children within the province was probably the most important change which had occurred.

It is almost impossible to report precisely the numbers of Franco-

Ontarians in different pockets of the school system in the province in 1960, and this in itself is a comment upon the situation which then still prevailed. In particular, few firm statistics are available concerning the number of francophone students attending English-language schools. A report of the Department of Education in 1962 suggests a total of some 85,000 French-speaking students in Ontario schools at that time, made up of approximately 3,300 in public elementary schools (some, but not all, of these being in what may be termed bilingual schools), 76,400 in separate schools (again, many of these were in what may be termed bilingual schools), and 5,600 in public secondary schools.[13] Figures given by l'Association canadienne-française d'Education d'Ontario two years before this put the total then at more than 88,000 students, some 4 per cent higher, and this figure would presumably have been still larger by 1962.[14]

Moreover, the definition of "bilingual" schools had become, if anything, less precise and more complicated with each succeeding decade. Such schools varied all the way from those in which every subject but English was taught in French to those in which every subject but French was taught in English, with a whole range of variations and special cases in between. However, in all but a few of these so-called bilingual schools, most of the textbooks were in English and most of the tests were in English.

What is quite clear, however, is the appalling rate of attrition amongst Franco-Ontarian students which then prevailed, substantially as it had done for many preceding generations. The Carnegie Study of Identification and Utilization of Talent in High School and College followed the secondary school careers of all the students enrolled in 1959 in Grade IX of almost all the public, private, and separate schools of Ontario. The Study revealed that much less than half of the French-speaking students reached Grade XI and only 3 per cent completed their schooling by graduating from Grade XIII without repeating a year. By contrast, over half the students from anglophone homes reached Grade XI and over 13 per cent completed Grade XIII without repeating a year.[15]

Many different factors contributed to this deplorable situation. For lack of French-language secondary schools, most French-speaking students had to transfer from bilingual elementary schools to English-language secondary schools if they wished to continue their education and many did not have sufficient grasp of English to make this abrupt and difficult transition. Many French-speaking students were from rural areas and small communities, from large families, from homes in which there was little cash income or in which the occupation of the father was comparatively low on a socio-economic scale, and from homes in which the parents had little formal education. Statistical studies indicate that, in all these family contexts, a child, of whatever language group, is more likely to fail or to drop out of school prematurely.

The quality of teaching was itself caught up in this vicious circle, with the supply of French-speaking teachers and the standard of their qualifications both very much limited by the difficult school experience through which many of them had to come. Going deeper than any of these considerable factors, however, was the fact that for many French-speaking students, and their families, success in the English-language schools of the province could mean cultural defeat and assimilation. The English-language secondary school system threatened their values and way of life. For them, education on these terms meant the sacrifice of their culture and of their identity.

All these factors, and many others, interrelated with one another and contributed to the disastrous rate of failures and drop-outs amongst Franco-Ontarian students in particular at the secondary school level. There was no reason to think that these students were intellectually inferior; rather, there was good cause to conclude that the basic objective of equality of educational opportunity was not being achieved for the children of a large and historically significant group which numbered some 10 per cent of the province's population.

ADMINISTRATIVE REFORMS

It is perhaps fair to say that the beginning of a period of extensive and fundamental reform in regard to the rights and opportunities of francophone Ontarians can be dated from the appointment by Premier Leslie M. Frost, on 17 December 1959, of the Honourable John Robarts as Ontario's Minister of Education. This period of substantive reform, touching eventually upon almost all aspects of the position of the Franco-Ontarian community, continued throughout the succeeding decade of the 1960s. During most of this decade, Mr.

Robarts was the Premier of the province, having been elected leader of the Ontario Progressive Conservative Party on 25 October 1961, and sworn in as Prime Minister of Ontario some two weeks later on 8 November. It is also perhaps fair to say that the programme of reform which he initiated usually had the warm support of the leaders of the other political parties in the Legislature, if not always of all their backbenchers—or his own.

The movement towards reform in regard to the position of Franco-Ontarians slowly gathered scope and momentum, reaching some notable peaks of legislative and administrative activity in the mid-1960s which were sustained for the rest of the decade. In the field of education, the first strong governmental impetus for reform arose from a number of wide-reaching studies, instituted by Mr. Robarts during his term as Minister, which examined almost every aspect of the numerous provincial programmes of assistance to education. This review of grants programmes had as its objective the creation of a more comprehensive plan of education to serve better the needs of the province in the coming decade. In particular, the means were sought to achieve a fuller equalization of educational opportunity throughout Ontario. This programme of fundamental review and reform was continued and enlarged upon by the Honourable William G. Davis, who succeeded Mr. Robarts as Minister of Education on 25 October 1962.[16]

In an increasing number of ways, attempts were made to adjust both the elementary and the secondary school programmes to serve more adequately the needs of French-speaking students. In particular, a greater use of French as a language of instruction was permitted in both elementary and secondary schools. Much of this change came about informally, as a matter of practice which was accepted and often encouraged by the Department. Some of it was the result of more formally recorded policy decisions by the Minister and his staff. In 1961 permission was given to some secondary school boards to have Latin taught in French upon an experimental basis. In 1963 a departmental memorandum authorized, at the discretion of the school principal, the use of French as the language of instruction in Grades IX and X. In 1965 the Minister announced that programmes of instruction in French could be extended to Latin, History, and Geography, throughout the secondary schools, at the discretion of the local school boards.[17] Arrangements were made with increasing frequency for textbooks and readings to be available in the French language, and greater use was made of radio and television to support the programme of francophone instruction.

On the administrative side, a number of appointments of Franco-Ontarians and other francophone staff members by the Department of Education improved communications between the Department and the French-speaking educational community. The introduction of the Ontario Foundation Tax Plan in 1963 brought a measure of financial assistance to the French-language programmes of instruction conducted by the separate schools of the province, and new administrative practices gave greater financial support to these programmes in the public schools.

More important than any of these developments, however, was the tremendous expansion of the *cours de français*. This special French course, named the *cours de français* to distinguish it from the French course taught to anglophones, had for many years provided a few French-speaking students in Ontario's secondary schools with the opportunity to take a more advanced and relevant programme of study in their native tongue. The extension of this course to many more schools and classes in the 1960s made it possible, really for the first time upon a large scale, for French as a subject to be taught in French to French-speaking high school students. This development went far towards ending the ludicrous anomaly, which had often prevailed, of French-speaking students being taught, in English, to read and speak their own French tongue. Despite the temptation to opt instead for the easier French course offered to anglophone students, there was a massive response by French-speaking students to the enlarged opportunities to take the *cours de français*. By 1966–1967, nearly 9,000 students were enrolled in the *cours de français* in the public secondary schools of the province, and a further 5,750 in Grades IX and X of the bilingual schools administered by the separate school boards.[18] This total probably more than doubled during the next two years, and by 1968–1969 there were some 27,000 students taking the course in French-language secondary schools, in addition to those remaining in independent and separate schools.[19]

At the same time as these arrangements for French-speaking students were occurring, there was a parallel growth in the opportunities provided to English-speaking students to learn French. At the secondary school level, a great deal of attention was directed to improving the quality and scope of French instruction. At the elementary level, permission was granted to local school boards to offer French in Grades VII and VIII as a recognized option for the first time in September 1966,[20] and they were encouraged to do so. Two years later, this permission was extended to include all elementary school classes from kindergarten to Grade VIII. A Director of French for English-speaking classes was appointed in 1964 and a committee of teachers, inspectors, and university professors was set up "to study and report upon possible procedures for developing an articulated programme of French-language instruction through the elementary and secondary grades of the Ontario school system."[21] Active assistance was extended in a variety of ways to local school boards in the planning and operation of their French classes. Visits by French teachers were scheduled and help was given through such practical matters as the supply of teaching materials and advice in regard to instructional techniques.

The result of these efforts was a vast and steady increase throughout the 1960s in the number of English-speaking pupils taking French in the public elementary schools. In 1962–1963, some 75,000 English-speaking pupils were taking French, representing about 6.5 per cent of the total enrolment of the public elementary schools. In 1967–1968, this had risen to 328,000 pupils, representing 25.5 per cent of the total enrolment. In 1968–1969, this had risen to 378,400 pupils. In 1969–1970, approximately 430,000 pupils, nearly one-third of the total enrolment in Ontario's public elementary schools, from kindergarten to Grade VIII, were taking French.

This massive enlargement of the programme of French instruction in the English-language schools, combined with the increasing number of classes and schools operating in the French tongue, posed new and serious problems in terms of the supply of French-speaking teachers in Ontario. Special summer and winter courses were instituted by the province to train teachers for these new classes. Sustained efforts were also made to recruit qualified instructors in Quebec and overseas.

The need for a great many more qualified French-speaking teachers to serve the now rapidly growing classes of French-speaking students in the bilingual schools posed even more acute difficulties. The very limited number of French-speaking students graduating, until recently, from the schools of the province in turn limited the number of potential, qualified French-speaking teachers. Moreover, the need was not only to engage many more francophone teachers, but to improve the qualifications of many of those who were already teaching in the bilingual schools. In 1963, of the teachers in the English-language public elementary schools, 95 per cent had a first-class certificate or better, whereas only 45 per cent of those teaching in the bilingual separate schools, where most of the French-speaking pupils were located, had these qualifications.[22]

The largest part of the answer to this problem must be found in the formal arrangements for teacher education within Ontario, and important steps to meet the need were taken when arrangements were made to increase the support given to the French-language Teachers' College in Ottawa and to found a second French-language Teachers' College, in 1963, in Sudbury. In 1967 the University of Ottawa established a separate Faculty of Education which, in addition to training francophone teachers for both the elementary and secondary schools, sponsors a growing range of research and postgraduate studies in pedagogy. In fact, with the establishment of its Faculty of Education, Ottawa became the first university in the province to provide a comprehensive programme of professional training for teachers of all grades from kindergarten to Grade XIII. Nonetheless, the shortage of well-qualified French-speaking teachers, both anglophone and francophone, continues to be one of the most difficult problems faced by the Ontario educational system. Only a huge and sustained effort will make it possible to meet the need.

During the years in which these developments in Ontario's school system were taking place, new and helpful relationships were being established with persons concerned with the problems of bilingual education in other parts of Canada. In particular, there was increasing consultation between representatives of the provincial Department of Education and their opposite numbers in the Province of Quebec, as well as with education officials in some of the other English-speaking provinces with substantial French-speaking minorities. In 1965 Mr. Davis invited Quebec's Minister of Education, the Honourable Paul Gérin-Lajoie, and some of his senior officials to spend several days in informal discussion of common problems. In subsequent years, despite the change of government in Quebec in June 1966, many individual and interdepartmental associations begun at that time were retained and enlarged upon. A degree of personal acquaintanceship, and to some extent a habit and ease of informal consultation, developed between education officials in the two provinces, which represent an important and constructive new factor in the educational affairs of both Ontario and Quebec.

LEGISLATIVE REFORMS

Despite the many changes and improvements in the period 1959 to 1967 which have been noted, the fact remained that in the year in which Canada observed the centennial of Confederation the large French-speaking community of Ontario still lacked a full equality of educational opportunity. Moreover, no specific statutory guarantee had as yet ever been given to the French-language schools of the province. Their very existence and virtually the entire programme of French-language instruction in Ontario were based upon practice and permission, rather than being a matter of right, based upon statute. In fact, none of the predominantly English-speaking provinces had up to that point ever based their school programmes upon the right of Canadian parents to educate their children in the official language of their choice within the public school system, as had, in effect, been the case in the province of Quebec since 1867. Fittingly enough, it was in centennial year that Ontario took this profoundly important step.

Premier Robarts chose the occasion of the Centennial Year Convention of l'Association Canadienne des Educateurs de langue-française, meeting in Ottawa on 24 August 1967, to announce the intention of his Government to provide, within the public school system of Ontario, secondary schools in which the language of instruction would be French. Reviewing with this gathering the many improvements and reforms of recent years, he noted nonetheless the continuing inequalities of educational opportunity for francophone Ontarians and declared that such a situation must not be allowed to continue. In his view "the potential contribution of Franco-Ontarians to our society is too great to allow them to dissipate their energies and abilities because they are denied adequate opportunities for furthering their education to the utmost of their abilities" and there was "an urgency to extend the availability of secondary school education in the language of the Franco-Ontarian community. . . . It is a fundamental necessity of 1967," he declared, "that the Franco-Ontarians be enabled to experience the full benefits of our educational system. Encompassed in this recognition of necessity is the proposal to extend what now is being done to provide, within the public school system of Ontario, secondary schools in which the language of instruction is French."[23]

He went on to emphasize that, since such schools would be an integral part of the existing public school system of the province, they would automatically receive the same financial support as all secondary schools, and he placed this proposal in the context of a public policy aimed at providing "equal opportunities in education for all our citizens" which had, indeed, been the stated objective of the programme of fundamental review and reform which he had himself initiated as Minister of Education in 1959.

To advise the Government upon the implementation of this proposal, a special Ministerial Committee on French-language Secondary Schools was established by Mr. Davis in November 1967. The Committee was chaired by Mr. Roland Bériault, a member of the Educational Policy and Development Council of the Ontario Department of Education. Early in the course of its study of the "procedures required to provide adequate opportunities in the public education system for those who are French-speaking," this Committee reached the conclusion that French-language instruction at the secondary level could not be viewed in isolation from arrangements at the elementary level. In consequence, the Committee broadened the scope of its study and, with the concurrence of the Minister, prepared proposals for legislation concerning French-language elementary schools as well as French-language secondary schools. Thus, the range of the review and of the subsequent changes undertaken by the Ontario Government in 1967 was substantially enlarged.

The special Ministerial Committee, which tabled its final report in November 1968,[24] covering a wide spectrum of matters related to French-language education in Ontario, presented an interim report in March of that year which proposed specific legislative measures to establish French-language elementary and secondary schools. These recommendations were favourably received by the Minister and the Government, and they formed the basis of three significant pieces of legislation introduced to the Legislature by Mr. Davis ten weeks later on 30 May 1968.

These three pieces of legislation were An Act to Amend the Department of Education Act, An Act to Amend the Schools Administration Act, and An Act to Amend the Secondary Schools and Boards of Education Act. The amendment to the Department of Education Act gave to the Minister of Education the power to make regulations prescribing the language of instruction which may be used in the elementary and secondary schools of the province. The amendments to the Schools Administration Act dealt with the legal provisions for establishing French-language elementary schools or classes, and with the language of instruction to be used by teachers in these schools and classes. The amendment to the Secondary Schools and Boards of Education Act added a new part to the Act to establish French-language schools and classes at the secondary level.

In regard to the secondary schools, the Minister expressed the view of the Department that the ideal situation would be the establishment of French-language composite schools providing all the options and programmes which were available to students in the existing English-language composite schools. He noted, however, that such schools were usually built for a student population of about one thousand and that, consequently, this goal could not be achieved everywhere that French-language instruction might be desirable because of the limited number of francophone students in some of the areas concerned.[25] To meet this situation, the legislation was designed to provide for a variety of alternatives: for French-language composite schools where there were sufficient francophone students, and for French-language courses and classes, or for complete French-language branches or sections, within a secondary school, where there were not.

A special committee, named the French Language Committee, was established within each divisional area to represent the views of the Franco-Ontarian community to the divisional board. Such a French Language Committee was to be established whenever and wherever ten or more French-speaking ratepayers requested it. It was to be composed of seven members, four of whom would be elected by the French-speaking ratepayers of the division and three of whom would be appointed by the Board. This Committee would assist and advise the local board on programmes designed to meet the educational and cultural needs of French-speaking pupils. In the view of the Bériault Committee, the concept of these French Language Committees was the cornerstone of the legislation, and it rapidly became clear that this assessment was correct. In October 1969, representatives of all the French Language Committees in the province came together to establish a Provisional Council of the French Language Advisory Committees of Ontario which could serve as an instrument for making representations in common to the Government and for examining together matters of mutual concern.

In his remarks in connection with this legislation, Mr. Davis again made clear, as Mr. Robarts had done in his address to l'Association Canadienne des Educateurs de langue-française, that it was not intended to create schools so exclusively French as to limit or restrict the opportunities of their students to learn English. The Premier had suggested that "a complementary and adequate knowledge of English is essential if the French-speaking person is to participate fully in the life of Ontario, of Canada, and, indeed, of North America." His views paralleled those of l'Association canadienne-française d'Education d'Ontario which, in a brief to the Ontario Government, had argued that "the secondary school graduate must . . . have obtained a knowledge of English so that he will be able to communicate effectively with his English-speaking compatriots, to compete on the labour market, and to take part in the political and social life of his province and of his country."[26]

"What we are striving to accomplish—indeed, are accomplishing—" declared the Premier, "is a process whereby the French-speaking student in Ontario will be taught in his own language and, at the same time, be equipped with a capacity and knowledge of English."[27] In so doing, the Government was not proposing to develop another system of secondary schools apart from and parallel to the existing provincial school system. It was, instead, seeking to extend the framework of Ontario's public school system to embrace secondary schools in which French-speaking students could be taught in their mother tongue. It was taking a constructive and practical step intended to provide a greater equality of educational opportunity for francophone Ontarians.

Mr. Davis had opened his remarks when presenting the three Acts embodying these reforms to the Ontario Legislature with the words, "The legislation which I have the honour of introducing today, Mr. Speaker, can be truly termed historic, not only for this province but also, I believe, for Canada."[28] It was a strong claim, but one which could fairly be asserted. In the view of the Royal Commissioners on Bilingualism and Biculturalism, it was a "legitimate" description of the importance of this legislation. "Instead of an almost clandestine *modus vivendi*," they observed, "French is to be permitted as the legal language of instruction in the secondary schools. The legislation is intended to ensure that French-speaking students will have the opportunity of receiving their education in French. It thus accords with the principle enunciated in the first Book of our *Report*—that Anglophone and Francophone parents should have the right to have their children educated in their own language—and represents a significant step forward."[29]

There is no doubt that the Royal Commissioners were right in their assessment of the importance of these pieces of legislation and of the spirit and intent which informed them. They were, however, perhaps less right in suggesting that they marked "a dramatic change in educational policy." The three Acts presented by the Minister in May 1968 were, rather, the coping stones in an arch of reform designed to uphold the educational rights of Franco-Ontarians which had been in the process of construction for nearly a decade.

In anticipation of this legislation coming into force in 1969, many school boards took early action to provide for at least a partial programme of French-language instruction at the secondary level, beginning in September 1968. In fact, the school boards in Cornwall, Haileybury, Hearst, Kapuskasing, North Bay, Ottawa, Timmins, and Welland all initiated plans in the spring of 1968, in keeping with the spirit of the proposed changes, as soon as they were known, to offer instruction in French for French-speaking students in a variety of subjects that fall. Several other boards followed suit during the summer. Events had moved rapidly indeed, and upon a broad front, since Mr. Robarts's announcement in August 1967. As the Bériault Committee noted in their final report in November 1968, "During the past year, we have witnessed with pleasure the way in which events have outdistanced, to a great extent, our deliberations and recommendations."

Much remained to be done, however, to carry through to its full practical application the spirit of the new legislation and many difficulties have already been encountered in connection with its implementation. In a number of jurisdictions there have been serious differences of opinion between the school board and the French Language Committee which indicate the need to clarify the role of these committees, and perhaps to give to them more precise and substantial powers in keeping with their responsibilities. Inevitably, there have been problems and tensions in several parts of the province as arrangements are being made to establish the French language classes and schools which were provided for in the legislation. *L'affaire Champlain*, which in late 1969 and early 1970 turned upon the problems involved in implementing the decision of the Ottawa School Board to establish a French-language high school that it judged to be needed in the city's west end, provided a clear illustration of the complex mixture of difficulties, and of emotions, that may be encountered.

The Provisional Council of French Language Advisory Committees presented a brief to the Minister on 21 January 1970, in which they noted some of the inadequacies in the present arrangements and made a number of recommendations for additional changes which would, in their view, improve further the quality and coherence of the educational opportunity available to the province's 120,500 French-speaking students. In particular, the Provisional Council recommended that a qualified person be appointed, with the rank of Deputy Minister, to be responsible for the total administration of the French-language branch of the Department of Education at all levels within the Ontario school system. The Council observed that "there are profound differences of opinion with certain School Boards of the province in the interpretation of the actual authority of the French Language Advisory Committees," and that "these differences often create an impasse between the parties concerned and result in time losses which delay the establishment of effective programmes to serve the Francophones." To remedy this situation the Council recommended the establishment of a provincial Grievances Committee to settle disputes which may arise between school boards and French Language Committees. The Provisional Council also proposed a re-definition of the responsibilities of the French Language Committees so as to make them decision-making rather than simply advisory bodies, recommending that they should be given responsibility for final decisions on "the establishment, orientation and administration" of French language schools and classes within their respective areas. The Brief concluded that

> it would be unfortunate indeed if, following the opening of French secondary schools in Ontario, the Francophone population of the Province should fear a sudden disinterest on the part of the Government authorities with respect to further improvement of the guarantees which gave new promise not only to French Ontario but to all of French Canada as well.[30]

Nevertheless, the assessment made by the special Ministerial Committee in 1968 of the importance of the steps which have now been taken may not be unreasonable: "The mould for French-language education in this province has now been formed. We believe that in the years to come, the quality of instruction in the French-language schools and the quality of the graduates will be the equal of any system in the country."[31]

BILINGUALISM IN HIGHER EDUCATION

Developments at the post-secondary level in Ontario during the past decade, in addition to the significant expansion of the bilingual teacher education programme already noted, also reflected a new awareness of the French fact and of the aspirations of the Franco-Ontarian community.

In 1967 Algonquin College of Applied Arts & Technology was established in Ottawa to serve the Ottawa Valley. The College offers a wide variety of courses at the post-secondary level, many of them leading to certificates and diplomas in technical, technological, and commercial studies. The proportion of French-speaking inhabitants in the five counties of this region of Ontario—Renfrew, Lanark, Carleton, Russell, and Prescott—which runs to nearly 25 per cent, is the highest of any region in the province. Plans were therefore made for this new community college to be bilingual. The founding board included three eminent representatives of the Franco-Ontarian community. It was agreed that official publications were to be bilingual; that teaching and administrative staff were to be substantially bilingual; that if ten or more students were attending any course, then arrangements were to be made for this course to be given in the two languages; that there should be second-language courses. To assist with the implementation of this broad plan, a co-ordinator of bilingualism was appointed. An eleven-member consultative committee was established to advise upon the problems of bilingualism at the College. A measure of special financial help was provided to assist with the extra costs of operating as a bilingual institution.

However, despite good intentions, the bilingual conception of the College attained only a very modest success in its first years of operation. Approximately 15 per cent of the student enrolment was French-speaking as opposed to the 25 per cent of the population which was francophone in the surrounding district, and many of these students had in fact come to the College from other parts of Ontario (13.1 per cent) and from Quebec (10.4 per cent). In particular, there were few Franco-Ontarian students attending the College from the rural areas, and these tended to take the apprenticeship courses, rather than the more exacting commercial and technological courses. This situation is to a large degree the result of the limited opportunities for vocational studies at the secondary level which have been available to French-language students, as well as being a reflection of the socio-economic problems which so many of them face. In November 1968, a research team under the direction of Professor Paul-André Comeau of the University of Ottawa was asked to examine the situation and to put forward recommendations to permit the attainment of a fuller bilingualism at Algonquin College. The report of the research team, presented in May 1969, advanced seventeen recommendations designed to achieve this objective.[32]

The University of Ottawa, one of the oldest institutions of higher learning in the province, with a long-standing and lively tradition of bilingualism, has made an outstanding contribution over the years to the welfare and progress of the Franco-Ontarian community, as well as to the French-English relationship in Canada. The University's financial strength, and its consequent ability to contribute still

more to the progress of the Franco-Ontarian community, was enhanced by the successful negotiations its representatives conducted
with the Government in 1964 which resulted in its full participation,
for the first time, in the system of provincial grants for the support
of higher education. In the 1968–1969 academic year, the students
of the University were, by mother tongue, approximately 50 per cent
French-speaking, 40 per cent English-speaking, and 10 per cent of
other tongues or nationalities; 41 per cent of the student body attended
lectures in French and 59 per cent in English. The Faculty of Law of
the University is the only one in Canada which prepares lawyers for
practice in both the civil law of Quebec and the common law of
English-speaking Canada. The University has also developed a
number of special programmes, at both the graduate and under-
graduate levels, designed to further the study of French-Canadian
culture.

In 1960 Laurentian University was founded in Sudbury to serve
in particular the needs of a large northern area of the province, including its substantial francophone population. While Laurentian
was conceived of as a bilingual university, concerned "with the maintenance and promotion of both the English and French languages
and cultures," it might more aptly be described at this point as duo-
lingual, rather than bilingual, since its French- and English-speaking
students tend to lead a parallel rather than an integrated existence.
Approximately one-fifth of its students are French-speaking at the
present time. With the growth anticipated in the French-language
Teachers' College now located on Laurentian's campus, and in a
number of the university's new and expanding programmes, the proportion of French-speaking students may increase in future years.
Laurentian established a School of Translators and Interpreters in
1968 which offers a programme leading to the degree of Bachelor of
Science in Language that is unique in North America.

At both of these bilingual universities students are limited to some
greater or lesser extent in their choice of courses depending upon the
language of instruction. The language in which courses are offered
varies from faculty to faculty, from department to department, and
even from instructor to instructor. At Laurentian University in particular, French-speaking students find, at least at this stage of the
university's development, that they must be prepared to operate in

English if they are to be able to take full advantage of the range of courses offered. Despite continued growth at the University of Ottawa and the founding of Laurentian University, the Ontario university system does not yet offer to Franco-Ontarians the opportunity to study in their own tongue the range and variety of courses in higher education which it has long been possible for English-speaking university students to take in their tongue in the Province of Quebec.

Both the University of Ottawa and Laurentian University now receive special supplementary grants each year from the province, over and above the regular provincial grants, to assist them with the added costs entailed in operating as bilingual institutions. Quite aside from these special provincial grants to Ottawa and Laurentian, the fifteen universities of Ontario gave notable support, again based upon provincial grants, to French-language education, which increased in every year throughout the 1960s. The number of full-time equivalent students taking courses taught partly or wholly in French, which was less than 2,500 in 1960, totalled 7,774 in 1967–1968. This rose to 8,983 in 1968–1969, to 9,989 in 1969–1970, and to well over 10,000 in 1970–1971. The decade of the 1960s thus saw a substantial expansion in French-language education at the university level in Ontario.

FURTHER CONSTITUTIONAL AND CULTURAL ASPECTS
OF ONTARIO'S QUIET REVOLUTION

Reform in the vital area of the educational rights of Franco-Ontarians was the most important single element in the quiet revolution in Ontario in the 1960s. However, there were many other facets to this revolution, and the radical changes noted in the field of education were paralleled by the development of new programmes and profoundly new attitudes in many other areas of provincial public policy during this decade.

Of particular significance was the establishment in January 1965, a month before the publication of the *Preliminary Report of the Royal Commission on Bilingualism and Biculturalism*, of the Ontario Advisory Committee on Confederation. This Committee, made up of eighteen people with some expert or scholarly interest in the problems of Canadian federalism, was asked to advise the Government of the province upon matters pertaining to the position of Ontario in

Confederation. The Committee, under the chairmanship of Mr. H. Ian Macdonald, then the Chief Economist of Ontario and subsequently the Deputy Treasurer and Deputy Minister of Economics, dealt with three broad areas: economic and fiscal questions, constitutional matters, and cultural and educational problems. The Advisory Committee and its sub-committees met regularly and frequently during the ensuing six years, initiating a large number of research projects and examining alternative approaches to the problems faced by Confederation. The terms of reference of the Committee had indicated that the Government was "desirous of seeking continuing advice in all matters which will assist it in performing its part in maintaining and strengthening the unity of Canada."[33] There is reason to feel that the Committee, working steadily and without fuss, has made a substantial contribution to this purpose.

To support the work of the Ontario Advisory Committee on Confederation, a Federal-Provincial Affairs Secretariat was established within the provincial civil service in 1966. This Secretariat was fortunate in recruiting the services of a group of able and concerned younger people who have applied themselves with great personal dedication to their work. The Secretariat has grown steadily in strength and in the scope of its responsibilities, which include the preparation of background material and working documents for the Advisory Committee, the conduct of research connected with many different aspects of intergovernmental affairs, the preparation and reports for the Government in connection with Ontario's participation in interprovincial and federal-provincial conferences, and the representation of the province on many intergovernmental working bodies.

The establishment of the Advisory Committee on Confederation and the Federal-Provincial Affairs Secretariat has given to the province, perhaps for the first time, the resources in terms of researched information and of increasingly expert knowledge and opinion which are necessary if Ontario's representatives are to be able to make their most effective contribution to some resolution of the extremely complex problems facing Canada.

The Advisory Committee and the Secretariat contributed substantially to the planning and preparations for the Confederation of Tomorrow Conference which was held in Toronto in November 1967.

Convened by Ontario in consultation with the other provinces, the Conference was chaired by Mr. Robarts and was very much an expression of his personal concern about the problems facing the country and the need to address these problems. It was his view "that we were then approaching one of those rare junctures in our history where a candid discussion of the sources of our grave national tensions was necessary for our country to survive."[34] The Confederation of Tomorrow Conference met this need on a number of counts. It served to indicate to Quebec, at a time when it was of critical importance to do so, the fact that there was both goodwill and a thoughtful awareness of its particular problems and point of view on the part of some other provincial leaders. The Conference also served to provide an opportunity for its participants to rediscover some greater sense of common interest and identity as they discussed a wide range of interdependent regional, cultural, constitutional, and economic problems, and recognized that they must face them together. All sessions of the Conference, which lasted three days, were open to the press and to radio and television. This was the first time in Canada that a major conference involving political leaders had been so completely open to the media. It had, consequently, an enormous impact upon the Canadian public, and did a great deal to inform people about the issues and facts and personalities involved in the current discussions about the country's future and to make clear the scale and immediacy of some of the problems.

The federal Government had been disinclined to begin upon the task of reviewing the state of Confederation, despite many signs that such a review was both necessary and urgent. In the absence of a federal lead in this matter, Ontario took the initiative by convening the Confederation of Tomorrow Conference and in so doing opened the dialogue which had to take place. Prodded by this Conference, and by the public interest it both expressed and aroused, the federal Government took up the initiative, as many provincial leaders had hoped it would do. It moved to convene, within less than three months' time after the Confederation of Tomorrow Conference, the first of a continuing series of federal-provincial conferences intended to examine the large basic constitutional problems which were before the country. The conception of the Confederation of Tomorrow Conference and the announcement of the decision to establish French-

language secondary schools within the public system of education
were parallel and related responses by Ontario to the constitutional
and cultural crisis which faced Canada. Together, they may well have
been the most helpful and constructive contribution made towards a
resolution of this crisis in the course of the year which marked the
centennial of Confederation.

The same elements of statesmanship and of a wider concern for
Canada's welfare were evident in the response of most leading Ontario politicians, of all three parties, to the several reports of the
Royal Commission on Bilingualism and Biculturalism. In a speech to
the Institute of Chartered Accountants of Ontario, a few weeks after
the publication of the *Preliminary Report* in February 1965, Premier
Robarts welcomed it "as a starting point for meaningful discussions,"[35] while expressing the hope that these discussions would not
focus too much on the report itself, rather than upon the larger
problems with which the report was concerned. He made clear on
this occasion, too, as he did on many others, his awareness of the
nature and importance of the events occurring within Quebec and of
the fact that these events would reach out and have a pervasive significance for all parts of Canada.

"This document is extremely important," he observed, "because it
brings to the attention of the public the fact that the so-called 'Quiet
Revolution' in Quebec is not a purely provincial matter but has implications for the future of Canada. . . . What is important is that a
revolution is now taking place in Quebec and that the effects of this
revolution are slowly and inevitably spreading throughout the length
and breadth of Canada."

"This is not surprising," he continued. "No major social or economic development can take place in any part of Canada without
affecting the rest of the country . . . and when change encompasses
the social, cultural and economic fabric of the whole Province of
Quebec, it is obvious that there will be repercussions throughout the
whole of Canada."

The Premier indicated then his concern "that the people of this
province should appreciate their immense responsibility to the future
of Canada." This realization of the potential importance of Ontario's
actions during a period of national tension was, fortunately, a constant factor in the thinking of most of the province's leaders through-

out the 1960s. There was, in particular, an understanding that Ontario was equipped to make a significant contribution to an improvement in the relationships between francophone and anglophone Canadians: by its geographical position neighbouring Quebec, with a shared boundary running for more than 600 miles; by its size and population which, alone amongst the predominantly English-speaking provinces of Canada, are of the same order as those of Quebec; by its resources and wealth; by its large and growing French-speaking population; by its close and continuing historical relationship with Quebec; and perhaps by virtue of the special place which it occupies in the mind and thoughts of Quebec as the substantial partner in its marriage with English-speaking Canada.

For Canada, this meant an increasing acceptance of the view that the duality of two major cultures is one of the bases upon which the country was formed,[36] and of the belief that "Canadians of French origin must be guaranteed certain basic rights and privileges."[37] For Ontario, it meant a growing recognition of the part played in the history and life of the province by the Franco-Ontarian community: "Men and women of French origin have played a significant role in the development of Ontario for more than three centuries, beginning with the explorers and fur traders of New France. This role continues today through the Franco-Ontarian community. . . . Its strength, vitality, accomplishments and potential are immense. Ontario— indeed all of Canada—is far the richer and stronger for the presence of these French-speaking residents."[38]

It was a natural development, arising from these views and from the previous actions of the Government, when on 22 July 1968 Premier Robarts moved in the Ontario Legislature:

Resolved: That, henceforth, every member of this House may, as a matter of right in this House, address the House in either of the two official languages of Canada.[39]

The Premier's resolution was seconded by the Leader of the Opposition in the Legislature, Mr. Robert F. Nixon, who supported it warmly on behalf of the Ontario Liberal Party, and it was also enthusiastically endorsed by Mr. Donald C. MacDonald, the leader of the Ontario New Democratic Party. All three pointed out that the resolution was really confirming in an official manner a practice which had already been for some time a part of the tradition of the Legislature, although a little-used one. But all were agreed upon the desirability of now placing this practice upon a more formally recognized footing. The resolution was concurred in unanimously, although it should perhaps be noted that a number of the members found it convenient to be elsewhere when the question was put.

The Journal and Proceedings of the First Legislative Assembly of the Province of Upper Canada record the fact that on Monday, 3 June 1793, the House adopted a resolution "that such Acts as have already passed or may hereafter pass the Legislature of this Province be translated into the French language for the benefit of the Western District of this province and other French settlers who may come to reside within this Province,"[40] and further made provision for the employment of "a French Translator for this and other purposes of this House." One hundred and seventy-five years later, the twenty-eighth Legislature of the Province, by this formal resolution in July 1968, once again recognized the place of bilingualism in its own affairs and in the governance of Ontario.

Throughout 1968 and 1969, in keeping with the spirit of this resolution and earlier developments, increasing attention was given by many provincial departments of government to providing, "wherever feasible, bilingual public services so that the people of Ontario will be able to deal in either the English or French languages with the various levels of government with which they come into contact."[41] To this end the facilities of the provincial translation bureau were expanded, and language courses were instituted for interested provincial legislators and civil servants. The initial response of both these groups to this new opportunity was encouraging. In the first year in which the courses were offered, some fifty Members of the Legislative Assembly attended regularly four days a week. A special course was arranged for them from 6 to 8 p.m., between the afternoon and evening sessions, which was the only time it could be fitted into the legislators' day. It was, consequently, necessary to serve dinner during the course and some uncharitable observers have not been above suggesting that this may have been a factor in the remarkable interest it aroused amongst the Members.

While interest in the course amongst the Members has declined

somewhat in subsequent sessions, many continue to work at it, and
the number of civil servants, for the most part at comparatively
senior levels, who are participating in the Government's programme
of French language classes has continued to grow. However, the need
for some greater proficiency in the two languages on the part of a
larger proportion of the provincial legislators and civil servants continues to be acute, as does the need for more skilled translators and
interpreters.

In February 1968, at the first meeting of the continuing Constitutional Conference, Mr. Robarts announced the establishment of four
task forces to investigate the feasibility of implementing the recommendations of the Royal Commission on Bilingualism and Biculturalism concerning: the administration of justice; the Legislature and
provincial statutes; municipal administration; and the provincial
public service. The studies of these groups were assisted by the
Ontario Advisory Committee on Confederation and co-ordinated by
the Federal-Provincial Affairs Secretariat. In March 1970 the Premier indicated to the Legislature that his Government had undertaken
to implement the principal recommendations contained in the reports
of the four task forces. However, the details of these proposals have
not yet been made public.[42]

One of the first projects of the Ontario Advisory Committee on
Confederation had been a study of the feasibility and possible value
of an educational and cultural exchange programme between Ontario
and Quebec. A report prepared for the Committee in 1965 strongly
recommended such a programme, to include eventually almost every
aspect of education and the whole range of the performing and creative arts. Noting the need for more and better communication
between French- and English-speaking Canadians, the report urged
that "immediate consideration be given by the Province of Ontario
to the establishment of an extensive and sustained programme of
educational and cultural exchanges, both with the Province of
Quebec and within this Province between its French and English-
speaking peoples."[43] The report further recommended that the possibility of similar educational and cultural exchange agreements
should, subsequently, be explored with other provinces or groups of
provinces.

While the formal Agreement for Co-operation and Exchange in

Educational and Cultural Matters between the Governments of Ontario and Quebec was not signed until June 1969, the spirit and intent of the report and many of its practical recommendations were implemented much earlier. Meeting in Peterborough on 20 October 1965, to lay two cornerstones, one inscribed in French and one in English, for Champlain College at Trent University, Premier Robarts and Premier Lesage referred to their intention to enter into negotiations to begin such a programme. The Speech from the Throne in each of the two Legislatures, in both cases delivered on 25 January 1966, confirmed this intention. In preparation, Ontario proceeded to establish its own Educational and Cultural Exchange Programme under the aegis of the Department of Education which, since 1967, has sponsored a broad range of activities and exchanges, both within Ontario and with other provinces, designed to foster improved communication and understanding between French- and English-speaking Canadians.

The formal Agreement of June 1969 went beyond the initial concept of an educational and cultural exchange programme and embodied a declaration of mutual faith and respect between the two provinces. Each undertook to provide, wherever feasible, public services in the English and French languages; to provide, wherever feasible, education in their own language to students of the French-speaking and English-speaking minority in each province; to provide students of the linguistic minority with the means to acquire a good command of the language of the majority; to exchange the texts of statutes, regulations, and government publications; to exchange information in the fields of translation and interpretation and to work together to provide facilities for the training of translators and interpreters; to foster contacts between representatives of local governments; to exchange information on methods of teaching English and French; to exchange public servants and to provide mutual assistance for the training of public servants. To direct this sweeping programme of exchange and co-operation, it provided for the creation of a Permanent Commission for Ontario-Quebec Co-operation with two co-chairmen, one to be named by each Government.

The Educational and Cultural Exchange Agreement was warmly received in both provinces and was, indeed, greeted by *Le Devoir* with the editorial statement that "it is not an exaggeration to call the signing, yesterday at Quebec, of the cultural agreement between our province and Ontario, an historic moment."[44] Approbation was not, of course, unanimous. A backlash was, in fact, never far beneath the surface in many sections of public opinion during the years in which the Province of Ontario was, with very considerable statesmanship on the part of its elected leaders, engaging in its own quiet revolution. There was widespread and often deeply felt opposition to the whole tenor of these changes in public policy, ranging from a vague uneasiness or suspicion to outright and determined hostility. This was an extremely serious factor which had to be borne in mind constantly by the Premier and by all political leaders in Ontario throughout the decade.

In addition to the Department of Education's Educational and Cultural Exchange Programme, many other elements within the provincial government system gave growing assistance to the Franco-Ontarian community and to an improved understanding and application of bilingualism in Ontario during the 1960s. The Province of Ontario Council for the Arts, established in 1963, helped to broaden the cultural opportunities available to Franco-Ontarians as a natural part of its work to nourish and assist the development of the cultural life of the province, as did, amongst many other concerned divisions of government, the work of the Community Programmes Branch and of the Youth and Recreation Branch of the Department of Education.

Beyond the growing number of activities sponsored by government in all its forms, however, lay a still more important development which was contributing to a better degree of mutual understanding between the French- and English-speaking inhabitants of Ontario and of Canada. This was the growth of an enormous number and variety of informal and independent exchanges between interested individuals, families, communities, schools, companies, and organizations of every conceivable sort. Such exchanges had, of course, occurred for years upon a small scale. However, during the 1960s they proliferated fantastically and a vast network of exchanges and associations developed between anglophone and francophone Ontarians and Canadians which had touched, by the end of the decade, almost every community in the province. Cities and schools were twinned; classes, families, and individuals corresponded and paired off; companies and government offices, alike, exchanged personnel.

There was an unprecedented teeming of tours and visits, and a near-plethora of cultural events. Indeed, one wonders how the province survived! Yet it is this massive citizen exchange which may prove to have been the most significant and salutary development of the decade.

Amongst the many private organizations working in the field of bilingualism in Ontario one, in particular, must be mentioned. This is l'Association canadienne-française de l'Ontario (ACFO). This Association, whose views and objectives were often shared and supported by the Ontario Advisory Committee on Confederation, served as a mainspring for much of the reform which characterized the quiet revolution in Ontario in the 1960s. Founded in 1910, on the eve of Regulation 17, as l'Association canadienne-française d'Education d'Ontario, this organization spent its early years in an essentially defensive posture, fighting for the very survival of the French tongue and way of life in Ontario. However, in the years after the Second World War, with Mr. Roger Charbonneau as its Secretary General, and more particularly during the 1960s with Mr. Roger Séguin as its President, the Association assumed a more forthcoming posture. By providing the organizational structure, the administrative arrangements and personnel, the publications, and a focus for the common concerns of Franco-Ontarians, it played an often decisive part in formulating proposals for policies and programmes which were subsequently accepted by the province. It was on the recommendation of the Association, supported by the Ontario Advisory Committee on Confederation, that the Premier appointed, in May 1967, a Committee of Enquiry, under the chairmanship of Mr. Roger Saint-Denis, to examine the participation of Franco-Ontarians in the cultural and artistic life of the province. The report of this Committee, presented in January 1969, is a major document in Canadian cultural history.[45]

EPILOGUE?

This outline of events is far from being a complete inventory of the many significant developments which have affected the position of Ontario's francophone citizens during the past decade, as well as the position of the province in regard to the French fact in Canada. But perhaps it may serve to illustrate and to support the contention that

Ontario, too, is experiencing a quiet revolution. This revolution—and I do not think the term is too strong—has already brought about changes of a fundamental nature in regard to the laws, practices, and attitudes affecting the language rights and educational and cultural opportunities afforded to the French-speaking inhabitants of Ontario. A great deal remains to be done before a full equality of opportunity and rights has been attained. However, much has already been achieved and some very significant steps have been taken toward this goal. In this process, the individual rights and the educational and cultural opportunities of all the people of Ontario have been enhanced.

In many ways Ontario's quiet revolution has paralleled and complemented the Quiet Revolution in Quebec. Less noted—in fact, passing almost without notice beyond the province and even within it—it may nonetheless prove to have been as important. It is important not only for the large French-speaking population of Ontario, for whom it represents virtually a new deal, but also as a decisive step by the country's largest English-speaking province towards a resolution of the tensions and issues which confront the Canadian Confederation.

Changes in the status of their francophone citizens, similar in spirit and import—if not yet always in scope—to those in Ontario, have recently occurred or are in the offing in most of the other predominantly English-speaking provinces. Together, these new developments and reforms at the provincial level, particularly in the field of education, may well be more significant in the long run than anything that can be accomplished at the federal level towards a resolution of Canada's bilingual problems. Remarkably little study of an historical and factual nature has been devoted to the position of the francophone minorities in Canada. It would be helpful to have—in fact it is now perhaps essential that there should be—a series of comparative and contemporary historical studies tracing the actual changes in recent years in the laws and practices pertaining to the language, educational and cultural rights and opportunities of the French-speaking minorities across Canada, and of the English-speaking minority in Quebec. Indications now are that such studies would reveal the fact that there have been profound changes in the traditional attitudes and policies towards French-speaking minorities in many parts of English-speaking Canada and that these changes, as in the case of Ontario, are being reflected in a massive renovation of laws and public practice.

The quiet revolution in Ontario is, nonetheless, a bold experiment. It is, indeed, on a number of counts a calculated risk. Amongst the risks involved is the possibility that the extension of minority language and educational rights could result in the creation of linguistic ghettos with Franco-Ontarians unintentionally locked inside, and with the Canadian community, in the process, weakened rather than strengthened. Or others may be right who argue, again with a pessimism I do not share, that the linguistic realities of North America are such that, even with goodwill and progressive legislation, the assimilation of the French minorities is inevitable. Regardless of these and other possibilities, both the demands of simple justice and the exigencies of our Confederation require that this experiment be made.

The question is bound to be asked: what will happen to the rights of the French-speaking minorities in Ontario and elsewhere in Canada if Quebec leaves Confederation? It is, of course, not possible to give a confident answer. Much would depend upon the manner and circumstances in which such a separation came about. Many thoughtful people accept it as a foregone conclusion that the consequence would be, at the least, a reversal of the trend to an enhancement of these rights which has been described in this paper. Indeed, some would foresee a sharp move towards the elimination of these rights in the heat of the emotional reaction which separation might well unleash. Undoubtedly there would be strong pressures in this direction.

However, I do not accept the inevitability of such a consequence, nor would I consider it desirable. Canada would face profound uncertainties and difficult challenges after any dismemberment of the present Confederation. In such a situation the tradition of cultural pluralism and diversity which has substantially distinguished the character, history, and values of this country from those of the United States would, I think, become more important to Canadians than ever before. Indeed, it might well prove to be the key ingredient in the will and in the capability of Canada to survive as a separate and distinctive nation in North America.

A fair and reasonable recognition of the cultural and educational rights of the French-speaking minorities is the indispensable cornerstone of this distinctive Canadian tradition of cultural pluralism and diversity.

NOTES

1. Dominion Bureau of Statistics, *1961 Census of Canada*, vol. I, pt. 2 (Bulletin 1.2–5), Table 35, p. 35–1.

2. Ontario, Department of Economics and Development, Economics Branch, *Ontario: French Ethnic Population, 1961, by County Percentage of Total Population, Quartile Distribution* (Toronto: February 1967).

3. D.B.S., *1961 Census*, vol. I, pt. 2 (Bulletin 1.2–9), Table 64, p. 64–1.

4. C. B. Sissons, *Bilingual Schools in Canada* (Toronto: J. M. Dent & Sons, 1917), pp. 73–79.

5. C. B. Sissons, *Egerton Ryerson: His Life and Letters* (Toronto: Clarke, Irwin, 1937), p. 26.

6. Ontario, Royal Commission on Education, *Report* (Toronto: King's Printer, 1950), pp. 401–402.

7. Canada, Parliament, House of Commons, *Debates, Official Report*, 1890, XXIX, pp. 746–748.

8. Franklin Arthur Walker, *Catholic Education and Politics in Ontario* (Don Mills: Nelson [Canada], 1964), p. 243.

9. Marilyn Barber, "The Ontario Bilingual Schools Issue: Sources of Conflict," *Canadian Historical Review*, XLVII (1966) : 235.

10. *Report of the Royal Commission on Education in Ontario*, pp. 422–423.

11. Margaret Prang, "Clerics, Politicians, and the Bilingual Schools Issue in Ontario," *Canadian Historical Review*, XLI (1960) : 281–307.

12. Canada, Royal Commission on Bilingualism and Biculturalism, *Report* (Ottawa: Queen's Printer, 1967–1968), Bk. 2 (Education), p. 51.

13. Ontario, Department of Education, *Report of the Minister, 1962* (Toronto: Legislative Assembly of Ontario, Sessional Paper no. 7, 1962).

14. L'Association canadienne-française d'Education d'Ontario, *Rapport général des fêtes du Cinquantenaire et du quinzième Congrès général* (Ottawa: 1960), p. 10.

15. *Report on Bilingualism and Biculturalism*, Bk. 2, p. 311.

16. Mr. Robarts continued to be Minister of Education as well as Premier until 25 October 1962, a full year after his election as leader of his party, when Mr. Davis was appointed to this portfolio. The post of Minister of University Affairs was created in the spring of 1964 and Mr. Davis was appointed its first incumbent on 14 May 1964. He continued to combine the two portfolios of Education and University Affairs throughout the rest of the 1960s.

17. Ontario, Legislative Assembly, *Debates, Official Report*, 3 June 1965, p. 3637.

18. *Report on Bilingualism and Biculturalism*, Bk. 2, p. 82.

19. Preliminary estimates of the Ontario Department of Education, February 1970.

20. Ontario, Department of Education, *French Program, Grade 7* [Curriculum I-15A7] (Toronto: 1966), p. 2.

21. Ontario, Legislative Assembly, *Debates*, 2 June 1965, p. 3577.

22. *Report on Bilingualism and Biculturalism*, Bk. 2, p. 82.

23. Ontario, Department of Education, Information Branch, "French in Ontario Schools," An Address by Hon. J. P. Robarts to l'Association canadienne des Educateurs de langue française, Ottawa, 24 August 1967 (Toronto: Queen's Printer, 1968).

24. *Report of the Committee on French Language Schools in Ontario*, (Toronto, 1968), p. 70.

25. Ontario, Legislative Assembly, *Debates*, 30 May 1968, p. 3641.

26. L'Association canadienne-française d'Education d'Ontario, *Mémoire concernant un Régime d'écoles secondaires bilingues en Ontario* (Ottawa: mars 1967), pp. 11–12.

27. Robarts, "French in Ontario Schools."

28. Ontario, Legislative Assembly, *Debates*, 30 May 1968, p. 3638.

29. *Report on Bilingualism and Biculturalism*, Bk. 2, p. 75.

30. Provisional Council of the French Language Advisory Committees of Ontario, *Brief to the Minister of Education* (Toronto: 21 January 1970).

31. *Report of the Committee on French Language Schools in Ontario*, p. 70.

32. P. A. Comeau, A. Carrier, F. de Kerkhove, C. A. Bonneau, *Les Franco-Ontariens et le Collège Algonquin* (Ottawa, 1969).

33. Ontario, Advisory Committee on Confederation, *Background Papers and Reports* (Toronto: Queen's Printer, 1967).

34. Constitutional Conference, Ottawa, First Meeting, February 1968, *Proceedings* (Ottawa: 1968), p. 19.

35. Remarks to the Institute of Chartered Accountants of Ontario, Toronto, 12 March 1965.

36. Remarks to the Advertising and Sales Executives' Club of Montreal, Montreal, 23 November 1966.

37. Robarts, "French in Ontario Schools."

38. Ibid.

39. Ontario, Legislative Assembly, *Debates*, 22 July 1968, p. 6101.

40. "Journals of the Legislative Assembly in Upper Canada, 1792–1804," *Sixth Report of the Bureau of Archives for the Province of Ontario* (Toronto: L. K. Cameron, King's Printer, 1911), p. 23.

41. Constitutional Conference, 1968, p. 33.

42. Ontario, Legislative Assembly, *Debates*, 4 March 1970, p. 234.

43. Ontario Advisory Committee on Confederation, *Background Papers and Reports*, pp. 283–297.

44. *Le Devoir*, Montréal, 5 juin 1969.

45. *Rapport du Comité franco-ontarien d'Enquête culturelle* (Ottawa: janvier 1969).

The Maritimes and the Problem of the Secession of Quebec 1967 to 1969

G. A. Rawlyk

THE MARITIME PROVINCES of Nova Scotia, New Brunswick, and Prince Edward Island cover an area of only 51,000 square miles, a little more than one per cent of Canada's land surface. In April 1969 the population of Canada was estimated to be 21,007,000, while that of Nova Scotia was 764,000, New Brunswick 626,000, and Prince Edward Island 110,000. For many Canadians, therefore, the seemingly unimportant Maritime area is considered to be an economic, political, intellectual, and social backwater. Events of crucial "national consequence" have apparently (or so it is argued) passed the backwater by. The main thrust of Canadian historical development after 1873, when Prince Edward Island finally entered Confederation, owed little, if anything (or so it seems), to events or persons in the three Maritime Provinces.

The Maritime Provinces have never fully recovered, in the psychological sense at least, from the traumatic experience of Confederation and the sudden end in the 1860s and 1870s of their Golden Age of "Wooden Ships and Iron Men." Before Confederation many Maritimers believed that their region had unlimited economic potential and also that theirs was the most sophisticated and best run of all the British colonies possessing responsible government. It was felt that the Maritimes had a special role to play in the evolution of a new British Empire.

The development of this sense of destiny and mission came to a sudden halt in the immediate post-Confederation period when the Maritime Provinces found themselves on the periphery of the dynamic westward transcontinental thrust of the new Canada. Largely by-passed by the flood of immigration into the interior of Canada, and lacking the natural and human resources for the new industrialism, the Maritimers witnessed the destruction of their special sense of destiny and mission. Who was to blame? The villain was obvious to the Maritimers—the federal government—Ottawa. The proof was there. Before Confederation there was widespread prosperity, and the entire region shared an optimism and a feeling of self-importance and pride. After Confederation there were prolonged periods of economic recession and a growing sense of collective inferiority and bitterness. The British North America Act was held by many to be responsible for this sudden and dramatic change in the Maritime Provinces. But there was also a reluctance to assume any kind of responsibility for the profound changes arising out of technological and industrial advances.

In the twentieth century, as economic, cultural, and political ties drew the region into a closer relationship with the rest of Canada, the cries of regional protest from the Maritimes became somewhat less shrill and despairing. Because of their unfortunate lack of adequate natural resources, the Maritime Provinces have become increasingly dependent upon massive federal government financial assistance. If any region in Canada feels that it will be adversely affected by the undermining of the federal government's power to redistribute financial resources, it is the Maritimes. If any Canadian region is attached to the constitutional *status quo* and is threatened by the spectre of Quebec's separation, it is the Maritimes. Although often unwilling or unable to articulate their sense of concern, many Maritimers give the impression that they are eager to be more Canadian than the most vociferous "Upper Canadian."

In the Maritime Provinces today, "professed liberalism" prevails among opinion-makers,[1] at least concerning the principle of cultural and linguistic equality for French-speaking Canadians. These men— newspaper editors, politicians, and entrepreneurs—appear to be sympathetic to what they consider to be the "legitimate" demands of the Quebec government and of French Canadians. However, Separatism, republicanism, special status, *deux nations* (in the political sense of the term), and associate statehood are flatly rejected in favour of maintenance of the constitutional *status quo* as far as jurisdictional arrangements between the federal and provincial governments are concerned. Both economic and emotional factors prompt the desire to maintain Canadian Confederation in its present form. The liberal, or accommodating, attitude towards the demands of bilingualism and biculturalism is "professed," but there seems to be little real understanding of French-Canadian grievances and aspirations; the economic problems resulting from regional disparity far overshadow the "Quebec problem" in interest and in fundamental importance as far as most Maritimers are concerned. Though there is seldom, in the views of the so-called opinion-makers, the degree of hostility towards Quebec as is expressed in some letters to editors or in the extremist approach of the Maritime Loyalist Association, the absence of critical attention paid to events in Quebec and the understandable obsession of the leaders with Maritime problems suggest that the principle of bilingualism and biculturalism is embraced more as an abstraction than a concrete, everyday reality. Indifference rather than enthusiasm or hostility characterizes the attitudes of most Maritime opinion-makers towards French Canadians and Separatism.

Concerning options open to the Maritimes if Quebec were to secede from Confederation, indifference and ignorance again probably describe the general view. The question, when asked, was generally greeted in a negative fashion—with amusement or disdain, surprise or bewilderment, and sometimes downright hostility—and responses, when pried from people interviewed (some refused comment), were on the whole rather superficial and poorly articulated. Editorial opinion in the Maritime newspapers rarely deals with political options available to the Maritime Provinces if Quebec were to secede. Indeed, Quebec Separatism, though vociferously opposed, apparently is not regarded as an imminent possibility. The Maritime "colonial mentality," with its love-hate dependency relationship with the federal government and "Upper Canada," is unable, and perhaps unwilling, to conceive of any possible political arrangement other than continued existence even in a fragmented Canada. Although the option of union with New England is sometimes invoked, it is done in a rather off-hand and ritualistic manner. It is clear that the vast majority of opinion-makers in the Maritime Provinces are determined to make any sacrifice to keep their region within Confederation.

If most Maritime opinion-makers and leaders have come slowly and perhaps reluctantly to a position endorsing biculturalism, they certainly do not hesitate to condemn what they conceive to be extreme French-Canadian demands. One Quebec nationalist doctrine that has sparked a great deal of adverse comment has been the controversial *deux nations* concept. The Diefenbaker-Conservative-leaning Charlottetown *Guardian* paid much attention to the Montmorency Conference and the Conservative Party's flirtation with the "two nations" notion, which it considered the prime cause of the party's defeat in the June 1968 general election. In the *Guardian*'s view, John Diefenbaker's fall was in part attributable to "his outspoken stand in denunciation of this pernicious doctrine. . . . There is reason to believe that the phrase was concocted for the purpose of confusing the issue, of placating Quebec extremists on the one hand while permitting others to accept it as a reaffirmation of what had already been embodied, a century ago, in the Confederation compact" (11 Sept. 1967). If the phrase is interpreted to mean nationality in the cultural sense, then there is little opposition to it; but if it is interpreted in the way that Jean-Noël Tremblay conceived it— "the nation is a socio-cultural and a political reality. . . . We must resolutely tackle the job of building our national state"[2]—then Maritimers will have nothing to do with *deux nations*.

The Halifax *Chronicle-Herald* warns of the danger involved in a doctrine which views Quebec as the political homeland of the French-Canadian people and an equal partner, politically and economically as well as culturally, with the rest of Canada: "No responsible political figure outside of Quebec believes it is right that associate statehood be granted Quebec. . . . Although there is sympathy for the proposition that the French language be given rights in the other provinces similar to those enjoyed by the English language in Quebec, it will evaporate if Quebec wishes to turn its back on Canada and become a French-speaking ghetto" (13 Sept. 1967). The *Cape Breton Post* blasts away at the basic iniquities inherent in the associate statehood constitutional position: "The implication seems to be that Quebec wants to have all the privileges of separate nationhood while, at the same time, enjoying all the benefits and privileges that are Canadian by natural right. A more selfish position couldn't be imagined" (13 May 1967). Most of those opinion-leaders inter-viewed, including Premiers Smith of Nova Scotia and Campbell of Prince Edward Island, also repudiated the *deux nations* formula. In the Nova Scotia House of Assembly in 1968, Premier Smith re-jected associate statehood in these terms: "[*Deux nations*] is a con-cept I don't understand and I don't accept. . . . I find it difficult to think that there is any room for it in Canada (Hear! Hear! Desk pounding)."[3]

Maritime opinion-makers also firmly oppose any form of special status for Quebec if by that term one means Quebec's obtaining a greater share of spending and jurisdictional powers than the province presently enjoys. Forays by Quebec politicians into the international sphere, in particular their desire to negotiate treaties with sovereign nations independently of the federal government in fields under pro-vincial purview, are considered illegitimate pretensions. The Halifax *Chronicle-Herald* flatly condemns any such action: "Quebec's claims in this field must be put down simply to an overweening provincial-ism which this country cannot afford" (5 June 1967). That Quebec politicians may be stretching the B and B slogan beyond acceptable limits is a suspicion expressed by the *Dartmouth Free Press*: "The rest of Canada has good reason to believe that Quebec politicians use their language and cultural differences as block blackmail to wring more and more fiscal and power concessions from the central gov-ernment" (16 Feb. 1967). Quebec's demands for a greater share of the federal-provincial distribution of power, according to the editor of the New Glasgow *Evening News*, is symptomatic of a provincialism which threatens the basis of Confederation: "At this time of mount-ing outcry for secession, for special status, and for increased regional powers not only for Quebec, but for other provinces as well, across the country, there is a pressing need for someone to speak for Canada as a country, not a mere loose federation of cantonments. . . . Quebec is merely the most avid, the most hungry, the most jealous, with added overtones of race and culture adding to her clamour" (18 Nov. 1967). The general position of Maritime opinion-leaders re-garding demands emanating from Quebec has been tersely sum-marized by the editor of the Charlottetown *Guardian*: "That Quebec wants to preserve her culture, language and manner is understandable and is fully recognized by all other provinces. But in pursuit of this course, the essential powers of the constitution cannot be defied or flouted" (2 Nov. 1967).

Finally, Martime opinion-leaders are, as one would expect, vigorously opposed to Quebec Separatism. Usually, economic arguments are put forward—Separatism would hurt the rest of Canada as well as Quebec economically. Indeed, the Fredericton *Gleaner* complains that even talk of Separatism is harmful because it frightens away investment: "Separatism could only be an act of suicide with results deplorable to both members of the body corporate" (27 Sept. 1967). René Lévesque—"a mealy-mouthed apostle of the destruction of Canada"[4]—Gilles Grégoire, Separatists in the French network of the CBC, and terrorist bombings in Montreal have all aroused the ire of Maritimers. The Halifax *Mail-Star* warns that if Quebec seceded the province "would indeed quickly fall under the control of the U.S.A." (15 April 1967). The Halifax *Chronicle-Herald* assails Separatists for not playing fair, "their political philosophies seem to be rooted in the treacherous consideration of race" (27 Aug. 1967). Another argument against the Separatist option is that a Parti Québécois regime would prove undemocratic and autocratic. The Fredericton *Gleaner* apeals to Premier Bertrand to "save democracy in Quebec" (23 June 1969).

Why are Maritime opinion-leaders opposed to any significant changes in the existing constitutional division of powers between the federal and provincial governments? One factor, patriotism, is revealed in the following statement from the New Glasgow *Evening News*: "If Canada awakens a glow in your heart, stand up and cheer today while it is still with us. There will still be a Canada tomorrow . . . but the collection of semi-autonomous regional states—will they still be called provinces?—won't be anything you'd recognize, and it is coming fast" (23 June 1967). Several indications point to a strongly embedded sentiment of national pride and Canadian identity among Maritimers. The distinctive Maritime trait of respect for history and tradition encompasses the Canadian as well as the provincial and regional experiences. Indeed, the Toronto *Telegram's* Canada 70 team found that of those Maritimers interviewed 62 per cent felt the most attachment to the nation, 16 per cent to their province, and 18 per cent to the Maritime region (the national averages were

70, 15, and 12 per cent respectively).[5] In an interview with political columnist Peter Newman, Premier Campbell maintained: "If anyone entertains any doubts about the allegiance of Prince Edward Islanders to this nation, all he has to do is come here and talk to them. We may be Islanders first, but we're Canadians before we're anything else."[6]

Expo euphoria and Centennial pride added to the usual Dominion Day celebration and evoked purple-prose editorials and letters to the editor. The Canada 70 survey team found (15 May 1969) that "many Maritimers almost choked with emotion when asked how important it was to them that Canada survive." The *Cape Breton Post* attested to the effectiveness of Expo '67 as a patriotic catalyst: "A story recently was told of a Prince Edward Islander at the fair caught in the act of actually weeping about it. He was so overcome with emotion that the magnificent display of Expo '67 in the total was 'Canada telling the world' " 26 (June 1967). The Yarmouth *Light-Herald*, a Nova Scotian weekly, resorted to hyperbole in its glorification of the Canadian nation: "The soul of our Canada is its freedom of mind and spirit in man. Here alone are the open windows through which pours the sunlight of human spirit. Here alone is human dignity not a dream but AN ACCOMPLISHMENT" (19 Sept. 1968).

Related to Canadian patriotism is an old and well-established sentimental force in the Maritimes, loyalty to the monarchy. The visit of the royal couple to Canada, and of the Queen Mother to the Maritimes, produced paeans to Canada's sovereign such as the Halifax *Chronicle-Herald*'s Dominion Day editorial in 1967: "The royal couple will provide a focal point beyond the immediately familiar, beyond ourselves, for our better hopes and aspirations. As Canada enters her second century, something very old—the institution of the monarchy—will help us to see ourselves more clearly, and thus help us to do a better job of building a yet very young country, whose promise is yet to be fulfilled" (1 July 1967). Although ties to the monarchy are probably weakening in Canada, especially among the younger generation, it is significant that the Canada 70 survey determined that "the largest combined regional proportion stating a loyalty to the Crown were found in Nova Scotia and P.E.I.—in each case 49 per cent" (2 July 1969). Though most Maritimers probably would prove less effusive in singing their praises of the Crown than the Halifax *Chronicle-Herald* editor, they do appear to take considerable pride in being British Canadians. This certainly helps to explain their opposition to measures such as Separatism and special status.

But the more important factor influencing the Maritime opinion-leaders' rejection of Quebec's demands to alter the constitutional *status quo* probably stems from economic self-interest. Maritimers display what can be termed a "paranoic" or, at least, an ambivalent attitude towards Confederation and the federal government. On the one hand, as Premier Campbell pointed out, they admit that membership in Confederation has brought cultural, social, and emotional benefits.[7] On the other hand, they complain with some justification that Confederation protected the infant industries of the Central Provinces at the expense of the Maritimers' lucrative north–south trade ties with New England. What can be termed the classical Maritime economic case against Confederation is summarized in this editorial comment in the Fredericton *Gleaner*:

> The great majority of our people are for Canada and for Confederation. But this does not mean that Maritime complaints are groundless or exaggerated. The Maritime provinces are a captive market, tied to the factories, banks, insurance companies and merchants of Central Canada by some hundreds of miles of inefficient railways and deplorable roads.
>
> Everything that we buy, whether in goods or services, enriches industrial Canada. By hard labour for inadequate return, we create a huge market. . . . Yet, when the Maritimes demand national investment in their area to build up their own productive potential, the rich men of Central Canada, influenced by their newspapers, call us beggars. (13 Dec. 1967)

To put this matter simply, Maritimers feel that Canada, represented by the federal government, owes them a living. If the existing constitutional division of powers between Ottawa and the provinces were altered to grant Quebec and other provinces a greater share of spending and jurisdictional powers, the have-not Maritimes would suffer economically because their equalization and development grants would be reduced. As a result, all three Maritime premiers, as well as those businessmen, mayors, and editors interviewed, insisted on a federal government strong enough to tackle the problem of regional economic disparity. In his address to the Confederation of Tomorrow Conference in Toronto, Premier Campbell succinctly expressed the Maritime position on constitutional change: "Canadian requirements as far ahead as one can see will necessitate a strong central government. Strength in this context means financial strength to provide a sufficiently large economic field within which a central government may exercise political and economic influence towards national ends. This implies certainly that the general erosion of federal financial authority must be brought to an end."[8]

The Charlottetown *Evening Patriot* addressed itself to the matter of constitutional change and the Maritime position with pragmatism and unusual candour:

> Our province has a permanent and monumental trade imbalance with up-the-river Canada. We buy more than we sell and the only way we can recover some of the money is through our equalization share of the tax bite which Ottawa puts on the profits to which we contribute. If the other provinces drive the federal government out of these tax fields, then the home office provinces of the firms we buy from will keep all the taxes and Ottawa will have less to send us in the various forms of federal assistance that now provides 65 per cent of our province's income. (1 Feb. 1968)

If there is any single factor which moulds Maritime opinions and perceptions, including attitudes towards Quebec and Separatism, it is economic preoccupation and concern for the "bread and butter issues." One need only glance at almost any editorial page or talk to any informed Maritimer to realize that regional disparity is considered the major problem of Confederation—even more so than French-English relations. That the issue of regional economic disparity is considered to be of greater consequence than Quebec's demands is cogently illustrated in a speech by Premier Campbell to the Montreal Branch of the Canadian Club on 20 November 1967. Recognizing two major threats to Canada's future, the constitutional and economic disparity issues, Campbell advocated striking a balance between the two. However, he left no doubt as to which he considered the more fundamental problem: "In all our discussions, in all our negotiations and in all our efforts towards accommodation, we must be ever guided and influenced by the higher objective, the political and economic unity of our country."

Part of the reason for the failure of Maritime opinion-makers to understand Quebec stems from their conviction that economic matters take precedence over every other issue. In the Maritime situation, it must be emphasized, this conviction is both natural and understandable. At times the cultural-linguistic aspirations of French Canadians seem frivolous by comparison. A graphic illustration of this feeling is a political cartoon by Chambers which depicts a Nova Scotian crawling up to Acadians newly returned from their cultural mission to France; on his back is a steel girder labelled *Sysco*, and he asks them, "He didn't happen to mention anything about steel, did he?"[9] When expressing their incredulity at the time and energy wasted by French Canadians in their non-economic endeavours, Maritimers use practical arguments such as: "Constitutions butter few parsnips" (Charlottetown *Guardian*, 27 May 1967) or "It is more important to get bread on all tables first, before we spend all our money making sure that everyone can discuss our economic problems—in two languages" (Saint John *Telegraph-Journal*, 17 Dec. 1968).

Apparently, because of their obsession with economic considerations, many Maritimers tend to look at the problems confronting Quebec from a simple economic point of view. They are tempted to distinguish between the ordinary Quebeckers and their leaders, portraying the former as being basically good, hard-working people like themselves, beset with economic problems. On the other hand, their so-called leaders advocate disconcerting concepts such as nationalism far removed from the real concerns of "the people." The Summerside *Journal-Pioneer*, generalizing from a successful exchange program conducted between citizens of Summerside and Chandler, Quebec, saw little desire for Separatism on the part of "the people," and blamed self-seeking Quebec politicians for Separatist and nationalist sentiment: "There is very little dissatisfaction in Quebec with regard to Confederation except on the part of the politicians and the intellectuals. The trouble is that many of the intellectuals have positions of influence in the communications media and the politicians are widely reported. . . . They can fan minority grievances until they become major constitutional questions" (22 Sept. 1967). The Charlottetown *Evening Patriot*, another Island newspaper, contends that the Quebec inhabitants are suffering economically because of their power-hungry leaders: "Politicians and intellectuals are so busy arguing about decorating the Christmas tree that there is nobody out in the kitchen to get the dinner on" (28 Nov. 1967). This attitude, however accurate it may be, reflects a lack of appreciation of the non-material, symbolic concerns and political susceptibilities. It contributes to the Maritimer's inability to view the problems of French Canadians in their proper perspective.

Other issues which touch on English-French relations, even in a peripheral manner, are also perceived from the hard-headed economic point of view. Though nearly all Maritime newspapers lauded Expo as a monument to Canadian pride and achievement, they vociferously opposed its being continued as a permanent fair because of the adverse effect it might have on the vital Maritime tourist trade. The Royal Commission on Bilingualism and Biculturalism, though its overall outlook and its specific recommendations are generally accepted, is considered wastefully extravagant and time-consuming. Quipped the Halifax *Mail-Star*: "Seldom have so many contributed so much to pay so few for so little" (5 April 1969). Another economic factor which exacerbates Maritime–Quebec relations is the feeling that the federal government ignores Maritime problems and concentrates on Quebec, where the more important bloc of votes is located. Complaining of a rise in express-freight rates, the *Truro Weekly News* commented: "At a time when the people of Quebec are concerned about propagation of their language and culture, which one cannot eat or wear, our existence in the Atlantic regions is flagrantly and arbitrarily doomed because of these added costs to our basic necessities" (5 Oct. 1969). A letter to the editor from a Dartmouth man probably reflects quite accurately the long-standing antipathy among Maritimers towards "up-the-river" Canada: "Joseph Howe was right and he knew Upper Canada would connive against us. . . . Quebec is proving that the squeaking wheel gets the grease" (Halifax *Mail Star*, 25 Nov. 1967).

The Maritimer's preoccupation with economic matters contributes to his attitude of indifference and, at times, hostility towards Quebec, the federal government, and the rest of the "have" areas of Canada.

The Maritime Provinces are psychologically as well as economically, and even to some extent, socially, far removed from the rest of Canada, and so it is not at all surprising that the liberalism *vis à vis* Quebec professed by Maritime opinion-leaders is largely unsophisticated and superficial. Although newspapers varied in their interest in and perception of events in Quebec, it was not uncommon to find gaps of several months between editorial comments. What interests Maritimers are events in their own region, particularly economic problems. In some newspapers even international and American affairs received more coverage than news from the rest of Canada.

It should be pointed out that the media of communication in New Brunswick are virtually controlled by one man, K. C. Irving, and that in Nova Scotia Halifax's two major dailies are owned by the same firm. The Maritimers, therefore, provide a captive audience for the opinion-makers who, in turn, accurately reflect the views of an influential business community. Though Premier Campbell has proven in the past to be receptive to Quebec demands and willing to grant bilingualism and biculturalism legitimacy, his main interest as expressed during an interview was, understandably, his government's new Comprehensive Development Program.[10] Mayor Corrigan of Charlottetown showed more desire to discuss the fine weather, good beaches, and booming tourist trade than Quebec Separatism.[11]

Another indication of the failure of some Maritime opinion-makers to understand fully the problems of Canada's French-speaking population is the common misconception they have concerning bilingualism and biculturalism. While the policy is generally understood to mean simply that every Canadian should have the opportunity to deal with his government's institution, courts, and schools in either French or English (provided a sufficient number are grouped together), some Maritimers think that "B and B" means that everyone must become bilingual. This misconception undoubtedly lies behind some of the opposition to the Official Languages Bill. Hon. Wendell W. Meldrum, New Brunswick's Minister of Education, recounted a conversation with a constituent: "A friend and a respected member of my community [said] 'Well, I see we're going to have to learn French.' "[12] How little "B and B" means to some Maritimers is illustrated in the following excerpt from H. J. Spence's speech in reply to the Speech from the Throne in the Nova Scotia House of Assembly,

16 February 1967: "What I mean here, even—I may be wrong—but I believe they called it bicultural, bilingual—or it could be vice-versa—I don't know! I wonder what good it's going to do? . . . It only cost $7,000,000. . . . I don't see it doing any good to change the name on the hotel! [Hotel Nova Scotian, Halifax] And maybe those are the boys that had it done."

The attitudes of Maritime opinion-leaders to this question range largely from sympathetic to indifferent, with a minority hostile. How the attitudes of the populace at large would place is, without closer study, difficult to determine, although it is probably a valid generalization that the opinions of the largely uninformed majority are more conservative than those of the more highly educated and more articulate members of the élite. It is also likely (although, again, this is an untested hypothesis) that younger Maritimers are more liberal in their approach to French Canadians. However, there are several sources of evidence that demonstrate the existence of a deep reserve of anti-French-Canadian feeling. One group which has probably received the greatest national exposure is the Maritime Loyalist Association, based in Salisbury, New Brunswick, just outside of Moncton. The Association announced that it would request injunctions against language bills proposed by the New Brunswick Legislature and the House of Commons. Many Maritimers, however, consider the MLA part of a tiny, lunatic fringe. Premier Robichaud rejected an unsolicited membership in the MLA with the words "Extremism of any kind is to be deplored and avoided."[13] Even a leading newspaper like the Charlottetown *Guardian* saw fit to feature the views of Patrick Nicholson, who consistently complained of the Pearson Government's "appeasement policy" towards Quebec: "English-speaking Canada has been forced to give up its Red Ensign because Quebec did not like it, has been saddled with the medicare plan, the Canada pension plan, yes, and even the family allowance plan, primarily as sops to Quebec . . . has had to carry the load of military service in war and peace because Quebec did not want conscription . . . English-speaking Canada has illegally been burdened with Bilingualism to cater to Francophonia" (8 Aug. 1967). The most common indicator of extremist sentiment is the "Plains of Abraham" type letter to the editor, such as the following by Otto Hubley of Halifax, a persistent author of anti-Quebec letters to the editor:

". . . we English-speaking real Canadians, supported by the Dominion Loyalist Association, will throw them all out and again take back and govern our country—the rightful title of which was transferred to our ancestors in 1759" (Halifax *Mail-Star*, 6 June 1969). An indication that not all is well between New Brunswick's two language groups is the following letter to the editor of the *Gleaner* by a Fredericton man:

> Any show of indignation on the part of the Premier [*re* Robichaud's refusal to join the MLA] must be tempered by the realization that the association he condemns came into being to counteract his desire, not for equality, but for stark supremacy of his race as it appears in the Acadian content in his cabinet . . . the regimenting and pushing of us all in the direction of biculturalism and bilingualism; and to hell with the financial condition of the province with its $42 million surprise deficit bill. (29 Jan. 1969)

It is evident, then, that not all Maritimers share even the professed liberalism of the majority of their opinion-leaders, and that indifference sometimes gives way to hostility towards Quebec. Maritime ambivalence in political attitudes (in part simply the gap between mouthing a principle such as "B and B" and actually living up to its concrete implementation) is well expressed by the Toronto *Telegram*'s conclusions: "When it came to considering how French Canadians should be treated, a fair-play attitude won out in the *Telegram*'s survey of the Maritimes. But there was also plenty of opposition to encouraging the spread of French into the region" (16 May 1969).

What would the Maritime Provinces do if Quebec were to secede from Confederation? Though the focal point of this study, the answer to this question proved far more difficult to obtain than the general impression concerning attitudes towards Quebec and French Canadians. What is noteworthy is not so much the substance of the responses to the various options suggested, but rather the absence of responses, the superficiality and, at times, the inconsistency of the answers, and the overall indifference or hostility expressed when the question was asked.

Most Maritimers seem to believe that the separation of Quebec would probably act as a catalyst for Maritime Union. But it is significant that Maritime Union is almost always mentioned as a panacea for economic ills, rather than as a positive reaction to the secession of Quebec. The possibility of secession is never really taken seriously, at least by Maritime newspapers and those opinion-leaders interviewed. The *Telegram*'s Canada 70 survey, on interviewing Premier Smith, reported that he considered the possibility of Quebec separation as "just that—a possibility, but not a probability."[14] The *Telegram* concluded that most Maritimers polled felt that Quebec would never really go all the way and separate; of those interviewed, 65 per cent felt that Quebec would remain within Confederation, as compared with a national average of 61 per cent.[15] Or, more important still, it may be that Maritimers do not want to think about Separatism and its possible effects. It is significant that the *Telegram*'s survey emphasizes that Maritimers, especially Nova Scotians, proved to be more militant and impatient with Quebec than Westerners, because of the fear of what would happen to the region if Quebec seceded (especially since the majority of those interviewed disliked the prospect of union with the U.S.).[16] For example, Henry Hicks, President of Dalhousie's University and a former Liberal Premier of Nova Scotia, has bellicosely trumpeted: "I would use force of arms to restore order and maintain peace in Quebec. . . . The United States had to fight to maintain the integrity of the union—if we don't believe in the integrity of this country enough that we wouldn't fight, then we don't deserve it."[17]

Union with the United States has always been a historical alternative for the Maritimes. The region had for centuries strong economic ties with New England; entry into Confederation, however, sacrificed much of the traditional north-south trade in return for an unbalanced east-west trade pattern that favoured the industries of Ontario and Quebec. Indeed, there is still clamour for free trade with the United States. Some Maritimers feel that, even if their region did not actually join politically with the United States, it would at least need some form of economic liaison if a sovereign Quebec interrupted the normal trade flow. One Summerside resident painted a rosy picture of union with the United States:

With such a move free trade would be automatic and would open up a fantastic market on our doorstep for everything we produce. As it is, the better off we become the more money we send to Ontario and Quebec. About 40 per cent of the people living in the Eastern states come from the Maritimes originally and would lean towards us when buying a very large percentage of the products we produce . . . we would pay 15 to 30 per cent less for what we buy and receive 15 to 30 per cent more for what we sell.[18]

Gerald Regan, leader of the Liberal Opposition in Nova Scotia, told the Canada 70 survey that "if there was a sovereign state in between the Maritimes and the rest of Canada, the ability of the federal government to understand and help us would be just that much less. Affiliation with the American union would become quite likely for the Maritimes."[19] Typical of the inconsistency and superficiality of Maritime views on these matters is the statement of the mayor of Charlottetown, who pointed out the natural geographical affinity between the Maritimes and New England, yet disliked the idea of union with the United States as a whole.[20] The editor of the Woodstock *Sentinel-Press* also mentioned the geographic and economic similarity between New Brunswick and Maine.[21]

There are, as well, non-economic ties between the Maritimes and the United States. One political opinion-leader singled out the strong emotional and family ties between the two maritime regions (his mother was from Boston) and claimed that the Maritimes have a different, and more sympathetic, philosophical outlook on the United States than does central Canada, where there is more fear of American economic domination and criticism of American foreign policy.[22] There are certain regions within the Maritimes—the Annapolis Valley, for instance—settled by both pre-Loyalist "Planters" and United Empire Loyalists which probably have retained a good deal of pro-American sentiment and social, economic, and religious ties with the United States.

But most Maritime opinion-leaders are not in favour of union with the United States if Quebec separates. The Toronto *Telegram*'s survey found that "despite the historic Maritime feeling towards New England and the fear of what may happen if Quebec separates, an overwhelming 230 [out of about 300 interviewed] were against Canada joining the U.S. The same number said it was not inevitable that Canada join her neighbour to the South."[23] One can assume that this attitude would apply to the subject of the Maritimes alone joining the United States as well. One reason for the opposition to the union with the United States is economic. Premier Campbell was not at all convinced that the Maritimes would have fared better economically if they had joined the United States rather than Confederation, pointing to the existing economic difficulties of the New England states.[24] A Saint John businessman offered a similar objection, asserting that if Maine is the United States' poor cousin, the Maritimes do not want to become an even poorer cousin state.[25] Another businessman rejected the economic argument in favour of union with the United States entirely, since he was afraid that union would, by opening the Maritime market wide open to American manufacturers, present unfair competition to Martime producers.[26] Mr. Stewart Trueman of the Saint John *Telegraph-Journal* summarized several of the arguments, economic and non-economic, against union with the United States. Traditional ties with New England, so strong a generation and more ago when a Maritimer could get on the "Boston Boat," arrive in New England and get a job the next day, have weakened in favour of stronger ties with the rest of Canada. The narrowing gap between Canadian and American standards of living has reduced the attractions of sharing the American prosperity. Crime and racial problems in the United States worry Maritimers. Emigration to the United States has declined in recent years, partly because of tightening barriers on immigration; more Maritimers now move to Ontario and other parts of Canada. Finally, Canadians have begun to be more aware of the Maritime area. Tourists from Ontario and Quebec, in increasing numbers, visit the Maritimes.[27] To some Maritimers, the differences between the Canadian and American life styles is a significant factor in their rejection of possible union with the United States. The editor of *The New Freeman*, a Saint John paper, expressed such a sentiment: "They [Americans] just exist; here we live."[28] Mayor Allan O'Brien of Halifax supports this view. "The penchant for conformity in the United States," he observes, "would be stifling to anyone who was used to the Canadian atmosphere."[29]

In a speech last year on the subject of Maritime options if Quebec were to separate, Premier Smith characterized union with the United States as "the least attractive alternative,"[30] and told the Canada 70 survey, in May 1969, that "it would mean an end to our way of life and sense of values. . . . We would be plunged into the melting pot which is the United States."[31] Premier Campbell indicated that he would be "appalled" at the prospect of the Maritimes joining the United States, partly because the Island would lose its distinctive identity.[32] New Brunswick's Premier Robichaud stated his views bluntly: "Only nitwits would advocate Canada joining the U.S."[33] Apparently, French-speaking Maritimers share their English-speaking compatriots' apprehensions about the different American way of life. Bernard Poirier, writing in *L'Evangeline* (Woodstock, N.B.), feels that closer relations with the United States can be achieved without the disadvantages inherent in full political union: "Géographiquement et économiquement parlant [union with the U.S.] c'est logique. Sans toutefois aller aussi loin, il y a moyen de collaborer plus étroitement avec notre grand frère sans pour autant sacrificier notre identité propre et nos manières de penser et d'agir" (1 May 1967).

Finally, at least one source of Maritime opinion, the *Cape Breton Post*, looks at the question from the American point of view and doubts whether the United States would want the Maritimes. Congressional representation would be out of proportion to the size of the region; there would be world-wide outcry against another example of American imperialism; the delicate balance between the Republican and Democratic Parties would be upset; and the United States would be saddled with three debtor states.[34]

Though there is some sentiment in favour of union with the United States if Quebec separated, there is little hope, in the eyes of most Maritime opinion-leaders, for an independent "Atlantica." The Maritime "mentality," with its shrewd awareness of political and economic realities, is unable to envisage an independent existence. Premier Smith considered this option "not very practicable."[35] The common fear was expressed by a New Brunswick businessman, who felt that a drastic drop in the standard of living would result if the Maritimes tried to go it alone.[36] The notion of an independent Maritime or Atlantic nation has never been seriously advocated in recent years in the Maritime press.

Although only three options apart from the present situation were suggested to those interviewed—union with the United States, independence (with or without full political union), and a sort of East Pakistan arrangement, separated from the rest of Canada by a sovereign Quebec—occasionally another option, union of French-speaking Maritimers with a separate Quebec nation, was suggested by Acadians. An Acadian history professor at the University of Moncton suggested that if Quebec separated, his first choice would be union of the Acadians in New Brunswick with Quebec, because certain assimilation (already an alarming problem) would take place in an almost entirely English-speaking Canada.[37] However, Jacques Filteau, editor of *L'Evangeline*, discounted this strategy because the Acadians, unlike Quebeckers, lack a state and because there is little love lost between Acadians and *Québécois*.[38]

All indications point towards preference for an East Pakistan arrangement for the Maritimes if Quebec actually did separate from confederation. Of course, most Maritime opinion-makers would deplore such a state of affairs; Premier Smith said to the Canada 70 survey: "I think the size of the population and the economic strength left would be still sufficient to maintain a viable country [but] . . . the most serious effect would be our extreme geographic separation from the rest of the country—that would be really difficult for the Maritimes."[39] The Charlottetown *Evening Patriot* lamented that "a separate, sovereign state of Quebec would cut off the Atlantic Provinces from the rest of Canada physically as well as reducing the federal financial assistance" (16 Oct. 1967). The *Cape Breton Post* stated that "the only feasible alternative is for the continued union of the provinces of Canada with an independent Quebec separating the two areas. . . . This would, as in Pakistan, lead to accelerated centralization and the Atlantic Provinces would be even more in the backwoods than they are now" (24 Jan. 1968). A P.E.I. daily summarized the problems that a separate Quebec would create for the Maritimes: "The excision of the Province of Quebec from the map of Canada would pose perhaps insuperable problems for the Atlantic Provinces, not only in the political area but in the flow of trade between central Canada and this region, in the movement of goods and people, and in the field of national defence and other federal government services" (Charlottetown *Evening Patriot*, 7 June 1968). It is no wonder that Maritimers refuse to think seriously about Quebec Separatism!

However, other options are usually considered even less attractive than continued existence as Canadians, albeit in a truncated confederation. It should by now be obvious that the Maritime region has strong ties with Upper Canada and the federal government, both economic (for example, 65 per cent of the budget of Prince Edward Island comes from federal funds) and emotional. In an interview, Premier Campbell made it very clear that his constituents have a strong sense of being Canadians, as well as Islanders, and that they have benefited greatly—socially, economically, and in terms of national pride—from membership in confederation.[40] The Mayor of Halifax argued: "I would favour the East Pakistan approach because in my view the Maritimes need to be part of a larger country for reasons related to the economy and the cultural development."[41] Improved communication, increased tourism, more attention paid by Ottawa to Maritime grievances—all these factors contribute to strengthen bonds with the rest of Canada. Richard Hatfield, Leader of the Opposition in New Brunswick, characterized the Maritimers' colonial status briefly: "Much of our destiny is tied, it must be frankly acknowledged, to the federal powers."[42]

The roots of what has been called the Maritime colonial mentality are deep and complex. The term "Maritime mentality" is not meant in any corporate or profound social psychological sense, of course, but simply as characterizing a cluster of consensual, recurrent attitudes. Naturally, there are variations and deviations from the norm, and it is quite possible that the social, moral, and political attitudes culled from the editorial pages of Maritime newspapers are more conservative than those of other opinion-leaders in government and business. On the other hand, it is likely that the conservatism of a paper such as the Fredericton *Gleaner* reflects the mores and attitudes of a large segment of Conservative, Protestant, English-speaking New Brunswickers.

A fundamental element in the "colonial-Maritime world-view" is its conservatism and almost Burkean resistance to the rapid revolutionary change that is typical of our post-industrial society. Dr. Alexandre Boudreau, director of the Memramcook Institute, castigated his fellow Maritimers for their anachronistic world-view and introspective regionalism and provincialism. He shrewdly observed that "we still act and think like nineteenth-century villagers in a world which accepts and recognizes no more boundaries."[43]

Professor H. G. Thorburn, writing in 1961 about New Brunswick politics, endeavoured to explain the political and social conservatism of the province. He described the social and political milieu thus:

> Loyalties to the local community are encouraged by the relatively static social situation in which families become attached to certain localities for generations and are identified as belonging to them. . . . These parochial loyalties make local improvements rather than provincial or national issues the main concern in politics. . . . The province has been a part of Canada for over ninety years now and has watched its relative position in the federation decline. When immigrants were streaming into Ontario and the West, New Brunswick was almost completely by-passed. Those who remained in New Brunswick were those who had a business, farm or other means of livelihood and who preferred the peaceful serenity of a community that changed only slowly. As a consequence, New Brunswick has retained much of its old social, economic and political pattern. . . . The two dominant parties stand for traditions, principles, attitudes and prejudices which resemble one another very closely. . . . The general atmosphere of tranquility and acceptance of the prevailing power relationships is sustained in the press of the province.[44]

Returning from a trip abroad, a Maritime business administration student looked at his birthplace in a new perspective: "One myth is that we take life slow and easy, and are a homespun lot, and thus slower economically. There are people in other areas who are homespun and friendly and who do a lot better economically than we do. We fall back on excuses, and economic changes won't come unless economic changes are made."[45] A man from Fairview, Nova Scotia, assailed Maritime dependence on Ottawa: "If Nova Scotians are to enjoy the standard of living found in the more progressive areas of Canada, they must be willing to face reality and step out of the nineteenth century into the . . . twenty-first century and earn their place in our Confederation instead of asking others to carry the burden."[46] These are, of course, by no means typical Maritime views, but they do draw attention to a basic trait of the Maritime mentality, a paranoic attitude towards Ottawa and Upper Canada. A graphic illustration of the dependency relationship with the federal government is the common use of the "family" metaphor when Maritimers refer to Confederation. The New Brunswick MP and former Provincial Premier, Hugh John Fleming, described the relationship between the provinces and the federal government in these terms: "Around the family conference table at meetings convened from time to time by the central government we should continue to advance our individual and provincial claims and aspirations."[47]

To continue the metaphor, Maritimers often feel like neglected, unwanted childern who suffer while the parent federal government caters to the rich Central Provinces and the spoiled brat, Quebec. The fact that most Maritimers are well aware of the degree to which their livelihood depends on help from Ottawa probably increases their bitterness towards a far-away power which fails to understand the problems of the eastern seaboard region. A consequence of the colonial relationship with Ottawa is a tendency to lash out against the external force as a scapegoat for Maritime problems. Professor Thorburn observes that "resentment, where it exists, is often directed outside the province; as a consequence, local and provincial interests escape reasoned criticism."[48] During the periods of economic crisis, an outpouring of political rhetoric blaming Ottawa for Nova Scotia's problems has been evident in the past: "The 'Paranoid Style' was effectively used by the Nova Scotia economic, social and political establishment to channel the deeprooted and sometimes violent frustrations of the ordinary farmers, fishermen and workers against Ottawa rather than against Halifax."[49]

The growing dependence on the federal government may have encouraged the growth of a Maritime inferiority complex. In his brilliant study of the psychological dimension of the colonial mentality, Albert Memmi suggests that the colonized eventually come, unconsciously, to believe and act according to the stereotypes of their colonial masters. "The ideology of a governing class," he contends, "is adopted in large measure by the governed class."[50] The Charlottetown *Evening Patriot*, angry at the typically condescending attitude of a national magazine towards Prince Edward Island, admitted that "we are a humble folk, partly because we have to be. In a small community, everybody knows us for what we are, so it is no use trying to put on airs" (14 Aug. 1967). Some Maritimers console themselves, because of their inferior economic position, by glorying in what Dr. Frank McKinnon terms a superior "standard of life" as opposed to a purely material standard of living.[51] The blessings of a slower pace of life, excellent recreational facilities, uncrowded cities and rural hospitality are contrasted to the impersonal, rat-race existence in far-off "large Upper Canadian cities . . . [with their] tinsel glamour."[52] The Charlottetown *Guardian*, in a rare respite from its usual griping about the mandarin-dominated, unresponsive government in Ottawa, rationalized the lower standard of living in the Maritimes:

> [life in Upper Canada] carries with it all the concomitant "privileges" of a nerve-wracking high speed, daily battle for existence in a business world where only success is tolerated. . . . If we allow the elements of that type of progress to attack our beautiful rural areas we can say farewell to the things of real value. (31 July 1968)

It is clear, however, that there are some Maritimers who do not wish to perpetuate what they consider to be the myth of their superior way of life. They feel that it is hypocritical, on the one hand, for Maritimers to glorify their bucolic way of life, while, on the other hand, they vociferously demand that Ottawa do something drastic to introduce an "Upper Canadian" standard of living in the region.

Of course, it is impossible to draw a straight casual line between aspects of the "Maritime Colonial outlook" and the proclivity of most opinion-makers towards continued existence even in a truncated Canada. However, as underlying factors, the various elements of the Maritime mentality—the psychological as well as economic dependency on Ottawa, the inferiority complex with respect to "Upper Canada," the social, political and moral conservatism and resistance to rapid change—help to explain Maritime attitudes towards the impact that the separation of Quebec might have on their region. Maritimers are apparently not accustomed to think in terms of what they *might* do *if* Quebec separated; rather, they prefer to concern themselves with the economic problems of the here and now. They find it difficult to envisage any constitutional arrangement other than that which has existed for the past century. They are proud of their distinctive way of life, even if its material aspect leaves much to be desired. Even the prospect of political union of the Maritime Provinces is rejected by most of the newspapers and many of those interviewed, partly because provincial loyalties and traditions are so strong.

Existence in a position of dependence on some other region or power is a basic aspect of the Maritime historical experience. As a result, the option of independence as a separate political entity is considered folly. Those opinion-leaders interviewed chose either of two dependency relationships, with the United States, or with the remainder of Canada. Continued existence within Confederation, even as a Canadian East Pakistan, is probably the majority preference because it accords closest with the *status quo*. The fact that, other than Premier Smith, no major political or academic figures or newspaper editors have publicly addressed themselves directly to the problems which a fragmented federation would present to the Maritimes helps to explain the negative attitude and superficial response of many of those opinion-leaders interviewed. If Maritimers do not take Quebec Separatism seriously, then they do not think much about the question; if they *are* worried about Mr. Lévesque and his friends, then they need to think about the future of the Maritimes cut off from their most important source of goods and services.

Maritime opinion-leaders show little genuine interest in events in Quebec. What occupies their attention and energy is the ever-present problem of regional economic disparity and the inadequacy of federal measures undertaken to combat what Maritimers with some justification consider to be an unjust legacy of Confederation. They accept, if at times grudgingly, the principle of linguistic and cultural equality for French Canadians, but they are not willing to accede to Quebec's demands for a greater share in the division of power between Ottawa and the provinces. Quebec may have a distinctive cultural and ethnic makeup, but politically it is just one province among ten. Separatist activities in Quebec are deplored, but receive little more than perfunctory condemnation in Maritime editorials; few Maritimers seriously consider secession of Quebec an imminent possibility. Despite a tradition of rhetorical whipping of the federal government and of the rapacious commercial activities of the tariff-protected Upper Canadians, Maritime opinion-leaders are well aware of the political realities of their position in Confederation. They are tied economically, and perhaps emotionally and psychologically as well, to Confederation, just as they have in the past been colonial outposts of New England and of Great Britain. Coupled with a failure to take Separatism seriously, this dependency complex leads most Maritimers to opt for continued existence as Canadians, even if their present isolation became intensified by the existence of a sovereign Quebec. For the federal government, such a situation might not prove as disastrous as one might expect. In a political cartoon featured in the *Gleaner*, former Prime Minister Pearson, surrounded by memos listing Maritime economic problems and confronted by a map of Canada depicting a separate Quebec, comments to Paul Martin: "On the other hand, Paul, it might be a blessing in disguise. It will create a buffer zone between us and the Maritimes" (26 Oct. 1967).

NOTES

1. The term "opinion-makers" is used in what may be considered a rather uncritical and unscientific manner. Nevertheless, it may be effectively argued that the editorial comment of the Maritime daily and weekly newspapers and other periodicals, as well as the public statements of municipal, provincial, and federal politicians, should throw considerable light on Maritime attitudes toward French Canada and Separatism during the period January 1967 to July 1969. To supplement these views, a number of influential Maritime newspapermen, politicians, and businessmen were interviewed in the Maritimes in July 1969. Most of the interviews and research for this study were done by my research assistant, Mr. Ken Battle. It should be pointed out that this essay was written in August 1969, before the Conservatives were swept out of office in Nova Scotia, and the Liberals in New Brunswick.

2. Quoted in the Charlottetown *Guardian*, 15 Sept. 1967.

3. *Nova Scotia*, House of Assembly, Debates, *Official Report*, 18 March 1968.

4. Halifax *Chronicle-Herald*, 8 Jan. 1968.

5. Toronto *Telegram*, 5 July 1969.

6. Summerside *Journal-Pioneer*, 27 Jan. 1967.

7. Interview with Premier Campbell, Charlottetown, July 1969.

8. Confederation of Tomorrow Conference, Toronto, 27–30 Nov. 1969. *Proceedings*, p. 21.

9. Halifax *Chronicle-Herald*, 24 Jan. 1968.

10. Interview with Premier Campbell, Charlottetown, July 1969.

11. Interview with Mayor Corrigan, Charlottetown, July 1969.

12. New Brunswick, Legislative Assembly, Debates, *Official Report*, 28 March 1968.

13. Quoted in the Saint John *Telegraph-Journal*, 25 Jan. 1969.

14. Toronto *Telegram*, 24 May 1969.

15. Ibid., 5 July 1969.

16. Ibid., 15 May 1969.

17. Quoted in the Toronto *Telegram*, 26 May 1969.

18. Letter to the editor, Charlottetown, 8 May 1969.

19. Quoted in the Toronto *Telegram*, 24 May 1969.

20. Interview with Mayor Corrigan, Charlottetown, July 1969.

21. Interview with the editor of the Woodstock *Sentinel-Press*, July 1969.

22. Interview with Mr. Wells, executive assistant to Premier Campbell, Charlottetown, July 1969.

23. Toronto *Telegram*, 15 May 1969.

24. Interview with Premier Campbell, Charlottetown, July 1969.

25. Interview with Mr. Joseph Likely, Saint John, July 1969.

26. Interview with Mr. Philip Oland, Saint John, July 1969.

27. Interview with Mr. Stuart Trueman, Saint John, July 1969.

28. Interview with the editor of the *New Freeman*, Saint John, July 1969.

29. Correspondence with Mayor Allan O'Brien, Halifax, July 1969.

30. Premier Smith, speech to a Halifax service club.

31. Toronto *Telegram*, 15 May 1969.

32. Ibid., 22 May 1969.

33. Ibid., 17 May 1969.

34. *Cape Breton Post*, 24 Jan. 1968.

35. Premier Smith, speech at a Halifax service club, reported in the Halifax *Chronicle-Herald*, 23 April 1968.

36. Interview with Mr. Philip Oland, Saint John, July 1969.

37. Interview with Prof. Theriault, University of Moncton, July 1969.

38. Interview with Mr. Jacques Filteau, Moncton, July 1969.

39. Quoted in the Toronto *Telegram*, 24 May 1969.

40. Interview with Premier Campbell, Charlottetown, July 1969.

41. Correspondence with Mayor Allan O'Brien, July 1969.

42. New Brunswick, *Debates*, 29 Feb. 1968.

43. Quoted in the Saint John *Telegraph-Journal*, 19 Nov. 1968.

44. Hugh G. Thorburn, *Politics in New Brunswick* (Toronto: University of Toronto Press, 1961), pp. 180–185.

45. Quoted in an article in the Halifax *Chronicle-Herald*, 25 Aug. 1968.

46. Letter to the editor, Halifax *Mail-Star*, 14 March 1968.

47. Canada, House of Commons, Debates, *Official Report*, 18 May 1967, 352.

48. Thorburn, *Politics in New Brunswick*, p. 185.

49. George Rawlyk, "Nova Scotia Regional Protest, 1867–1967," *Queen's Quarterly*, LXXV, No. 1 (Spring 1968), 108.

50. Albert Memmi, *The Colonizer and the Colonized* [Tr. by Howard Greenfeld] (Boston: Beacon Press, 1967), p. 88.

51. Frank McKinnon, "The Island's 200th Birthday as a Political Entity," *Atlantic Advocate*, May 1969.

52. *Cape Breton Post*, 10 Jan. 1968.

The Prairie Perspective

J. A. Archer

IT WILL NOT BE the prairie West that precipitates the disintegration of Canada. Westerners, prairie Westerners, feel deep economic concern with, and strong emotional ties toward, the modern Canada they did so much to create. Prairie people, however, will reserve their right to opt into or out of any new Canada that would emerge were Quebec to separate. Any such drastic change in the rule book could provide the spark for independent status, and it might well do so were the spark to light in an atmosphere already charged with discontent, puzzlement, and a sense of alienation. Westerners are quick to resent the charge that they are *anti*-Quebec. They are *pro* a federal Canada and point with pride, a complacent pride, to the wide-open doors of opportunity which the settlement of the prairies opened to all Canadians and to thousands of people from other countries.

It should be remembered that it was the successful settlement of the prairie West that made Canada an economic whole, adding breadth, depth, economic muscle, and optimistic exuberance to the nation. If Ontarians and Maritimers flocked west to settle Manitoba, and later Saskatchewan and Alberta, while the *Québécois* did not, it was unfortunate; the French Canadians who did come were fine farmers. There were no barriers against them. Settlers came from "Old France," Germany, Hungary, and the Ukraine. But few came from Quebec, though good land was already scarce in that province and farmers' sons were seeking land.

It was not to be, and the West developed as part of English-speaking Canada, not pro-Ontario, not anti-Quebec, but preoccupied with

the business of home building and seeking in one language and in
secular schools the ready means to mould a multitude of tongues and
cultures into a new society. It might have been so different. Certainly
Quebec's factories ran full throttle to meet the demands of the burgeoning West. Financial houses in Ontario and Quebec prospered.
Provincial and national treasuries felt the infusion of fresh income.
But the Quebec farmer did not share in this burst of energy and this
soaring confidence of the spirit. He was not part of that saga of
courage, resolution, hardihood and accomplishment. Neither his
voice nor his views were current coin in a new West that scoffed
at "old" ways and rebelled against the financial and economic fetters
of Eastern Canada. Today there is a new challenge from Quebec.
The province has burst out in new-found energy and dynamism;
Quebec farmers are in revolt against the strictures of the city man,
and Quebec young people seek a sudden way to technical know-how
and administrative control. The West, true to its own tradition, can
only applaud the energy and respect the enterprise. What a pity it
does not wholly understand the motive or the goals. But who was
there in the West to interpret the new revolution in Quebec?

The area now known as the Prairie Provinces—Manitoba, Saskatchewan, and Alberta—first came under an organized jurisdiction on
2 May 1670. On that date King Charles II granted "The Governor
and Company of Adventurers of England Trading into Hudson's
Bay" the sole right of trade and the power of holding and alienating
land in Rupert's Land. The Hudson's Bay Company, as the concern
came to be called, claimed rights by charter to all the land drained
by streams finding their outlet in Hudson Bay. This stance seems to
have won tacit acceptance from the legal fraternity and royal officers,
but practical application of the monopoly was disputed by the French,
and after 1763 by the Montreal-based North West Company. A bitter
fur trade rivalry ended in 1821 with the amalgamation of all fur-
trading companies active in the area under the name of Hudson's
Bay Company.

For nearly a half century the "Great Lone Land" was under company rule. In the main this rule was fair: the liquor trade was restricted; missionaries were aided; settlers were tolerated; the Indians
were not maltreated. But the Northwest could not remain a fur
preserve, nor did the British Government intend that it should. In

1868, following negotiations with the newly created Dominion of Canada, the British Government ratified an agreement by which the Hudson's Bay Company surrendered all claims to Rupert's Land to Canada in return for a cash settlement of £300,000 plus a substantial grant of land. Canada thus acquired a vast wilderness empire far removed from Cartier's Quebec or Macdonald's Kingston. In fact, Canada, herself but lately a colony, acquired a colonial empire.

The Canadian Government was shortly caught up in the problems of governing a distant fief. Neither distant Ottawa nor more distant London informed the inhabitants of the Red River Settlement of the meaning of the changes. Indian, Métis, and white settlers were agitated, while sharp cleavages developed over proposed changes in the status of the Northwest. There was uncertainty, anxiety, neglect, and finally bloodshed. Historians have found a central figure for the turmoil in the person of Louis Riel, a man of mixed blood, a visionary, and a man of action. Eastern Canadians have persistently misunderstood the significance of the Red River Rebellion, seeing it from the constricted viewpoint of their own limited horizons. Riel was neither an evil man nor a saint. The Métis he led were not French rebelling against British. Essentially, the Red River insurrection was the futile resistance offered by a small, rather primitive community against the aggressive economic forces of a more powerful civilization. The Métis, whether French or Scottish, did not want to be absorbed by the Canadians. They did not understand the new system of land tenure and they feared the coming of the railway. They did not want to join the United States. They simply wished to be left alone, to speak French or English, to be Protestant or Roman Catholic, to hunt buffalo, to farm, and to live the good life of their forefathers. But it was not to be. In 1870 Riel's provisional government fell before the onset of British and Canadian soldiers, and Manitoba became a province under terms set by the Parliament of Canada.

With the establishment of Manitoba as a province, the remainder of the area came directly under the rule of the representative of the Canadian Government. Canada could not leave her newly acquired territories unprotected and unpopulated. The United States had offered the Hudson's Bay Company a large sum of money for Rupert's Land in 1868, and there were prominent Americans who advocated the taking of the Northwest by force. Manifest Destiny had an earthy taste in American mouths, but a strident croak in Canadian ears. Canada decided that her western hinterland would remain Canadian—by determination and energy, and, if necessary, by force.

Within the compass of national policy, the projected transcontinental railway linking British Columbia to Eastern Canada was rerouted to cross the prairie land near the United States–Canadian border. It had formerly been surveyed to follow the fertile crescent of the Saskatchewan River system. The international boundary line was surveyed from Ontario west to the Pacific. The township system of survey as applied to the United States frontier lands was adopted, and surveyors began laying out the West in square sections. A liberal homestead policy was adopted to attract settlers, and the North West Mounted Police was formed to keep law and order and thereby lessen opportunity for outside meddling. Treaties were made with Indians to ensure peaceful settlement of the Canadian Northwest.

In some respects the Canadian plans went well: the Mounties kept order, the boundary was surveyed, and the Indians moved peacefully to reservations. There was a painfully slow movement of settlers into the prairie West, but towns did come into being along the main line of the Canadian Pacific Railway and at strategic trading crossroads elsewhere. There was a gradual evolution of government. But again, distant Ottawa failed to heed or to appreciate the voices of hunger, discontent, and protest that swelled in the West, voices that were duly reported by police officer and government official responsible for "peace, order, and good government" in the Territories.

In the main, the disaffected were again the Métis and their Indian allies. These people had turned to farming in the late seventies after the disappearance of the buffalo. Many had trekked out of Manitoba after 1870 to settle on the banks of the Saskatchewan, there to establish a rude democracy under Gabriel Dumont, their elected leader. They settled and farmed strips fronting the river, expecting that squatter's rights would be recognized. In spite of repeated petitions for title to their river lands, for recognition of their assembly as a local government, and for schooling in the French language, nothing was done to reassure farmer, delegate, or priest that the "Métis Nation" would not be swallowed up, dispersed, or assimilated by the threatened advance of a Canadian tide of settlement. By 1884 fear and anxiety over the future induced the Métis leaders to seek out Louis Riel and to persuade him to return to aid his people.

Many white settlers supported Riel in 1884, for the whites, too, had grievances. This should have alerted Ottawa to the need for action. The reports of administrators and police officers warned of trouble. There was danger of an Indian uprising as hunger and hopelessness crept over the land. What could have been solved peacefully in 1882 or 1884 meant bloodshed in 1885, and an abortive uprising ended with the defeat of the Métis at Batoche. Riel was hanged, and Quebec, seething with anger, felt that the noose had been intended for the Catholic heart and the French tongue. The Orange Order of Ontario averred that hanging was a natural end for traitors. In the West, while there was relief that the danger of an Indian War was passed, there was also a feeling that Ottawa had again resorted to the army to cover up the result of years of deliberate neglect.

Much of the frustration, many of the doubts of the eighties, were forgotten in the golden years of success which came at the turn of the century. For a variety of reasons, many of which had no direct connection with Canadian policies, the prairie land of Western Canada became a lure which attracted a swarm of settlers. Free land was there—free land and a free life. There was also a French-Canadian prime minister, a Western minister of the interior, a flood of landseekers from Eastern Canada, the United States, the British Isles, and continental Europe. The whole prairie region was clamorous with ploughing, sowing, building, making homes in a new land, adapting old ways to new ways, fighting prairie fires, facing blizzards, working long hours that one's children might have a better chance. And the settlement of this last great land frontier was successful beyond all dreams.

All those born on the frontier, or reared there, or who have spent years in the prairie West as part of the pioneering process, share the Western heritage. Whether a Westerner by birth, option, or adoption, every product of that heritage knows that it was the successful settlement of the prairie West that made Confederation work. When Laurier exclaimed that the twentieth century belonged to Canada, the Westerner might have added that he and his kind had made Canada a nation capable of meeting the challenges of the twentieth century. This feeling of successful participation in nation building, supported by the physical evidences of success, has influenced the Westerner's views on the role of governments in society and the relationship between regional and federal government, district and provincial government. The Westerner is prepared to cope with the natural hazards of wind, drought, hail, and insects. He has learned to cope with modest tariffs, unpredictable freight rates, arbitrary interest rates. He knows that the answer to pressure is counter-pressure and that the antidote to arbitrary power is countervailing power. He knows also that you should grease a wheel when it squeaks.

Western farmers expect governments to act in their interests. There is little of *laissez faire* in their view of the governmental function. Tariffs, freight rates, and interest rates have been fixed by governments. Governments should be involved, also, in such vital matters as the grading, transportation, and marketing of grain. The government, in its proper role, is the extension of the local community and is created to accomplish those tasks that loom too large for the individual. The government should be concerned with highways, schools, and health services. Westerners have ever put their faith in written platforms to be adopted by political parties. They have ever been surprised, angry, and militant when platforms have been lost in the labyrinth of political expediency.

Western rural society came out of the formative years of pioneering indelibly marked by the process of adapting to a stern environment and a ready-made mould of national policies. Co-operation, neighbourliness, a delight in mechanical things, and an admiration for material advance—these were but part of the large image of Prairie Man. He was a doer rather than a philosopher in those early days. He was less British and more Canadian than his Ontario counterpart, for he was a man of many cultures. Part of him, at least, came to the Canadian West from Europe expecting to learn to speak English and hoping to find a school that his children could attend, for he wished them to have the opportunities that had passed him by. If he thought of the French-speaking Canadian it was as a neighbour, another stranger in the wilderness, not distinguishable as Canadian by his language or handicapped by it, for the European has an appreciation, or tolerance, of languages.

The pioneer farmer in the Canadian West differed markedly from his earlier American counterpart. The American pioneer outran civilization and drew law, government, and the trappings of society after him. The Western Canadian settler came into a region where the environmental challenges were very great but where the framework of law, order, and government were set out to await the coming of the user. If the prairie settler didn't know when he first arrived that there was a tariff barrier, a railway, freight rates, a shortage of easy money, he was quickly made aware of these prime facts of existence. Through hard and bitter experience he learned that the only effective power in the matter of schools, telephones, roads, was the provincial government or its agents. In both Alberta and Saskatchewan he fashioned governments to his liking. He had little fear of making government an owner, for he saw government as an extension of himself. The federal government was distant, obviously controlled by the populous East and as obviously perverse in its policies. He could not fashion it after his image, though he tried to reform it. The best he could hope for was to pressure it to control the grading and marketing of wheat, the incidence of freight rates, and the level of tariffs. Pressuring the federal government was a necessity, and succeeding Western farm leaders learned the techniques and the timing well.

In all this the Westerner was acting as any sensible person would who hoped to provide for his family's economic well-being. He applied himself directly to controlling the instruments open to his hands, and he sought countervailing power to offset the power of the vested interests ranged against him in Eastern Canada. With a single-minded purpose he had settled the prairie West, populated this last agricultural frontier, made industries hum elsewhere in Ontario and Quebec, and made Canada a nation from sea to sea. His was an uncomplicated credo. It was a good thing to grow food for a hungry world; conversely, it was an evil thing that hindered the process of getting that food to the consumer. If this smacked of smugness and self-righteousness, then what of the men who grew no wheat yet made fortunes by speculating in it, who knew nothing of hard physical toil yet battened on the avails of usury!

It would be but simple truth to say that few people in the Prairies gave serious thought to the bicultural nature of Canada during the half century 1895–1945. There were crises to remind all concerned that religious issues roused heat and that religious convictions carried over into education matters. The Manitoba School Question, the Territorial Ordinance of 1901, the educational settlements of 1905, were all milestones along the road from bilingualism and biculturism to a secular public school system with provision for privately supported religious schools. These were usually Roman Catholic institutions. The tide ran strongly in favour of secular schools, modelled on the Ontario pattern. Religious symbols aroused a brief storm in the early thirties, and thereafter the tide ebbed. By 1960 it had set the other way, a movement which began of its own momentum and was already flowing when the sharp voices of Separatism were raised in modern Quebec.

The Prairie Provinces found common ground in their views of the role of the federal government in Confederation. Within its own boundaries, each province developed individually. In this latter respect, and at the risk of generalization, it might be said that Manitoba was more influenced by Ontario than was Saskatchewan or Alberta. Saskatchewan represented the wheat-growing West and the West of the co-operatives, while Alberta was much influenced by the influx of American settlers and American financiers. As provinces, the three differed widely in outlook, in political allegiance, and in resources.

In their views on Confederation they were and are much more as one. The West did not join Canada in the same manner as did Prince Edward Island and British Columbia. Manitoba was created a province by the federal government and the boundaries were arbitrarily extended later. Alberta and Saskatchewan were created provinces under terms differing from those applying to other provinces. The control of natural resources of the Prairie Provinces was withheld at the time of joining Confederation, to be used for the purposes of the Dominion. The prairie West entered Confederation after the ground rules regarding railways, tariffs, and land settlement had been laid down. Protests against discriminatory treatment and bargaining for better terms have been exercises carried on within the general framework of Confederation. While the West has flirted with the idea of secession when in dire distress, it is not from a yearning for a status enjoyed earlier but rather a reaction to a federal union the burden of which at the moment seemed intolerable. The whole instinct of the West, nevertheless, is to keep Canada a political whole.

The West has looked with favour on the federal system, viewing it as a workable device by which local decisions are made at one level and national decisions at another. It sees the need for a strong central government, sufficiently powerful to control financial policy, trade and commerce, and the armed forces, and to provide a supreme court as arbiter in constitutional disputes. The West knows that Canada is neither a geographic nor an economic unity, though it is a political entity. Compromise and countervailing power are necessary, then, if the divergent demands of the various regions are to be met and a policy bringing rough economic justice to all is to be effected. Over the years, the West has forged political alliances on various occasions federally with Quebec, with Ontario, and with the Maritimes in an effort to influence policies, to blunt the oppressive, and to support the constructive, as these are interpreted in Prairie constituencies.

The West has viewed with considerable admiration and some envy the seemingly unerring instinct which Quebec voters show in aligning that province with the winning party federally. Only—so it seems to Westerners, at least—only when there has been a stampede of voters or an aberration from the norm has Quebec been out of step with the general mood of Canada. The West knows with a sure instinct that Quebec must have a strong economic base from which to bargain. Since World War II, Ontario has outstripped Quebec, her nearest rival, in economic advance and has become the unchallenged power base in Canada. Since the Duplessis period, Quebec has undergone a profound social and economic revolution. Westerners view with profound respect the giant strides made to modernize the province. The retraining of a labour force and the rebuilding of an economic base take time and money, and the process is fraught with frustrations. Many Westerners see the noise and turmoil of Separatist rallies partially as an expression of impatience over slowness of reforms and partially as a countervailing measure to shake further economic concessions from Ottawa. This much they understand. It is when the confrontation with Ottawa moves into areas which the West sees as being of national concern only that Westerners become anxious for the future of a strong central government. It is when marches, slogans, and rallies give way to bombs and rioting that Westerners recoil from a new, menacing, unfamiliar element in an old game.

Nevertheless, this unfamiliar element in Quebec strikes a responsive chord in some breasts. The West itself has experienced a growing sense of being alien in the past few years. No longer is it a centre of prime political power. No longer is there a power bloc based on the old clearly definable bases and exercising the old recognizable pressures. The wise men in the seats of power today are all from the East, and the language they talk is deflation, integration, urbanization. Where, now, the power and magic of wheat? Who, now, will be spokesman for the West? Not since 1919 has the Prairie voter felt so impotent, so alien in the country he set going, so much an appendage to an Ontario body politic. It is almost enough to make him think back to the days when his only allies were the Laurier Liberals from Quebec. But then who really knows the new Quebec—and what do the *Québécois* want?

It is a pity, many thinking Westerners will tell you, that Quebec seems to demand so much so fast. Give us time to see how each change fits, they intimate. Ontario can afford to make concrete changes to meet the wishes of large French-speaking minorities in that province. New Brunswick is at cross-purposes because things were done too fast. The West, so these people say, is ready to consider changes— but don't expect Westerners to act in quite the same way as Easterners. To begin with, it is natural that Ontario should take special cognizance of its French-speaking people. These came in from Quebec, and Ontario and Quebec agreed on certain things in common when the idea of Confederation was mooted. The Acadians were in New Brunswick before the United Empire Loyalists, and there are many of them. There was a French–speaking element in Winnipeg in 1870, and this group deserves special consideration. But, apart from this group and two or three other areas where French settlements appeared early, there is little sense in making provision for French schools. There would be more sense in Ukrainian schools, or German schools, or Hungarian schools—but these other groups wanted to learn English and even disobeyed their elders and voted for secular schools. So runs the argument. The farther west one goes, the more violent the tone of argument becomes. Manitoba has taken steps to provide for French schools. Saskatchewan provides for the use of French as a language of instruction in certain school districts. Alberta has generally shown more reluctance to move in this direction.

The West is nevertheless vitally concerned over Quebec's place in Confederation. Evidence of this concern is revealed through the reaction of Westerners to various aspects of biculturalism. Separatism, "two nations," language rights, and "special status" appear to be the burning issues. One must bear in mind, however, the difficulties facing anyone who attempts a definitive explanation of a Western viewpoint on specific issues. He may read the newspapers, but it is the sport of Westerners to prove the "leading journals" wrong. He may interview political figures and captains of industry, and he will hear what the interviewed "hopes" will be true. He may talk to all manner of ordinary people, and he may then come extraordinarily close to the grass roots opinion. But if it rains, the grass changes colour.

The newspapers provide an obvious index. Prairie editors have very definite views, and it is certain that no daily newspaper in the Prairies would look kindly on an independent Quebec. None favours "special status," however each may interpret that term, though some might be willing to accept this were the choice special status or separation. The *Winnipeg Free Press* has paid more attention to the French-English issue than have other dailies in the Prairies, and it is as strongly opposed to any kind of special position for Quebec as it is unalterably opposed to separation. On the other hand, unlike some of its counterparts elsewhere, it supports the recommendations of the Royal Commission on Bilingualism and Biculturalism and it favours the Official Languages Bill. The majority press opinion in the Prairies would be willing to see more rights given to French Canadians but is opposed to special concessions for the Province of Quebec.

The "one nation" theme, interpreted usually as a "no basic concessions to Quebec" theme, is widely supported by editorial writers. While most would agree that all other provinces should be willing to accept constitutional changes which would further protect Quebec's rights, there has been no editorial support for granting treaty rights to Quebec. Premier Daniel Johnson was roundly attacked for advo-

242   *J. A. Archer*

cating that Quebec have the right to make certain agreements with
foreign countries. President de Gaulle was compared to Hitler, to
Mussolini, and to Stalin for his reference to a "free" Quebec. It was
not surprising, perhaps, that the press should object to interference
by the head of a foreign state in Canadian affairs. But the hysteria of
the response was surprising in the light of no comparable response to
American interference in the domestic affairs of Caribbean nations.
Indeed, some papers appeared to dislike de Gaulle as much for his
anti-Americanism as for his *"Québec libre"* speech. The *Edmonton
Journal,* for example, was relieved that the de Gaulle affair had not
disrupted our friendship with our southern neighbour.

The attitudes of the press and of government spokesmen to the
outcome of the constitutional conferences of 1968 and 1969 were
essentially similar, though the press seemed more willing to make
concessions to French Canada than were the politicians. Certainly in
Alberta the press was inclined to support concessions and chided the
premier for being unyielding. Premier Weir led the way in offering
substantial concessions to Manitoba's French-speaking minority. Press
and politicians were nearly unanimous in stating that there was room
at a constitutional conference for negotiations on specific cultural
matters—and, of course, on finance—but that there were certain
fundamental matters which were not negotiable. These non-nego-
tiables were the concept of two separate states, or the "two nation"
theory as understood by English-speaking Canadians,[1] special status
for one provincial government not granted to the other provincial
governments, foreign affairs, national defence, banking, communications, and trade and commerce. It was quite clear that the provincial premiers and the English newspaper publishers were willing to
grant concessions to French Canadians even if they opposed basic
concessions to Quebec.

Newspaper comment on the selection of Pierre Elliott Trudeau as
Liberal leader was almost entirely favourable. It was felt that Trudeau would be more than a match for the Separatists and their
collaborators in France. Trudeau could "bridge the gap between the
two major language groups in Canada." This enthusiasm carried
over into the federal election of 1968. One newspaper declared that
its support for Trudeau was "based primarily on his unequivocal and
consistent advocacy of one Canada." Yet the New Democratic Party,

advocating special status for Quebec, held its strength in Winnipeg and gained ground in Saskatchewan. It is probable that economic factors played a much more important role in the Prairies than did the national unity question or the French-English factor. Nevertheless, the pro-Liberal press in the Prairie Provinces hailed the Liberal victory under Trudeau as a victory for "one nation" and a blow against the Quebec nationalists. One prominent journalist, in predicting that Trudeau's victory in Quebec would strengthen his hand against the nationalists or Separatists, warned English Canadians that they must recognize French language rights as their part of the bargain.

This manner of interpreting the election results had its dangers. Many Westerners entertained the fond hope that the election decision had given the quietus to the Quebec nationalists and that the future of Confederation had been decided. Another unfortunate result was that the Liberal appeal in the West had been interpreted as essentially an anti-Quebec appeal. Trudeau, a French-speaking leader with a French name, would stand up to Quebec better than would Pearson, an Anglo-Saxon. While it was true that the "one nation" theme was stressed and economic issues glossed over, in the mind of many an Easterner, the economic plight of the Prairies, albeit worsening, was yet of secondary importance to the vital issue of national unity. The fact that Separatism is still a force in Quebec and that English Canada is being pressed to implement further concessions has created something of a backlash. This is apparent in the reaction to the Official Languages Bill.

Early in February 1969, the Prairie premiers, meeting for a session of the Prairie Economic Council, sent Prime Minister Trudeau a telegram questioning the constitutionality of the proposed Languages Bill and asking him to refer it to the Supreme Court for a ruling. Premier Thatcher of Saskatchewan declared that if the federal government did not seek a ruling, the Prairie Provinces would. He is reported to have added a strong objection "to the civil service of our province having to speak French." He added the comment that it would be too expensive for the courts to be bilingual. Clearly, there was a misconception in the West concerning the provisions of the bill which the politicians did little to clarify. There was a widespread belief that the provisions would apply universally rather than being confined to regional units where at least 10 per cent of the people spoke French. It is difficult to judge whether the opposition to the bill was a ploy to force a change in the agenda for the constitutional conference, substituting financial for constitutional matters. By May 1969, the daily press and leading provincial politicians were modifying their opposition to the bill, advocating instead a gradual implementation of its clauses.

A poll taken by the Canadian Institute of Public Opinion and published in May 1969, revealed that nearly two-thirds of the Westerners polled disapproved of the bill while less than one-third approved. A further poll taken at about the same time showed that some 40 per cent of those polled in the Prairies thought Prime Minister Trudeau had been against the West generally; nearly 40 per cent thought he had shown favouritism to Quebec while less than half thought he had treated all provinces equally. If such polls can be taken to indicate attitudes, one must surmise that Prairie people feel that the federal government has not solved immediate economic problems and that too much emphasis is being laid on language and culture and too little on basic economic issues. The *Western Producer,* certainly one of the most widely read farm newspapers, commented editorially on the Official Languages Bill in June 1969. With so many bread-and-butter problems to be faced, people "quite naturally regard cultural legislation as a luxury at such a time." The editorial goes on, however, to comment that the bill is not very revolutionary, though it might cause administrative problems in a multi-ethnic society. It simply means that Canadians "may address their federal government agencies in the official language of their choice." The bill, therefore, is reasonable, and "failure to provide a minimum bilingual service would benefit the separatists and lead to two nations."

None of the above answers the ultimate question, what will the West do if Quebec leaves Confederation? It would appear that Westerners have not yet faced up to this issue. Discussion on the possibility of Quebec's seceding at some early—or distant—time is current coin in Quebec and in Ontario, perhaps even in the Maritimes. Westerners view the possibility as undesirable and unthinkable— perhaps undesirable, hence unthinkable. Dr. Lewis Brand, a former Saskatchewan M.P., and a candidate for the party presidency of the

Progressive Conservative Party, remarked, "Westerners believe you cannot have Canada without Quebec. If Quebec goes or becomes a separate state, then what do western Canadians have to look to? So they've come to realize that maybe it wouldn't be such a bad idea to become a western state."[2] Westerners can prove that Quebec will be the loser economically, politically, and culturally, were the province to secede. They raise the probability of an internal split in the province if the issue of separatism is forced. With wonderful assurance they prove that the federal system best provides that protection so necessary to a cultural minority who are near neighbours to a powerful American nation. Such exercises prove nothing, convince no one, achieve nothing. They are significant, however, of the deep-rooted instinct of the Prairie people to keep Canada whole. Also inherent in all this is the knowledge that Separatism in the West is something that would only have to be seriously considered *after* Quebec withdrew.

Articles on Separatism in Prairie newspapers invariably portray Separatists in an unfavourable light. Lévesque's independence manifesto of 1967, which called for economic co-operation between Canada and an independent Quebec, was termed unrealistic because of the backlash which would result in Canada were Quebec to secede. Any notion that there might be voluntary co-operation after secession was "altogether unthinkable in Canada."

> What Quebec wants, in Mr. Lévesque's terms, is that Canadians of every race and political complexion should give up the country they are heir to, for something less, something less durable and something much less viable, than they supposed their national inheritance to be. And what the Quebec theorists of Mr. Lévesque's stamp do not appear to appreciate is that such a notion is altogether unthinkable in the rest of Canada. Nations do not voluntarily dissolve themselves, even if the dissolution means no immediate economic loss.[3]

Separatism was consistently portrayed as being an economically disastrous course for Quebec. Little was said of the effects of separation on the rest of Canada. Prairie newspapers rarely discussed the role of American and Anglo-Canadian capital in Quebec, save to praise the past and to fear that Separatist talk might dry up the springs. In this respect one can only surmise that newspaper publishers are more continentalist in outlook than are the elected representatives of the people, for the representatives have been concerned with the relationship of American capital to control of the Canadian economy and its ultimate effect on political self-determination.

A few years ago, a Prairie premier was quoted as saying that if Quebec were to separate, his province might join the United States. This indiscretion met with so cool a reception that it was not repeated. Western separatism has not so far been argued as a goal for action but rather has been referred to as a dramatic possibility for the one region which has the potential viability to separate. Practical politicians in the Prairies know that such views are voiced by a minority, usually by men with strong economic ties with the United States. Such pro-Americanism is strongest in Edmonton and Calgary. The moderate agrarian view, as expressed through the wheat pools, is that all provinces would be the poorer if each went its separate way. No province can sell wheat alone, or beat poverty alone, or build cities alone. All need Canada and Canada needs all. This is probably the message closest to the ideas and emotions of the average Westerner. It would probably never occur to him that the United States decided many years ago that it would not take in a further tier of northern states without offsetting additions in the south. Perhaps the United States wouldn't accept offers on the part of the Prairie Provinces to enter that republic. What a blow to Western pride that would be!

Westerners as a whole have little understanding of the emotional roots of Quebec nationalism. Western opposition to anything resembling special status and the extremely antagonistic attitude towards Separatism is an indication that Prairie opinion would not be inclined towards economic or political co-operation with an independent Quebec. In the Westerner's view, a separate Quebec would probably go bankrupt and end up as a dictatorship of the Right. This would mean that, for a period at least, Ontario would dominate the Canada remaining—a bad thing for the West. Some sort of counterpoise to Ontario would have to be built, perhaps one government for the Prairie region. The Lethbridge Conference (May 1970) on "One Prairie Province" showed that there was little enthusiasm for any such step short of some drastic realignment in the federal structure. Westerners feel that outlets to the seaboard by way of the St. Lawrence will continue to operate freely since the seaway is international. In any event, facilities at Vancouver and Churchill could be enlarged to handle Prairie grain crops.

In all this there is no threat, no hint of marching or forcing a position or wresting a corridor from Quebec. The thought of internal strife is alien to the Westerner. Were there to be civil disorders in Quebec itself, defections, coercions, and brutal repressions, attitudes could change. There is no thought of such an eventuality today. Indeed, next to Prime Minister Trudeau, René Lévesque is the most popular French Canadian in the West, according to the polls before the Quebec election.

There is another element in the equation which affects the situation today and may affect it profoundly tomorrow. This element is the present attitude of a goodly number of Westerners to Ottawa, to Eastern Canada, and to Confederation itself. "Alienation" is the word most often used today to describe this attitude. This is not a new phenomenon. In the West the seeds of alienation were planted early. The roots go deep. The West believes that Central Canada—Eastern Canada in Everyman's language—was the real beneficiary of Confederation. The Prairies are not grateful for the colonial heritage. Westerners do not regard the financial institutions of the East as partners or helpmates. A permanent and disadvantageous tariff policy is no cheerful legacy. There is a widespread feeling in the West that Eastern politicians, financiers, and businessmen have no real understanding of conditions in the West and have no desire to learn. The resentment might only smoulder were the Prairies dependent on the bounty of the East, but Westerners feel that the West is economically able to stand alone. Alienation, condescension, and flippant advice come perilously near to insult in such a situation.

The West feels alienated, snubbed, and ill-used. The feeling is much more widespread than in 1919 or during the thirties. Farmers are angry—angry that Easterners have clearly bungled the marketing of wheat. A few years ago cabinet ministers urged them to grow wheat promising that it would be sold. The Toronto *Globe and Mail* stated editorially on 18 July 1969: "In 1966 they [the Prairie farmers] were assured by the annual meeting of federal and provincial agriculture ministers and their officials that Canadian wheat exports would stay at a high level until at least 1970. . . . These were assurances that were being reiterated—while they were also, in some quarters, being contradicted—as late as last year." Today cabinet ministers from Ontario and Quebec appear to have no real appreciation of the problems facing agriculture and no long-term policies to better a chronic situation. Meanwhile, Eastern editors sagely advise farmers to switch to cattle or oats or bees! Western oilmen feel that they are deliberately excluded from the rich Eastern Canadian markets—the victims of arrangements made by Eastern distributors with American producers. Western financiers have felt the rebuke of so-called colleagues in banking circles in Eastern Canada. There is a general, widespread belief that what Montreal or Toronto, Quebec or Ontario wants, Ottawa will grant—be it subsidy to dairymen, maintenance for Air Canada, or aid for Expo. Back of it all is the maddening, frightening knowledge that in terms of political weight the Prairies no longer qualify even for the welter division. Mistress in her own house, the West would be a power to be blandished.

An Ontario daily of long-standing reputation referred to the Western grievances and the fact that Ottawa has taken the West for granted. In doing so, the editorial writer quoted the Minister of Agriculture, H. A. Olson:

There is "a deep feeling of isolation from the rest of the country" in Western Canada. Mr. Olson, Liberal member for Medicine Hat, said that in addition to the feeling of isolation there is "a backlash of sorts" in the West. "There is a feeling that the Government is far more concerned with what happens in Ontario and Quebec, and always has been, than with the West," he added. "I think most of the people out there think they're strong enough now that they could get along as a separate entity from the Manitoba border. . . ."

The editorial goes on:

At the centre of the economic disaffection are the prairie farmers with full barns of wheat and no prospects of them being emptied in the near future. The oil industry in the West is running below capacity, while the eastern market is closed to them. There is a feeling that . . . an airport in Montreal is given the green light while money for an astronomical observatory in B.C. is voted down; Man and His World is revived with Dominion Government help while no comparable consideration is given to the promotion of tourism in the West.[4]

Quebec, to the degree that it is Separatist, is Separatist on emotional grounds. Economically, Quebec is bound closely to a united Canada. The West, where separatist at all, is separatist on economic grounds. Emotionally the region is deeply Canadian. There is, then, no real understanding or appreciation of the dynamic forces boiling up under the surface in either area. The West sees Quebec as a gainer economically from Confederation and either misjudges or refuses to believe the mounting evidence of Separatism. Faced with an actual separation, the West would not act in haste, for sound economic policies are not formed of snap judgements made in times of stress. If a separate Quebec meant little disturbance and the door were left open for a return, the West would probably opt for a continued Canada without Quebec. But the bargaining over national policies of the new Canada would be hard and sharp, unless the West were sure of some means of countering Ontario's economic, financial, and political power, it would consider going its own way.

The West can document its own case in cold economics, and in hot anger can demand a fair shake from the Ottawa government. It can list empty promises made by prime ministers in 1910 and in every election campaign since. It can invoke statistics and economics to prove that it has paid the price for membership in Confederation. Part of that price, as worked out by Winnipeg economists, is $6.87 for every family every year for tariffs alone. The West can show an impressive list of instances when Ottawa aided Quebec—Expo 67, Air Canada base to Montreal to Winnipeg's loss, Man and His World, and Westerners will further maintain that Alberta was denied a chance to enter the Montreal oil market. If there is any single thing that stands in the way of a cordial understanding of Quebec's dilemma, it is that what Quebec wants Quebec gets from Ottawa at the expense of the West. It is difficult to sell an Official Languages Bill to a section of the country that feels that Ottawa is preoccupied with Quebec and uninterested in the West's economic plight.

There is a widespread disbelief in promises of federal cabinet ministers. "A Just Society—Just for Quebec," as one headline stated. Westerners flatly reject the assurance that anyone professing a willingness to learn French will qualify for any "senior post in the federal civil service." The belief is that the civil service, save for junior clerks, perhaps, will be recruited from Central Canada and, more than ever, administrative decisions will favour Ontario and Quebec. This, together with the knowledge that politically Ontario and Quebec can carry any decision in Parliament, makes Westerners writhe in exasperation and anger.

What, then, is the Prairie perspective? Westerners still opt for a federal Canada. Anger, exasperation, and the feeling of alienation have not yet broken down the traditional expectations that governments can and will respond to regional arguments boldly argued. When economic justice has been done, then there will be a more acceptable time to pursue such necessary and proper goals as biculturalism. But biculturalism in the West will be ordained, legislated, and practised in the light of the history and traditions of the Westerners. It cannot be imposed by the action of a political majority representing regions other than the West. While most Westerners are ready to widen the avenues open to those whose language is French, or those who would become proficient in French, the same Westerners will remind the listener that land was indeed free to all who would come to the prairies, and if those who came from Quebec were few in number, Quebec leaders today cannot fairly condemn Western leaders for carrying out the expressed wishes of their constituents. Yet there is little of such fruitless argument. The West hopes Quebec will find a satisfactory role in the Canadian federation. While Westerners do not always appreciate the roots of Quebec nationalism or Separatism, their instinct is to compromise for the sake of a whole Canada. Should Quebec leave Canada, however, Westerners may very well decide that separation for them is also an option to be considered. If that decision is made in the present mood, there is a very real possibility that the West would shun Ontario, seek some accommodation with British Columbia, and strike out independently.

NOTES

1. In an editorial of 21 December 1967, the *Winnipeg Free Press* declared that all "practical" problems must be negotiable but that the question of two nations was a non-negotiable matter: "French Canada should know at once that it is useless to prepare any constitutional amendment which would establish two nations within Confederation." The editorial went on to declare that the English-speaking provinces would be better off to accept separation than a "two-headed constitutional monster" that could not work.

2. *Weekend Magazine*, 12 July 1969, p. 14.

3. *Winnipeg Free Press*, 21 September 1967. Editorial.

4. *Kingston Whig-Standard*, 15 July 1969.

British Columbia
and the Canadian Federation

R. M. Burns

I have been faithful to thee, Cynara! in my fashion.

Ernest Dowson

FEDERATIONS are seldom the end result of any logical evolutionary process. More often they evolve from the dreams of their founders and from the pressures for immediate political solutions to geographic, economic, political, and social problems. Certainly this was true of Canada to a great extent, and in British Columbia long-range questions were pushed aside by the pressing problems of the day from which union with Canada offered some hope of respite.

To understand, and even more to appreciate, British Columbia's sometimes quixotic actions in the Canadian federation today requires a breadth of familiarity with the resources, geography, politics, and people of the province. For nearly one hundred years of the province's life as part of the Canadian nation, British Columbia has been remarkably consistent in its attitude to federal issues and relationships.

Perhaps more than any other province, British Columbia since pre-Confederation times has been in some form of emerging colonialism, seeking to establish its independence from parental control, yet at the same time reluctant to relinquish the sometimes intangible benefits which the filial association brings. Even today, the image of the "spoilt child of confederation" occasionally is to be seen.

British Columbia has had a special, and often a unique, role in the Canadian scene. The nature of Canadian federation has been a con-

Acknowledgement is made of the assistance in documentary research of W. Douglas Costain of the University of British Columbia.

tinuing political issue in British Columbia over the years, but the problems of dominion-provincial relations have not been the products of partisanship but of more fundamental factors of geography, and economic and social backgrounds. Perhaps most of all they have been the product of the development of those unlimited natural resources, for which all successful British Columbia leaders have been quite prepared to take full personal credit.

The development of the British colonies on the Pacific Coast into the province of today was not a consistent process or one conducted in an atmosphere of agreements and amiability. British Columbia from its early settled times has been an area of wide variation of resources and interests. This is inevitable in a land of pocket settlements separated by endless ranges of high mountains. People, particularly people in other parts of Canada, tend to think of British Columbia as a homogeneous unit centred on Burrard Inlet or the Empress Hotel in Victoria. This illusion often extends to the residents of those places as well. But the people in the rest of the province do not make this mistake. British Columbia is not a homogeneous unit any more than is Canada. Its interests and its attachments have varied from region to region from earliest times. Perhaps, in a manner, this worked to the advantage of Canada, for the focus of interest has often thus been diverted from Victoria and directed to the broader national scene.

Political attitudes and relationships are not developed in a vacuum. Even with the diversities of emphasis, every area of the province has to some degree been under the influence of those factors which we have mentioned. In the province they have been of such significance over time that they have moulded the political forces rather than having been factors which political forces have utilized for their own ends.

While British Columbia, from its early times, has had more than its necessary share of internal dissension and divisions, nevertheless the core factors of its existence have played an important role in preserving a consistent provincial identity. From earliest colonial days to the present time, even in the face of a lack of supporting evidence for the dream fantasies, there has been a tendency in the province to think of itself as an outpost of Empire—first of Great Britain, then of Canada—from which the "riches of the Indies" have flowed to enrich the fortunes of those who remained behind. As one experienced observer has noted, even today British Columbians like to visualize themselves as pioneers resisting to the end the rape of their birthright by the grasping of effete financiers of the East. Even the lowliest clerk in the concrete jungle of Vancouver's West End sees himself as a sort of logical heir to the pioneers who made the Canadian West.

A brief look at the nature of British Columbia's founding and early development can help us to understand something of what has happened and how the present state of affairs has come about. In the beginning, the Pacific Coast of Canada was first explored and then settled from the sea. For many years it was the object of a colonial struggle in which the United States, Russia, Spain, and Britain were all involved at various times. In the early stages it was merely a haven for seamen trading to the Orient, and later the area of operations for the fur-traders of the North West Company and the Hudson's Bay Company. Somewhat later it was a part of man's eager search for instant wealth through gold. Even in the vast interior, with the exception of early explorations like those of Mackenzie, the ties with the East were tenuous, separated as it was from the centres of settlement by the mountains, the prairies, and the vast wilderness of the Canadian Shield.

There was little in the province's early history as a British colony to link it in any way with the British possessions in eastern Canada. It was an outpost of colonial settlement and its ties were by sea to Europe, to the Orient, and to California. It would not have taken very different circumstances for the history of British Columbia to have taken a very different turn. If the Gold Rush of '58 had not petered out so quickly, if the tide of U.S. settlement had flowed somewhat faster to the Northwest, if the fur companies had been less aggressive in the consolidation of their interests, the story might have changed. As it was, the interest and influence of Macdonald and Cartier, with their dream of an empire from sea to sea, provided the acceptable alternative. For without this incentive, it does not seem probable that the Colonial Office would have exerted the influence that would make the colonies part of Canada rather than allow them to drift into the orbit of U.S. control, as they likely would have done eventually in the absence of an acceptable alternative in union.

But union with Canada, however, unreal and artificial as it might have appeared, did provide that alternative. The leaders in the colony were faced with the evident desire of Great Britain to be relieved of some measure of responsibility for this questionable asset and, besides, they were faced with the problem of economic survival brought about by the pressure of the economic depression of the late 1860s in British Columbia.

There are good reasons to believe that, if financial conditions had permitted, the united colony would have successfully resisted Canada's advances for some time. As it was, the offers of increased public works expenditures, especially the promises of railway construction, had an important influence on a government burdened by the public debt and with few alternative prospects in view. These, along with the positive pressures of the Colonial Office exercised through Governor Musgrave, made the ultimate union an inevitability. Perhaps the unexpected generosity of Cartier in offering a railway, instead of a wagon road from Fort Garry, was a major factor in undermining the resistance of those who favoured continued attempts at Pacific independence. Cartier's takeover technique was well in advance of his time.

No one in this country needs to be told today that political union does not necessarily make for unity. Continuing delays in the implementation of the terms of union increased friction, and Canada and British Columbia, especially in the period of Alexander Mackenzie's term as Prime Minister, entered into a long and often bitter controversy about their political relationships. In the absence of any strong emotional background, the failure in the realization of material benefits was of that much greater effect. In a sense, this had partisan overtones, for the bringing of British Columbia into confederation had been a Conservative act and Mackenzie was not disposed to approve of Macdonald's inpetuosity. But what was probably more significant than any partisan reaction was his bitter opposition to what he regarded as the extravagances of the railway terms. But at the provincial level, while most provincial representatives from British Columbia supported the Conservatives, politics were essentially personal in nature, and the attitude toward Canada depended substantially on the attitudes and interests of the government leaders.[1] For example, under Walkem in the period from 1874 to 1883 it was largely a state of active political warfare, and in 1876 a secession resolution was introduced and passed in the Legislature, although with little practical effect. Subsequently, with Macdonald's return to power and the assumption of the premiership by William Smithe, a conciliatory attitude prevailed which was consolidated by the completion of the Canadian Pacific Railway and the settlement of many disputes about the terms of union, at least for the time being.

If there was a brief respite from the quarrels over the terms of union, there was another point of difference to take its place. From as early as 1872, but assuming importance only in the later part of the century, there was a growing resistance in British Columbia to oriental immigration, particularly of the Chinese.[2] They had first come to British Columbia from California in the pre-Confederation days of the Gold Rush, and later by direct route from China when imported as labourers for the construction of the C.P.R. The British Columbia governments were persistent and consistent in their efforts to close off the influx by the harassment of restrictions on numbers and by heavy head taxes. While the government of Canada had some sympathy for the provincial view, it was not prepared to accept the extremities of the British Columbia position, and several of the Acts and Orders of the Province were disallowed. The issue was largely resolved in 1902 when Canada raised the head tax to $500, in effect eliminating the problem of mass immigration from the Orient which had been the main object of the provincial concern.

It was noted before that the early struggle over the terms of union had been more or less settled with the completion of the C.P.R. and the adjustments under the Settlement Act of 1884. At that period the province seemed generally to be satisfied with its place in the Canadian federation, financial manœuvring ceased for the time being and British Columbia was not a participant in the first Interprovincial Conference which Mercier, the Premier of Quebec, called in 1887 in an attempt to seek support for the strengthening of provincial powers.

But the period of tranquility was to be a short one. By the early 1890s the B.C. representatives in the federal Parliament were seeking a greater voice in the determination of national policies, and the provincial government was putting its case for improved financial returns based on the alleged imbalance between federal revenues and expenditures in the province. This was an early start on a favourite British Columbia topic, which has provided for countless words in many provincial submissions in the intervening years.

Essentially, the position taken by the British Columbia governments over the years has been based on a reiteration of a number of claims, some valid, others merely political sounding-boards. On the whole, British Columbian leaders have been reasonably consistent in their efforts to secure some better financial arrangements than have been available to them under the original terms of union. The claims have been based more or less on the same factors, although the emphasis has varied from time to time.

In the earlier part of the period, the main emphasis was on the financial factors of the revenue-expenditure imbalance and upon the conditions under which the province had entered union. The constant attempts to secure subsidy adjustments had precedent in earlier successful efforts elsewhere, in Nova Scotia in particular. As the economy developed, other claims were advanced, including such matters as railroad developments, coastal fisheries, shipbuilding, and the tariff and international trade.

While the province did secure some redress in a special adjustment of $100,000 a year for ten years at the first Dominion-Provincial Conference of 1906, on the whole there was a continuation of the irritations of the often minor grievances which had complicated the relationships of Canada and the province.

The province's final efforts in the period before World War I were contained in two memoranda or briefs prepared in 1913 and 1914. Essentially the same in content, they reiterated many of the arguments on economic disabilities as well as the favourite and time-honoured complaints about the terms of union which had been the meat of the province's disputes with Canada for many years. While the province won a moral victory in the appointment of a Royal Commission to consider these matters, World War I prevented its operation and put an effective damper on British Columbia's campaign for better terms for the war years and for some time thereafter.

In the 1920s a number of Dominion-Provincial Conferences were held and this part of the fabric of intergovernmental relations began to assume importance. British Columbia continued to advance its claims and two new arguments became prominent. The entry of the Dominion into the field of the income tax in 1917 as a war measure and the problems of the Pacific Great Eastern Railway became subjects of continuing discussion then and for subsequent years. It was in this period that the question of equitable freight rates first assumed prominence. One cause of dissension was removed with the return of the Peace River Lands to the province in 1930.

The problems of the Depression diverted attention from the endemic problems of union to the more immediate and pressing demands of unemployment and actual physical distress. But with the change of government in 1933 there was renewed attention by the new Premier, T. D. "Duff" Pattullo, to the fundamental issues. Pattullo, perhaps by political instinct, anticipated the era of Keynes which was soon to have an important impact on government policies in Canada and, in the election and in his demands on the government in Ottawa after his election, he laid heavy emphasis on the need for strong governmental intervention in the economic life of the country. His slogan of "work and wages" found little fertile ground in the Ottawa of Prime Minister R. B. Bennett.

In the early Pattullo years the most divisive influences since the days of Walkem came to the fore. Premier Pattullo, whose ideas of the nature of public economic responsibility were substantially in advance of his time, was frustrated by his inability to secure federal co-operation in the economic affairs of the province in the manner that he considered appropriate and necessary, not only in a period of economic depression and high unemployment, but as a necessary element in continuing stable growth. When he failed to receive what he thought an appropriate response to his demands for a program of "work and wages," he threatened that British Columbia would "go it alone," although he was never very precise on just how this was to be done.

In many ways this was more an expression of the exasperation of the times, for while Pattullo was undoubtedly a man who enjoyed power, he was essentially a Canadian, although, like so many British Columbians before and since, it may have seemed to be a bit on his own terms. During this period there was some suggestion that party politics were an important factor in the influencing of the relationships between the British Columbia and Dominion governments.

Certainly R. B. Bennett and Pattullo had little in common politically or personally, and no doubt some elements of parties and differences played a part. But it would likely be a mistake to attach very much significance to this fact then, or at any other time in British Columbia history. The conflict has been more fundamental: generally the age-old differences between benefactor and beneficiary, parent and child, unable to agree on the conditions of the aid or the terms of their relationship. The friction has been intensified by a belief prevalent in British Columbia that the province's difficulties could be settled if a fair deal could be made with Canada. The truth is that British Columbia's problems have been much deeper than that and are generally merely highlighted by the difficulties in the development of national policies adequate to the particular case and the particular time.

The appointment of the Royal Commission on Dominion-Provincial Relations in 1937 gave the province an opportunity to present in detailed and formal fashion all the grievances which had been part of its differences with Canada over the years. The British Columbia brief was a detailed recapitulation of most of the arguments which had formed the substance of British Columbia's case over many years. The recommendations which concluded the official presentation covered all the usual points of tariffs, freight rates, and the federal invasion of the income tax field. The special position of British Columbia and the need for financial adjustments, of course, received the usual attention.

But the Pattullo Government went further in its proposals. It entered into areas of dominion-provincial relationships which had received limited previous attention, and in many respects it antici-pated areas of intergovernmental relationships which were to dom-inate the scene in the years to come after the war in such mat-ters as constitutional amendment, broader provincial taxing powers, full federal responsibility for old age pensions and unemployment in-surance, increased co-operation in the fields of health, welfare, and vocational training. Strangely, there was an echo from the past in a proposal to prohibit oriental immigration on ethnological grounds. Thrust into the recommendations in isolation, that recommendation was perhaps a forerunner of things to come in the treatment of Japanese-Canadians a few years later, in 1942.[3]

While the British Columbia position did not give ground on any of the earlier points on which its disputes with Canada had been based, it nevertheless did adopt something of a new stance which was closely related to the concepts of co-operative federalism which was to assume increasing importance in the postwar years.[4]

In the circumstances, it is perhaps surprising that Premier Pattullo took the strong position that he did at the Dominion-Provincial Conference of January 1941, in opposing the implementation of the Rowell-Sirois Report. In this he was aligned with the premiers of Ontario and Alberta. While, in retrospect, Pattullo's disagreement with the recommendations of the Royal Commission and with the timing of the proposals makes more sense now than it appeared to have done in 1941, his alignment with the mavericks of Canadian politics, Hepburn and Aberhart, made his role as a loyal Canadian suspect. Perhaps he was only criticized for his unwillingness to conform to the approved pattern of war-time conduct for provincial premiers. In any event, the statement of W. A. C. Bennett, then a private member, that he would have done better to negotiate than to have walked out, is hard to refute. The fact is that Premier Pattullo's timing was bad, and the political company he kept was worse. In politics such errors are hard to rectify. Mr. Pattullo tried but failed.

The proof of Mr. Pattullo's error is an important fact in any consideration of the British Columbia role in Confederation. There is no doubt at all that his stand at Ottawa was almost universally unpopular with the press, with most of his colleagues, and with the public. The loss of his majority in 1941, in an election that he should have won and expected to win easily, cost him the premiership and the leadership of the Liberal Party and led to the Coalition Government under his Finance Minister, John Hart, which assumed office in December 1941.

In the eyes of most political observers of the time all this was clear proof of the fact that, while British Columbia is always willing to press its case against Canada, in times of stress there is a basic Canadian strain which predominates and submerges all the narrow provincial interests of less strenuous times. In other words, when the chips are really down British Columbians are Canadians first, if a choice must be made. The question that needs to be answered now is, does this still hold good?

The basic consistency of the British Columbia relationship is illustrated in a rather interesting way by the approaches employed by the two men. John Hart had been a long-time friend and colleague of Pattullo and in many ways they provided the ideal team of Premier and Minister of Finance. They were quite different personalities, however. Pattullo believed in the direct approach. Hart was a believer in the soft word backed by a strong will and superb bargaining sense. But even though he substituted finesse for the frontal attack, essentially there was no change under his leadership in the provincial attitudes.

It was not practicable in the war years for a province to assert its independent attitude. Only in Alberta did Aberhart find this in any way possible, and then only within closely defined limits. In the postwar reconstruction period, the federal priorities were clearly evident; the provinces had little choice but to continue their secondary roles. The federal domination of the Reconstruction Conference in 1945–46 clearly showed that, even though the provinces retained a veto power, the essential activities of government in the war and early postwar periods were controlled from Ottawa.

British Columbia in the postwar period, under John Hart and later under Byron Johnson, continued to press its case for better treatment, with particular emphasis on its higher costs and its greater contribution to the national economy. But in spite of consistent maintenance of its position, it was prepared to accommodate itself, where profitable and necessary, to the realities of federal control. In these years, while there was greater emphasis on financial aspects than on the economic problems of tariffs and trade and the inequities of the terms of union, the pattern of the relationship remained more or less true to form.

In view of the somewhat fundamental nature of the political credo of the Social Credit Party which Mr. W. A. C. Bennett had adopted in 1952, one might be excused for expecting that he would, as Premier, have adopted a position more related to basic provincial rights. But Mr. Bennett had been a free-enterprise conservative before he ever heard of Social Credit. Mr. Bracken may not have been able to make over the Conservative Party, but there is no doubt that Mr. Bennett successfully converted the Social Credit Party in British

Columbia to his own ideas in a way that would have done credit to the personal politicians of the pre-McBride era.

The probable truth of the matter is that Premier Bennett, like most successful Canadian politicians, was and remains a complete pragmatist who has never let himself be confused by political principles which have a habit of standing still as time passes them by.[5] One cannot help but be struck by his similarity, in many ways, to two of his predecessors, Sir Richard McBride and "Duff" Pattullo. Margaret Ormsby has noted that McBride sensed that "British Columbia had some distinctive quality, not quite Canadian or British or American or even a blend of all three—he dreamed of developing its vast natural resources through grandiose schemes which would make it almost an empire in itself."[6] He was, as Miss Ormsby further notes, "a provincial patriot, an incurable optimist, a 'booster' and a promoter, an admirer of the industrialist-capitalist system, he had shared all the local fears of Socialist theories and all the local racial prejudices."[7]

Except in the last respect, the similarities are strong. The important difference, in both cases, is that Mr. Bennett has had a great deal more to work with and has had the pleasant task of operating in sweeter years of almost unremitting boom.

In the context of our interest here, these facts are important only as they relate to our main theme of British Columbia's relationship with the nation. If British Columbia under Mr. Bennett had adopted a more aggressive and independent attitude than under his predecessors, it would not have been to surprising or too illogical. After all, he had no continuing political affiliations with those in power at the centre, nor was the province financially a ward of the central government. But, regardless of all this, nothing has really changed in the nineteen years of his regime, although the surface manifestations may sometimes indicate otherwise. There have been changes in emphasis, a greater reaching for independent authority and a desire to deal more in the manner of political equals. But this seems to be more a product of the basic change in the whole federal-provincial relationship than in any specific change on the part of British Columbia alone.

Starting with a brief submitted to the Government of Canada on

Federal-Provincial Co-operation on Economic Development in December 1953, and continuing on to the present day, one finds a thread of argument that is straight from the fabric of the past, although there is a greater reliance on rhetoric and a lesser reliance on economic facts than used to be the custom. But perhaps the facts have all been produced and there is nothing more to say. There tends to be a greater emphasis on the broad plans for economic growth and less on particular points of dispute. There is often a myopic concentration on the needs of the province for greater taxing power quite regardless of the effect of such demands on the national existence. But, all in all, these are but variations on themes that have been played for a good many years by politicians of various persuasions. "The more things change. . . ."

But if the basic approach has not changed, it would be quite wrong to infer that there has been no reflection of Mr. Bennett's personality and acute if somewhat unorthodox political style in the relationships between Victoria and Ottawa.[8] No man, given the power he has enjoyed (and that seems the right word), could fail to impose some elements of his own personality on the political scene. And while basically, as stated, the relationship with Ottawa have followed a pattern—if sometimes an erratic one—the style has changed. Maurice Western in the *Winnipeg Free Press* of 29 August 1969, writing of Mr. Bennett's recent provincial election victory, refers to the Premier's relationship with the federal Government in these words: "Neither the Liberals nor the Conservatives have any reason to look with affection on Premier Bennett. Except for Jean Lesage in his heyday, no provincial magnate has done more to create trouble for successive national governments. Mr. Bennett has been an unpredictable force in Canadian politics. At times disarmingly accommodating, at others hostile. Often he has simply ignored Ottawa, treating it virtually as the capital of some not-very-important foreign country."

All this may be so, and probably the comment is well founded. But one may be forgiven for wondering sometimes if, in the final analysis, this "trouble-making" is not just one more manifestation of British Columbia's rather defensive detachment from the Canadian federation, expressed through a somewhat ebullient and sometimes politically erratic personality. Perhaps, in a sense, his success provincially but not federally is an expression of the split personality of the province within the Canadian union.

But if British Columbia has no real desire to harm the Canadian federation or to relinquish its place in the union, sometimes its activities and its demands have been of a nature incompatible with the effective continuation of a strong and effective federal state.

There have been times when the British Columbia case has been founded in the traditional approach but has contained claims that, if taken at face value, could only be regarded as complete negations of the federal idea and a determined attempt to destroy the central authority. Financial demands have been stated in terms that have paralleled or exceeded the most extreme demands of Quebec. Issues like those of the Columbia River, Roberts Bank, and the off-shore mineral rights have been phrased in the most provocative terms. Political partisanship may not have been an important element, but in its place we have seen mutual personal animosity which has often distorted differences far out of proportion in a manner certainly not consistent with the public interest.

If the provincial Government has on occasion been provocative and unco-operative, the Government of Canada has often made its own contribution to continuing misunderstanding. The process, as noted, seems quite capable of developing regardless of the extent of the partisan ties between the federal and provincial governments. Sometimes the lack of apparent willingness to accept the nature of British Columbia's place in the Canadian federation on the part of the province's federal representatives has been as hard to appreciate as the difficult and often parochial activities of the provincial leaders. Perhaps part of the trouble is in the very basic fact of British Columbia's detachment and its limited involvement, often by apparent choice, in national affairs. Perhaps the rather irritating British Columbian habit of boasting *ad nauseam* about its great wealth while, at the same time, raising cries of public poverty has sometimes contributed to the obvious lack of sympathy and understanding elsewhere in Canada. Be that as it may, it has often seemed as if the governments of Canada and British Columbia alike were determined to reach a basis of mutual misunderstanding at all costs on all possible occasions.

And yet this is all wrapped in a paradox. Mr. Bennett, who is seldom reluctant to twist the tail of the Ottawa lion when occasion offers, could be classed on his performances as a provincialist, if not a potential separatist. But he frequently claims with fervour (and almost certainly sincerity) to be a staunch and loyal Canadian. And Mr. Bennett, I think, represents the current British Columbia mind and attitude today as much as any one person is likely to. This is the man who, at the Federal-Provincial Conference of November 1963, said, "We, like all Canadians, are citizens first of a country and not of a province" and who, at the Constitutional Conference of February 1968, said, in part: "I say as the Premier of British Columbia, but especially as a Canadian citizen, that while there are problems in this nation there is no crisis! And we cannot tackle any of these problems in a spirit of crisis; we must do it quietly as reasonable people, as Canadians one with another, and not in any spirit of crisis at all." All through most of his public statements we find this theme of the province's devotion to the Canadian idea, if not always to its execution.

Is this just a political aberration, a façade, a manœuvre? Or is it a genuine expression of the ambivalence of British Columbia's attitude to its place in the Canadian union? Do the leaders and the people of the province believe in this duality of their part in federation, and, if they do, have they stopped to examine the implications of such a role for the continuing future of Canada? No one can answer that question with any confidence, but I doubt if the people themselves, even those most directly involved, ever really get down to an objective examination of their ideas, their motives, or their actions.

The confusion that exists in the minds of people generally is illustrated by an episode in 1965, not important in itself, but only in that it could happen at all in the province. In fact it still remains largely unexplained. In May 1965 one of Premier Bennett's cabinet ministers created quite a public stir with a rather confused statement that if the province could not get an adjustment of its grievances with Ottawa, it would have to consider the possibility of separation. Actually, idle threats of secession are not new. There have been such statements in the past and, no doubt, there will be others in the future. What is interesting is that on this occasion, while the statement was disowned by colleagues in the Cabinet, and harshly criticized by the press and the public, the Premier himself is reported

to have side-stepped the issue and did not disavow the statement
expressly, although he gave it no support.

The only really significant thing about the incident is that while
Premier Bennett handled the matter with caution (and his minister
may well have been "flying a kite" or establishing a bargaining
climate) he obviously concluded that, while squabbling with Ottawa
is usually well received in the province, ideas of secession and separatism provide little political capital and may very well be harmful.
Certainly there has been no recurrence of these attitudes, and the
assumption of those who should be informed in such matters is that
Mr. Bennett knows a non-starter when he sees one. The lesson of
T. D. Pattullo in 1941 has not been forgotten.

Of course, much of this speculation on attitudes of the people in
British Columbia is without current documentation. Provincial
elections seldom seem to be concerned with such issues, but rather
more with personalities, the "good life," and the dangers of socialism.
Perhaps it could be argued that Mr. Trudeau's success in British
Columbia in 1968 was a sign of the people's choice of a Canadian
role, but the issues, and even the alternative, were singularly limited.
If there is substance at all in these views of the British Columbia scene,
separation from Canada is not now, and has not been in the recent
past, a very live issue with which we should concern ourselves.

Always politically, less often emotionally, British Columbia is part
of the Canadian federation. But the extent of her integration is more
open to question. It is doubtful that the people collectively feel
themselves an integral part of Canadian life to the extent that the
people of Ontario, or even the Prairies, do. Nor do they have the feeling of dependence that seems to prevail in the Atlantic Provinces. In
some ways, I suspect, the people of Quebec may feel a stronger relationship to the Canadian whole than do many in British Columbia,
despite the current degree of alienation that is apparent in certain
circles in that province.

In terms of geography, history, trade, and in some respects, in a
way of life, the people of British Columbia often feel a sense of detachment from the rest of Canada. In its attitude to life, the province
has been and largely remains a bit like the daughter who returns to
the family for special occasions. Even though some of the factors,
especially that of geography, have been altered by the developments

of the times, they still retain some psychological influence, if nothing more. Under most of its leaders in recent times British Columbia has been chiefly concerned with its own affairs and the pursuit of its own destiny, rather than with establishing itself as a vital and integral part of the Canadian nation.

Federalism is essentially much more than a co-operative system and a marriage of interest. It is co-ordinative and competitive, and much of British Columbia's relationship with Canada is based on that distinction. Even in political life her politicians have been unable to become assimilated successfully in the larger Canadian scene. Outside of Sir John A. Macdonald's brief term as a refugee member for Victoria, there has not been a prime minister or even a party leader from the province in national politics. Even more surprising is the fact that no British Columbia cabinet minister has ever held a continuing position of predominant influence in a national government. To speak of the domination of Central Canada is not enough. There have been political figures of the first rank from the Maritimes and the Prairies as well as from Ontario and Quebec. Nor need we presume that it is a lack based on inadequacy. Rather, it is likely related to that sense of detachment and self-sufficiency to which we have already referred and which has weakened the fabric of Canadian political life in British Columbia. Even within their political parties the federal-provincial diversity is exploited, as witness the attempts of W. A. C. Bennett to displace Herbert Anscomb as Conservative leader with the support of the federal party wing. British Columbians seem to have developed in an unconscious sort of way a treaty-like relationship with the rest of the country, rather than being an integral and influential element in the nation of which they could be an increasingly vital part. British Columbia, considering its status, has made a relatively unimportant contribution in recent years to the development of new approaches to federalism in Canada. That this is apparently a matter of deliberate policy rather than a lack of capacity makes the deficiency all the more telling.

If all that has been said is true, the observer of the scene might be excused for asking just what it is that has kept the province within the union in the past, and how likely it is to continue in the future. There seem to be so many reasons for the hybrid Canadianism that appears as a product of British Columbia detachment that some have regarded the dangers of separatism there as being as real in prospect as they are in the Province of Quebec.

Perhaps on cold facts this could be so except for what are two rather important distinctions. In the first place, the British Columbia attitude is more negative than positive. It is one of disinterested detachment, a sort of acceptance of the Canadian idea but without any great sense of responsibility for it or feeling of need to make a contribution toward it. A positive role may be assumed willingly in time of crisis, as was so well illustrated in both 1914 and 1939, but it takes that sort of stimulant to awaken the latent interests that exist. Secondly, there still exists a sentimental attachment to the Canadian idea, based among some (ever fewer in number) on the British connection, in others on the fact that they came from other provinces of Canada and from abroad to a part of Canada on the Pacific Coast, not to a province. Macdonald's dream of an empire stretching from sea to sea is still a valid concept for those who still can dream, and it takes more than the irritations of fiscal and economic disagreements for the dream to be allowed to fade.

But if one is to leave, there must be somewhere to go. To break away from the established tradition of nearly a hundred years can become increasingly difficult, failing some positive factor which forces the decision. British Columbia has celebrated more centennials in the past few years than any other province, and each one has provided a further link between the future and the past.

What of the United States? As we have seen in earlier history, the influence from the south was always an important factor in the province's growth. In many ways the connection of the people of British Columbia with the south remains strong. In many parts of the province, the American influence is more pervasive than in any other section of Canada. Premier Bennett is even reported to have attended conferences of the Governors of the Western states on occasion. But though the American influence is pervasive, the distinctions remain. People may visit California for their holidays, they may cross the boundary to Blaine, or spend a weekend in Spokane as if no national lines existed. They may watch American television stations beamed into the Vancouver market, or have cottages at Point Roberts, and even sell their best land to Americans for summer places and their companies for profit. But the influence is superficial and without real

depth, perhaps now more than ever before. It is not easy to judge
how people might react under the changed conditions in which a
choice would have to be made, but there is little to suggest that political union with the United States offers any likely alternative, now or
in the foreseeable future, to Canadian union. Today the growing
interest in the Orient and the involvement of Japan in B.C. commerce
is a factor increasingly to be considered as a factor in assessing future
attitudes.

As things stand, British Columbians would very likely prefer to
leave well enough alone. Most of them are reasonably content with
the *status quo* (*vide* the last election); and making money and
enjoying the "good life" of the glossy magazines is much more to the
liking of the influential classes than any deep concern with the problem of social, economic, or political change that would occur should
any untoward change in their constitutional relationship take place.
In effect, British Columbians rather like having their cake and eating
it too, in being part of the Canadian nation but without making any
of the conscious efforts or accepting the obligations which would make
the relationship a real and living thing. The perhaps now out-dated
English phrase, "I'm all right Jack," has been fairly descriptive of
the attitude to the Canadian federal system. Nothing has really
changed in British Columbia since early times. The land of limitless
resources remains, and the people retain or soon acquire, no matter
whence they came, their fantasy-like belief in their province's limitless destiny. The thirties are long gone, and to the postwar generation,
familiar only with inflation and continuing boom, everything seems
possible and probably is. As long as British Columbians see it this
way, as long as the material elements of the "good life" continue
to occupy their ambitions, it will remain a sort of adjunct to Canada,
looking west and south rather than east, never out but never entirely
in, never disintegrative but never a positive element in the nation's
growth to maturity. The course is ever upward, but in the limited
confines of a provincial world. Which may be quite all right if that is
the limit of your horizon.

But what of a Canada that changes and loses the character that
has made it unique over the first hundred years of its life? How do
the people of British Columbia regard Quebec? What responsibility
do they feel for some reasonable accommodation to the demands

of Quebec in order that we may resolve the difficulties of the problems of English- and French-speaking Canadians?

The truth of the matter seems to be that they think about it very
little at all. As Premier Bennett pointed out to the 1968 Constitutional Conference, those speaking French are a very small minority
(1.6 per cent) of the people of British Columbia and are greatly out-
numbered by those of ethnic origins other than Anglo-Saxon. It is
very difficult indeed for a people who have no contact with a culture
or a language to regard the preservation of that culture or the life of
that language as a matter of importance in their lives. The limits of
understanding are dangerously narrow.

Essentially the Government and the people of British Columbia
alike seem to regard the whole question as one of the St. Lawrence
Valley, a problem in which the Premier of Ontario might concern
himself, but one in which the Premier of British Columbia has only a
peripheral interest. Whether or not this is a supportable attitude is
one of personal conviction; but when you get across the prairies and
the mountains, the problems of St. Léonard and the activities of René
Lévesque and of the F.L.Q. somehow shrink in proportion.

If this were not enough, there is in the minds of a good many
people a more positive element that enters into the question which
could be difficult to adjust to. One finds that many are convinced
(and not only in British Columbia) that in some cases the problems
of French language and culture have been used by various groups in
Quebec, official and unofficial, as tools in the process of securing
acceptance of demands in areas of intergovernmental relationships
little connected with the stated purpose. Whether or not this suspicion is justified, the fact that it is there does little to improve the
depth of understanding.

But even though their appreciation of French-Canadian needs
may not be all that we might wish, most people of British Columbia
regard Quebec is an important and valuable part of the rather
nebulous traditional concept of Canada to which they give allegiance.
The impact is certainly less than in Ontario or New Brunswick or
even Manitoba; nevertheless, it is a real part of the Canadian scene,
if often an awkward and an irritating one.

It would not be wise to assume too much, for it is doubtful that
British Columbia would pay any unlimited price for the retention of

Quebec in Canada, or would accept a relationship that was a one-sided union in name alone. The people of British Columbia neither understand nor seem inclined to accept on faith the "two nation" policy by which Mr. Douglas and Mr. Stanfield attempted to lend flexibility to their positions in 1968. Perhaps this may be illogical, for they themselves may be accused of a form of hyphenated Canadianism of a somewhat different sort, but the view remains.

Given these circumstances, should a situation ever arise where Quebec was prepared to leave the Canadian union, the odds seem to be that the role and influence of British Columbia would be a limited one. Under certain circumstances she might be prepared, in irritation, to echo the words of a certain well-known political scientist: "In the name of God—Go."[9] It would be true that any such departure would be accepted with deepest regret both for the loss of that province itself and for the effects of the departure on Canada's future. But the reaction would be a passive one and the price that would be paid to hold Quebec would likely be relatively small.

The consequences of a Quebec departure are wrapped in all the uncertainty of future political events. But should it happen, there are a number of alternative courses of action which might develop. Perhaps the most likely in the minds of most observers would be a strong effort to maintain a viable English-speaking nation in Canada. In this the province could play an important part. Under existing conditions the residual influence of the Canadian connection could operate favourably in that direction. But should it prove that such a country, whether federalized or, perhaps more logically, as a unitary state, were not a practical concept, other alternatives would have to be weighed. In these circumstances it does not seem very likely that the more limited concept of a Western Canadian Union or an Alberta–British Columbia merger would have very much attraction.

It has already been suggested that for now, at least, a United States connection would be unlikely, although the ultimate end is more in doubt. We are thus left with the solution, which is not too far-fetched in the minds of many British Columbians, that the province should, as T. D. Pattullo once suggested, "go it alone." One need only refer again to the interview with P. C. Newman wherein Mr. Bennett is quoted as saying that "if we ever did separate from Canada, we would become the Dominion of British Columbia and stay in the Commonwealth." On the surface the idea is feasible. Whether or not it would stand up in the difficult world of today and tomorrow is a matter for much more thorough thought and analysis than has yet been given to the problem.

No one can say today how British Columbia would go, or for that matter how any other part of Canada would react, should the present federal structure begin to disintegrate. But regardless of the likelihood of that event, the detachment of British Columbia from the fabric of Canadian nationhood is real and under any circumstances a weakening influence. Whatever the political demands of the future may be, a prime objective should be the drawing of the Pacific Province into a role as a major partner in Canadian federation.

NOTES

1. W. N. Sage, "Federal Parties and Provincial Political Groups in British Columbia, 1871–1903," *British Columbia Historical Quarterly*, vol. 12 (1948): 151–169.

2. F. W. Howay and E. O. S. Scholefield, *British Columbia From Earliest Times to the Present*, 4 vols. (Vancouver & Montreal: S. J. Clarke, 1914), ch. 32.

3. See *Report of the British Columbia Security Commission, 1942.*

4. See the various British Columbia submissions to dominion-provincial conferences, particularly: *British Columbia in the Canadian Federation*, a submission presented to the Royal Commission on Dominion-Provincial Relations by the Government of the Province of British Columbia (C. F. Banfield, King's Printer, Victoria, 1938); and *Statement by Premier Pattullo*, Dominion-Provincial Conference, January 1941 (Ottawa: King's Printer, 1941).

5. The literature on Premier Bennett is limited, but the writing is increasingly frequent in the press and periodicals. The only full-length study is that of Patrick Sherman, *Bennett* (Toronto: McClelland & Stewart, 1966).

6. Margaret Ormsby, *British Columbia: A History* (Toronto: Macmillan, 1968), p. 336.

7. Ibid., p. 371.

8. The sometimes peculiar ambivalence of Mr. Bennett's attitudes is illustrated in an interview with P. C. Newman, published in the *Victoria Daily Times*, 18 February 1967. In this interview, Mr. Bennett at one stage blames Ottawa for most committable political offences but ends by reaffirming his abiding faith in Canada. Perhaps the key to his position on many things is contained in the quoted remark, "We make policies for the hour."

9. See the article by Eugene Forsey, "Concepts of Federalism: Some Canadian Aspects," in J. Peter Meekison (ed.) *Canadian Federalism: Myth or Reality* (Toronto: Methuen, 1968).

Postscript

Richard Simeon

SINCE THE PAPERS included in this volume were written, two events which may have profound implications for the future of Confederation have occurred in Quebec. First was the Quebec provincial election of 29 April 1970. The large majority won by the Liberals under Robert Bourassa led most English-Canadian observers to interpret the returns chiefly as a plebiscite on the future of Quebec in Canada which the forces of national unity had won resoundingly. For a brief moment, it seemed, English Canadians persuaded themselves there was not so much to worry about after all, even though there was that 22.8 per cent vote for the Parti Québécois to provoke sober second thoughts. The complacency was rudely shattered in October, when the train of events touched off by the terrorist FLQ kidnappings and the murder of Hon. Pierre Laporte plunged the country into political crisis, and raised once again the unsettling question: can we survive?

It is too early to place these events fully into perspective, or to assert with any confidence what their implications for the future of Quebec and Canada are. Some might argue that both events, in different ways, have strengthened the federalist forces. Others see them as more likely to move many Quebec citizens at least a step or two farther down the road towards a Separatist stance. In the long run, which of these positions is more correct may well not be so important as what both events reveal about developments within the province. What happens within Quebec is going to be far more important for Confederation than what happens in exchanges between Quebec and federal politicians.

Both events seem to reflect an increasing level of internal conflict and division within Quebec and an increasingly complex pattern of cleavages. These divisions are the long-delayed product of a process of social, economic, and cultural change. Their effects are likely to persist for a long time, so that the prognosis for Quebec is more domestic division and turmoil, of which the election and the kidnappings and their aftermath are but two examples. Those concerned with the future of Canada must understand these developments, even though they may be powerless to affect them. In this essay I will try to give one interpretation of the recent events from the perspective of a concern with the causes and consequences of social conflict.

English Canadians have tended to see Quebec as a homogeneous entity, as a unified whole, in which a relatively passive and acquiescent population deferred to strong political and religious élites. As a result, it seemed reasonable to talk of "Quebec opinions" or "Quebec demands" as if there were one clearly identifiable set of interests involved. The pattern of accommodation which evolved to deal with English/French-Canadian disputes was the federal-provincial conference, whose logic was that the government leaders of a united province would bargain with other governments. This pattern both reflected and contributed to the image of Quebec as a unified whole. The image, in some ways a convenient one, was probably never wholly accurate. Nevertheless, despite the social changes going on beneath the surface, this perspective was broadly correct during the years of rule by Maurice Duplessis and even in the years of the Lesage Government.

When English Canadians did consider the effect of basic changes in Quebec society, as during the "Quiet Revolution," they tended to stress how this seemed to lead to increased conflict between English and French Canada. But even more important, as we now see, is that these changes lead to increased conflict within Quebec society.

The dimensions of the increased conflict have yet to be clearly mapped, but the indications are numerous, and can be seen in many areas of Quebec life. A glance at the newspapers shows that political rhetoric seems to be much more intense and ideological in Quebec than elsewhere, though other factors may contribute to this. Mass demonstrations have become a common feature of Quebec life. The St. Léonard schools dispute brought the linguistic issue down to the individual level and into the street. The postal workers strike and the Montreal taxi strike, among others, demonstrated an intensity of political content in labour disputes rare elsewhere. Two anti-élite parties, the Ralliement Créditiste and the Parti Québécois, have rapidly won substantial support. Community action groups have achieved considerable success in organizing working-class citizens, especially in the depressed areas of Montreal. Internal conflict—and with it sporadic violence—appears to be both more intense and more widespread, whether one compares it with Quebec's own past, or with other parts of Canada today.

This pattern stems from the consequences of profound social changes in Quebec, which have been going on for a long time, but which only relatively recently have manifested themselves in political life. Social change has several consequences which are likely to lead to disunity, breakdown of traditional allegiances, and increased internal conflict. First, it leads to increased differentiation among social groups, who develop their own political and economic interests and perspectives. Second, such changes as urbanization, development of the mass media, and increased education lead to greater awareness of group interests and to a more direct realization of the benefits enjoyed by other groups, as is especially the case in Montreal, where the residents of the slums of St. Henri can see flaunted before them the glitter of Mayor Drapeau's Montreal. The same forces lead to a breakdown of the social cement provided by the traditional value system, in Quebec represented by Church and family. Increased mobility—geographically, socially, and occupationally—makes these traditional value systems far less powerful. And with their breakdown comes a marked decline in the deference that citizens show towards the traditional élites who embodied the value systems and were legitimized by them. No longer are voters so willing to listen to the advice of their "betters"; they are more prepared to listen to new leaders, who more accurately reflect their new interests, values, and grievances. A survey conducted by La Société de Mathématique Appliquée in 1966 found that 43.5 per cent of voters felt there was room for a third party in Quebec.[1] Groups once passive are thus mobilized into new forms of political awareness and action. Sociologist Guy Rocher recently wrote:

In the course of Quebec's evolution in recent years, a new pheno-menon has appeared, which has not yet received the attention it deserves: this is the more and more marked role played by certain sectors which may be called marginal. It is in these milieux that social and political demands are expressed with the most vehe-mence; here are recruited the new forces of opposition to the estab-lished powers; here one senses the awakening of new contending energies which are still unformed and ready to let loose an anger which will persist a long time.[2]

These marginal groups include both the rural and the urban poor. Traditional parties, unions, and other institutions have never effec-tively appealed to or spoken for them. Recently, Rocher suggests, new grass-roots movements have begun to organize; the earlier passivity, dependence, and indifference are being replaced by growing political awareness and a revolt against the élites who have ignored them for so long. "The anger which is rumbling in the marginal milieux has only begun to express itself." We can thus expect many new forms of political action by groups with intense grievances and resentments.

Social change is not equally beneficial to all groups: the emergence of a modern industrialized Quebec has given status and power to the new middle classes; it has left behind those who remain in small villages operating marginal farms, and those who populate the urban slums. The changes can also have profound psychologically unsettling effects on those caught up in them. Individuals break away from old patterns and try to find a place in the new, often only at the price of great conflict with parents and others, a process described by revolutionary Pierre Vallières in *Les Nègres Blancs d'Amérique*.

These changes do not fully explain the exact nature of the new patterns of political cleavage and conflict which emerge. What alliances will be formed, which parties will grow strong, and what directions they will take depend also on much more immediate fac-tors—on such things as the economic conditions of the day and on the quality and nature of the political leaders who emerge to give shape and direction to the new forces. But the changes described do help create a climate, which in this case acts to increase internal divisions and conflict.

This perspective helps cast some light on the implications of the

Quebec election and the crisis of October–November 1970. It was common to regard the election as something of a referendum on separation. English Canadians, particularly, saw the result as a victory for national unity. Claude Ryan, editor of *Le Devoir*, calculated, by juggling various figures, that fully "three Quebeckers out of four have expressed their preference for the federal formula." On the other side, Parti Québécois partisans correctly suggested that if one looked only at French-speaking voters, the party's popular support was well above the 22.8 per cent of the vote it actually received. Such playing with numbers, however, greatly oversimplifies the nature of the election and its implications.

Political events, especially in such a complex and changing society as Quebec, seldom resolve themselves into a neat choice between two clear-cut alternatives. Certainly many voters cast their ballots according to party stands on the constitutional issue. English Canadians, virtually unanimously Liberal, are one example. Similarly the question was obviously very important to many French-speaking intellectuals—students, professors, professionals—who probably wielded much more influence than their numbers alone would imply because they provided many of the energetic and enthusiastic campaign workers who were so successful in building PQ support in many areas. Others, too, were undoubtedly motivated by the issue of federalism, but the fact remains that it is very hard to measure the issue's significance. As the polls show, a great many PQ voters were not Separatists. Some observers have suggested that this means the party's support should not be considered an accurate measure of Indépendantiste support. They are right, but by the same token, it would be equally wrong to regard the voters of other parties as staunchly federalist; many of them also voted for other reasons. This point is clearly illustrated in Table I.

The Créditiste vote, for example, appears to reflect basically an "anti-modernist" sense of grievance among more traditional segments of the population. The party presently mobilizing this discontent is federalist; there is no special reason why it could not be channelled in a more nationalist direction, and the PQ is presently attempting to do so. Thus, as a referendum on separation, the results are very ambiguous. The most detailed analysis of the election concludes that "internal

TABLE I

Vote Intention and Constitutional Position

Political Separation of Quebec along with economic association with Canada

	Lib.	PQ	Créditiste *(Per Cent)*	UN
YES	17	70	26	41
NO	72	24	57	50
UNCERTAIN	11	6	17	9
TOTAL	100	100	100	100

SOURCE: Adapted from Lemieux *et al., Election de réalignment,* Table 4.8, p. 88. Data from poll conducted by S. Peter Regenstreif, April, 1970.

political problems had more weight in the electors' decisions to vote than external [constitutional] politics," though this varied in different regions.[3] Clearly more than one question divided the voters.

More important, the results indicate the growing complexity of cleavages in Quebec society. They also seem to indicate a growing political mobilization in the province. Turnout rose to 85 per cent from 75 per cent in 1966. The Liberals benefited from the increased participation in predominantly English-speaking constituencies, where voters were stimulated primarily by the constitutional issue. Elsewhere, especially in Montreal where the increase in turnout was most striking, the PQ most successfully mobilized those previously not voting.[4]

Much more data are needed to map the current pattern of cleavages, but some of the more important ones stand out. First, of course, is language. As *Le Devoir* put it in a headline, the results in Montreal revealed "une île, une région, mais deux sociétés." Of the four parties, only the Liberals had any cross-language appeal, though Michel Brunet has calculated that less than three in ten French-speaking Quebeckers voted Liberal. In addition, one has the impression that language disputes—as the recent General Motors strike at Ste. Thérèse indicates—are no longer the major preoccupation of intellectuals concerned with the abstract question of cultural survival; they now involve the immediate interests of ordinary citizens.

Second is what appears to be a growing and more intense class cleavage, especially in Montreal. Here, perhaps, lies the greatest significance of the rise of the Parti Québécois. The major areas of PQ strength were the working-class French-speaking areas of Montreal. To mobilize such widespread support so quickly among voters who are traditionally hard to organize is a major accomplishment. The leadership of the PQ remains rather an uneasy coalition of nationalists of differing left- and right-wing stripes, but the overall thrust of the party is clearly akin to the New Democratic Party on socio-economic matters, and it may not be stretching the point too far to suggest that the PQ is the first party of the Left to have gained substantial support in Quebec. The social changes mentioned above, especially if combined with continued economic problems, may well produce a far wider clientele for a mass working-class party, especially if, like the PQ in the provincial election, and like the Front d'Action Politique more recently, it pursues imaginative strategies such as development of neighbourhood offices and community action groups which can mobilize and channel working-class grievances. A nationalist party of the Left, with a working-class base, and with ideologies and activists drawn from the rapidly growing ranks of university and college graduates, could prove very potent. A growing proportion of these graduates are of working-class origin, and their alienation will increase if the economy cannot provide the white collar jobs for which their education has trained them, or led them to expect. Such a party would be nationalistic because the highly visible economic dominance of English Canadians makes it easy to link them with economic dissatisfactions. But it would also divide French Canadians themselves, pitting the working class against many middle-class Quebeckers, who themselves would be torn between their economic and cultural interests.

A third cleavage revealed by the election may be called rural versus urban, or perhaps more accurately, a centre–periphery cleavage. In a sense this aligns the more "modern," developed areas of the province against the more traditional and less developed. These areas have not benefited from the social and economic changes, and are the ones most threatened by the breakdown of the traditional order. The PQ and the Liberals may be said to represent the more "modern" segments of the population, the Créditistes and the Union Nationale the less modern. Both have their strongest bases in the rural areas, and both have complained about many modern developments while defending the threatened values of family and religion.

Another cleavage is between the parties of protest (the PQ tapping urban, working-class grievances and those of the young students; the Créditistes, rural grievances) versus the established parties. Together, the protest parties won 35 per cent of the vote, suggesting widespread alienation, and a new willingness of the dissatisfied to break away from past allegiances and voting habits. Whether these defections will be permanent is an interesting question: certainly the likelihood seems to be a long period of relative fluidity in voting patterns before new loyalties establish themselves.

A further cleavage which seems to cut through Quebec society is less easy to document, though it has prompted much comment. This is the division between young and old. In rapidly changing societies deep generational differences are to be expected as the young more rapidly discard old values and attitudes and take on new ones which may be different from their parents'. This again seems to be a persistent theme of much of the radical writing. It was also reflected in the election results, with the PQ drawing almost half the vote in the 18–24 age group, but less than 20 per cent among those 55 and over.[5]

Finally there is the cleavage of federalism versus separatism, with a great many shades of opinion on both sides. Again this is just as much a division within Quebec as it is a division between Quebeckers and other Canadians. As with the language issue, nationalism in Quebec, which has traditionally been seen as an élite middle-class phenomenon, has recently penetrated to the working class, as economic grievances have become linked to ethnic ones.

The cleavage lines vary in different regions of the province. In Montreal, the constitutional issue appeared more salient though opposition to the incumbent government was also strong. Here the polarization was between the Liberals and the PQ. In the central region, where the Créditistes profited most from dissatisfaction with the government, domestic issues predominated over constitutional ones.[6]

These cleavages are obviously related to each other in complex ways, and to some extent they cut across each other. For some groups, the cleavages seem to reinforce each other, that is, those who are on the "losing end" on one are on the losing end of others. Perhaps the extreme case here is the citizen who is young, French Canadian, lives in Montreal, and is a member of the working class or identifies with it. This is the group most likely to become mobilized to support extreme protest groups, working-class parties, and the like. For them, the nationalist issue becomes fused with the economic issue; the two are virtually inseparable and feed off each other. In the various manifestos of the Front de Libération Québécois, for example, it is impossible to tell which is the more important theme. When cleavages overlap in this way, conflict is likely to be more intense and to be much more difficult to resolve. One's opponent on one issue is likely to be one's opponent on all the others. He may then be defined not as opponent, but as enemy, who must be defeated however extreme the means and high the cost.

To summarize, as Quebec society itself has become more diverse and complex, so have the internal lines of division. Where once social and economic distinctions within the population were obscured or mitigated by a unifying value system, now there is fragmentation as that value system and its representatives have become largely discredited. No alternative system of values has arisen to replace the old. Previously passive groups have become mobilized. Thus the apparent internal unity is shattered and a complex party system, representing some of the widely varying interests of different groups, has arisen. These changes have already produced a higher level of conflict than one finds in most provinces, and have made it impossible to speak of Quebec, except geographically, as a single entity.

The specific directions that the new lines of conflict will take depend, of course, on many more immediate factors. It is not so much the fact of division itself, but the intensity of division which is most important. This will depend on at least three factors: first, the kinds of political leaders who emerge, for they will to a large extent define the interests of their followers and channel their activities. The second factor may be institutional changes. For example, the introduction of proportional representation would be likely to decrease the alienation of those groups who rightly felt cheated in the April election, but at the same time would give party leaders little incentive to create a new consensus based on reconciling the interests of many groups. Instead PR would encourage new parties to enter the arena and old ones to cultivate and stress group differences. Third, and most important, will be the activities of government, at all levels, in dealing with basic social and economic problems. Continued high levels of unemployment, or the continued unequal distribution of income (according to the Economic Council of Canada, income in Quebec is distributed more unequally than in any other province) and continued large gaps between the living standards of English and French, rural and urban, will produce increased conflict.

All of this provides a perspective for looking at the recent kidnapping affair. The kidnappings themselves did not represent the sudden outbreak of violence in a heretofore peaceful state. Rather they were an escalation, undoubtedly encouraged by the success of similar tactics elsewhere, of what had already become a familiar pattern of scattered violence in the province since early in the sixties. What was different this time was the audacity and severity of the crimes, and, more important, the nature of governmental reaction to it.

That there should be increased levels of conflict does not necessarily mean that it should be accompanied by violence. Indeed, the violence embraces only a tiny proportion of the population, and we need other, perhaps more psychological, theories to explain why some individuals turn to violent means to express their grievances. Nevertheless, when there is intense disagreement and many hold strong grievances, there is fertile soil for violence, both on the part of the disaffected and on the part of those whom they oppose. In addition, for each person who engages in violent acts, there are many who do not, but who share the goals of the violent and condone their tactics.

The significance of the crisis can be interpreted in two distinct but related ways. It was, first, a crisis for Confederation and for French/English-Canadian relations. But even more, it was a crisis for Quebec society itself. Once again, English Canadians were forced into awareness of the existence of forces prepared to go to desperate lengths to achieve independence. Many English Canadians blurred, if they did not obliterate, the distinction between moderate and violent Separatists and were prepared to use the events as a signal to crack down on all forms of nationalism. Similarly, some French Canadians saw the sending of troops and the use of the War Measures Act as evidence that English Canada would use force rather than tolerate separation in any form. But the crisis never did become a confrontation between the mass of English Canadians and the mass of French Canadians; it did not divide the country on ethnic lines. Revulsion against the kidnappings was as intense in Quebec as elsewhere. The Gallup poll reported that 89 per cent of English Canadians supported the Government's use of the War Measures Act; so did 86 per cent of French Canadians. The federal Liberals gained in popularity all across Canada including Quebec, where, said the Gallup poll, "the popularity of the Liberal party is at a new high." Furthermore, despite the disputes about who was really in charge and where the initiative came from, the drastic government efforts to deal with the FLQ were a *joint* effort of the Montreal, Quebec, and federal Governments.

The FLQ terrorism and the reaction against it therefore involve much more than a crisis for federalism. The FLQ directed its attack not simply at the federal system, but at the whole social, economic and political make-up of Quebec society. It did not so much endanger the federation, as it did public order, established authority, and the existing economic system. It was these aspects of the crisis that were stressed by leaders like Montreal Mayor Jean Drapeau, Quebec Justice Minister Jérome Choquette and others in their public statements. The sin of the Front d'Action Politique (FRAP), which was mounting a strong campaign in the Montreal municipal elections, and which was bitterly attacked as subversive by Mayor Drapeau, was not its separatism but its economic and social ideology and its mobilization of the dissatisfied.

It is hard to assess how much of a real threat the FLQ posed to Quebec society or whether there was a real possibility of a massive insurrection. The evidence so far revealed suggests that the FLQ was not very large or well organized, though as a dedicated splinter group, it had—and still has—considerable capacity for disruption. The extreme reaction to the events both by government and citizens perhaps tells us more about them than it does about the FLQ. The most likely explanation for the response is that many groups felt threatened and insecure even before the October events. Many English Canadians had a sense of the fragility of Confederation and of the ease with which it could be destroyed. French Canadians feared the bewildering new climate of *contestation*, alienated students, militant workers and the decay of old values. In such an atmosphere of self-doubt, it takes little to trigger the feeling that the edifice is about to come tumbling down, and that all possible powers must be used to save it. The "party of order" triumphs—at least for a while.

Whether the autumn events will lead to the further growth of Separatism is not clear. In the short run, Separatist support may have weakened by the association, however unfair, with the use of violence. (The PQ candidate in the February by-election in Chambly did, however, increase his vote slightly.) The FLQ actions may have convinced some wavering federalists to support that option more firmly. On the other hand, the governmental reactions have probably led some wavering nationalists towards a firmer Separatist stance.

The events produced a special agony for Quebec intellectuals, appalled at the use of violence, but equally appalled at the sight of federal troops patrolling the streets, at the suspension of civil liberties, at the use of mass arrests often without much apparent reason, and at what appeared to many of them as federal intrusion into Quebec's own crisis. For them, the events were not something to be assessed and analysed from afar. Instead they created an intense and complex personal crisis, in which they were pressed to make virtually impossible choices. How these dilemmas were faced, and what choices were made, is not known, but in the long run they may be vital since the intellectuals play a central role in defining the alternatives and opportunities of the changing society.

The middle has become an increasingly uncomfortable place. There is likely to be a hardening of the lines and a decline in the influence of the moderates, whether they be Separatists like René Lévesque or federalists like Claude Ryan of *Le Devoir*. Some committed Separatists have become convinced that the English Canadians have demonstrated that they would not tolerate a Quebec decision to separate and would use force to prevent it. If this feeling is widespread the future of the *democratic* Separatist movement would be weaker. Some English Canadians may welcome this, on the assumption that a more militant movement would have less chance of building widespread support. But the price would probably be in the long run even more violence, and more repression. At any rate, Separatism of whatever sense will remain a central factor in provincial politics, and electoral success of the PQ, especially if the Bourassa Government fails to improve economic conditions, is by no means an impossibility.

It is still too early, however, to assess what the results will ultimately be. The issue of separation is now inextricably intertwined with all the other issues dividing Quebec: questions about the relationship between generations, classes, and ethnic groups, about civil liberties, the economy, and all the rest. It is impossible any longer to discuss Separation versus Confederation as an abstract issue independent of the social and political context of Quebec. The choices made on any of the other issues will decisively affect Quebec's choices on the constitutional question.

Intense conflict and fragmentation, not consensus, characterize Quebec politics today, and will continue to do so. The election results and the FLQ kidnappings and their aftermath both reflect and will contribute to this pattern. Militant opposition will continue, as, perhaps, will correspondingly militant attempts to repress it. Widespread agreement on any constitutional option is therefore very unlikely to emerge in the near future. It is impossible to say how the complex political currents now flowing will resolve themselves. In any case, English Canadians have limited ability to influence the final outcome. But their goodwill and understanding, their willingness to meet Quebec half-way or more than half-way, can provide a more reasonable climate of opinion for the continuing dialogue.

NOTES

1. Vincent Lemieux, Marcel Gilbert and André Blais, *Une élection de réalignment: l'élection général du 29 avril 1970 au Québec* (Montreal: Cahiers de *Cité Libre*, Editions du jour, 1970), p. 41. This is the most complete and imaginative analysis of the election available, and fully reports data from three pre-election surveys.

2. Guy Rocher, "La marginalité social: un nouveau réservoir de contestation," *Le Devoir*, 30 Dec. 1970, p. A-17. My translation.

3. Lemieux *et al*, p. 97.

4. Ibid., pp. 150–151.

5. Ibid., p. 66.

6. Ibid., p. 168.